This book comes with access to more content online.

Test your knowledge with four full-length
practice exams!

Register your book or ebook at
www.dummies.com/go/getaccess.

Select your product, and then follow the prompts
to validate your purchase.

You'll receive an email with your PIN and instructions.

Securities Industry Essentials™ Exam with Online Practice

by Steven M. Rice

Securities Industry Essentials™ Exam For Dummies® with Online Practice

Published by: **John Wiley & Sons, Inc.**, 111 River Street, Hoboken, NJ 07030-5774, www.wiley.com

Copyright © 2019 by John Wiley & Sons, Inc., Hoboken, New Jersey

Published simultaneously in Canada

For general information on our other products and services, please contact our Customer Care Department within the U.S. at 877-762-2974, outside the U.S. at 317-572-3993, or fax 317-572-4002. For technical support, please visit https://hub.wiley.com/community/support/dummies.

Wiley publishes in a variety of print and electronic formats and by print-on-demand. Some material included with standard print versions of this book may not be included in e-books or in print-on-demand. If this book refers to media such as a CD or DVD that is not included in the version you purchased, you may download this material at http://booksupport.wiley.com. For more information about Wiley products, visit www.wiley.com.

Library of Congress Control Number: 2018960626

ISBN 978-1-119-54500-2 (pbk); ISBN 978-1-119-54501-9 (ebk); ISBN 978-1-119-54502-6 (ebk)

Manufactured in the United States of America

V10019838_071520

Contents at a Glance

Table of Contents

Introduction

So you want to be a securities industry professional such as a stockbroker? The good news is that a career in the securities field can be extremely lucrative and rewarding. The not-so-good news is that anyone who plans to become a stockbroker and sell securities in any of the 50 states must first pass the Securities Industry Essentials (SIE) exam and one of the top-off exams. Even the SIE exam alone is quite a challenge for most people. To pass the SIE, you have to commit time and effort.

I passed all my securities exams the first time with very high scores, but they all required weeks of study and sacrifice. Those who aren't totally prepared on exam day are in for an unpleasant wake-up call. I always had a few students in every class who had enrolled after they already failed one of their exams. Most of them initially expected the same easy ride that they'd experienced in high school or college. Not only were they wrong, but they also had to pay a significant amount of money to reregister for the exam and wait another 30 days (a mandatory FINRA rule) before they could retake the exam.

Back to the good news again. You're obviously interested in doing well, so you probably won't be one of those people. This book can help you pass the Securities Industry Essentials exam and achieve your goal.

About This Book

This book should be all you need to pass the exam, although I certainly encourage you to view other materials and take whatever exams you can get your hands on.

I cover the topics that appear on the test, offer formulas as needed, provide definitions, and go over the foundational information you need to know. I also include lots of tips and a few memory tricks. But the real benefit of this book is finding out how to study and think through problems as well as you possibly can. That's why I help you choose a study program, explain how to handle specific question types, warn you about common mistakes, connect concepts, and show you how to pull questions apart and get to the bottom of what's being asked. You then get to apply this knowledge in two full-length practice tests so you get a taste of the SIE exam experience.

This is a reference book, and most sections are self-contained. In other words, you can read a section and understand it without looking over the text that comes before it. When some background information is helpful, I give cross-references to related topics. Therefore, you can pretty much jump in and out whenever you find topics you like (and when you find those you don't). And like all good tour guides, I also point you to some other sites of interest — topics you can explore further on your own. If you're short on time (as you probably are) and aren't ready for a break just yet, you can skip the sidebars, those little gray boxes that contain interesting but nonessential information.

Foolish Assumptions

While writing this book, I made a few assumptions about you and why you picked up this book. For starters, I assume that you're looking for a no-nonsense study guide to supplement your textbook or prep course — one that provides a ton of example questions and some sample exams. Look no further! Whether you're preparing to take the test for the first time, retaking the test after a less-than-stellar performance, or looking for a refresher before you recertify, this is the book for you!

Icons Used in This Book

To make this book easier to read and use, I include some icons to help you find and fathom key ideas and information.

 This icon highlights example SIE test questions (which I follow with helpful answer explanations).

 This icon is attached to shortcuts and insider advice for studying for and passing the SIE exam.

 This icon points to information that's especially important to remember in order to do well on the test.

 This icon warns you away from actions that can harm your work and drop your score.

Beyond the Book

In addition to the material in this book you're reading right now, this product also comes with access to some really useful online material. For additional tips and tricks, check out this book's free Cheat Sheet by going to www.dummies.com and typing "*Securities Industry Essentials Exam For Dummies with Online Practice* cheat sheet" in the search box.

You also get access to an online database of practice exams. The two exams in this book are online, and you can also take two additional exams for even more practice.

To gain access to the four online exams, all you have to do is register. Just follow these simple steps:

1. **Register your book or ebook at Dummies.com to get your PIN. Go to www.dummies.com/go/getaccess.**

2. **Select your product from the dropdown list on that page.**

3. **Follow the prompts to validate your product, and then check your email for a confirmation message that includes your PIN and instructions for logging in.**

If you do not receive this email within two hours, please check your spam folder before contacting us through our Technical Support website at `http://support.wiley.com` or by phone at 877-762-2974.

Now you're ready to go! You can come back to the practice material as often as you want — simply log on with the username and password you created during your initial login. No need to enter the access code a second time.

Your registration is good for one year from the day you activate your PIN.

Where to Go from Here

Although you can read this book from start to finish, you can certainly work your way through in more creative ways. Where you start is up to you, though please, please don't start with the tests! Give yourself a good grounding in the content here, and then use the tests to evaluate your understanding and show you where to focus your studies. You can flip to the topics you think you understand fairly well to boost your confidence or skip directly to whatever's giving you trouble — let the index and the table of contents be your guides. If you have a good understanding of how to take the SIE exam, from how it's structured to how to tackle questions, then you can go directly to the chapters in Parts 2 or 3, which address types of securities. If you're feeling shaky on the legal aspects, check out the FINRA rules and regulations in Part 4. Everyone, however, can probably benefit from Part 1's test-taking basics and info on study plans. Wherever you go, feel free to take detours to your textbooks, flash cards, FINRA websites, and any other resources for more information. Just remember to come back so you don't miss anything here!

1 Getting Started with the SIE Exam

Review the computerized exam format and the procedures for registering to take the SIE exam.

Select the right study course and materials to prepare yourself for exam day.

Understand how to organize your study time efficiently and effectively — even when your time is limited.

Examine test-taking tips to maximize your chances of selecting the correct answer choices.

Discover what to expect on test day (because the only surprises that day should involve the triumphant return of your social life).

IN THIS CHAPTER

» Introducing the SIE

» Taking a look at companion tests

» Registering to take the exam

» Uncovering topics tested on the SIE exam

» Mastering the computerized exam format

Chapter **1**

Introducing the SIE (Securities Industry Essentials) Exam

ongratulations on your interest in becoming a financial professional! But before you can lose yourself in the energy of the office, the eager voices of your clients, and the warm glow of success, you have to face the SIE as well as one of the top-off exams such as the Series 7. In this chapter, I give you an overview of the SIE exam, including its purpose, structure, format, scoring, and some helpful tips to guide you through the registration procedure.

What Is the SIE Exam, Anyway?

Initially, the information in the Securities Industry Essentials exam was included in books that covered the Series 6, Series 7, Series 22, and so on. The Financial Industry Regulatory Authority's (FINRA's) idea was to strip the similar information from these exams and create the SIE exam. What I've found is that besides stripping the information from these other exams, unfortunately for you and other exam takers, FINRA added a lot more information. What this means is that you will have to study a lot of information to answer 75 randomized questions.

The SIE exam tests your basic knowledge of the securities industry and is open to anyone age 18 or older. Association with a securities firm is not required — individuals may take the SIE exam prior to or after being hired by a firm. You will need to know certain terminology used in the securities industry, different securities products, how the market is structured, how the market functions, different regulatory agencies and their purposes, as well as regulated and prohibited practices.

Since unsponsored individuals are allowed to take the exam, you can take a step toward becoming a securities professional prior to being hired.

The exam's purpose is to protect the investing public by ensuring that the individuals who sell or give information about securities have mastered the skills and general knowledge that competent practicing representatives need to have.

The SIE exam itself is a computer-based exam given at Prometric (www.prometric.com/finra) test centers throughout the United States. The 75-question exam, administered by the FINRA, is 105 minutes in duration. A score of 70 percent or better gets candidates a passing grade and puts big smiles on their faces.

The sections later in this chapter explain the setup of the SIE Exam and give a rundown of how to register for the exam. If you have other questions, contact the FINRA Support Team at 240-386-4040 or visit www.finra.org/industry/qualification-exams.

Profiling the SIE Exam-Taker

The SIE exam is a co-requisite exam for people who want to become an investment company rep, a general securities rep, a direct participation programs (DPP) rep, a securities trader, an investment banking rep, a private securities offerings rep, a research analyst, or an operations professional.

The purpose of the SIE exam was to strip the information that was similar in all the aforementioned exams to make it easier for individuals to add additional licenses to their resume. So, in order to become a securities professional, you need to pass the SIE exam, one of the exams listed in the next section, and typically the North American Securities Administrators Association (NASAA) Series 63 or 66 exam.

People who have a long and sordid history of embezzlement, forgery, and fraud are generally disqualified and precluded from taking the exam. Candidates must disclose any prior criminal records, and the FINRA reviews each application on a case-by-case basis.

One's Not Enough: Tackling the Co-Requisite Exams

The SIE exam is just your starting point. In order for you to become an industry professional, you will have to take one of the co-requisite exams and in most cases, the Series 63 or Series 66 state exams. As far as which co-requisite exam(s) you'll have to take, that depends on the job you want and/or are hired to do. After you pass the SIE exam, the financial institution that hires you will tell you which exams you need to take and help you schedule them.

REMEMBER

In addition to taking the SIE exam and one of the co-requisite exams listed below, you'll likely have to take either the NASAA Series 63 exam or NASAA Series 66 exam. These exams go into state securities laws as compared to federal securities laws, which are focused on in exams like the SIE. The difference between the Series 63 and Series 66 is that the Series 66 allows holders to become investment advisers also. Your employer will let you know which one they want you to take. More and more broker-dealers want their agents to take the Series 66. Don't worry too much; neither of them are the beasts that some of the other listed exams are.

Series 6: Investment Company and Variable Products Representative Exam

The Series 6 is the license required by most banks and insurance companies. This license allows the holder to sell products such as mutual funds, variable annuities, and variable life insurance (along with having an insurance license). To see the complete outline of what is covered, go to www.finra.org/sites/default/files/Series_6_Content_Outline.pdf.

Series 7: General Securities Representative Exam

The Series 7 is the license exam that most people will be taking. This is the license required by most broker-dealers. The Series 7 allows you to sell equity securities, mutual funds, bonds, direct participation programs, options, and so on. To see the complete outline of what is covered, go to www.finra.org/sites/default/files/Series_7_Content_Outline.pdf.

Series 22: DPP Representative Exam

If you're planning on focusing your career on selling direct participation programs (DPPs), the Series 22 is the one for you. This license allows you to solicit and sell limited partnership interest in DPPs like real estate programs, oil and gas programs, equipment leasing programs, and so on. To see the complete outline of what is covered, go to www.finra.org/sites/default/files/Series_22_Content_Outline.pdf.

Series 57: Securities Trader Exam

The Series 57 license allows holders to execute trades in securities. Typically a Series 57 licensed individual works in the trading department executing trades for persons or firms. To see the complete outline of what is covered, go to www.finra.org/sites/default/files/Series_57_Content_Outline.pdf.

Series 79: Investment Banking Representative Exam

The Series 79 Investment Banking Representative exam allows holders to work in the investment banking realm. As such, the holders' functions would include advising or facilitating equity or debt securities offerings through public offerings, private placements, and mergers and acquisitions. To see the complete outline of what is covered, go to www.finra.org/sites/default/files/Series_79_Content_Outline.pdf.

Series 82: Private Securities Offerings Representative Exam

If you're planning on selling securities privately as compared to publicly, the Series 82 is the exam you'll need to pass. The Series 82 tests you on the knowledge needed to perform functions of a private securities offerings rep, including the solicitation and sale of Regulation D private placement securities as part of a primary offering. To see the complete outline of what is covered, go to www.finra.org/sites/default/files/Series_82_Content_Outline.pdf.

Series 7 + Series 86 + Series 87: Research Analyst Exam

If you love taking exams, this is the one for you. You not only have to pass the SIE exam but also the Series 7, Series 86, Series 87, and either the Series 63 or Series 66 — yikes! However, if you want to be a research analyst, this is the route you'll need to go. A research analyst is required to prepare written and/or electronic communications that show an analysis of company securities and industry sectors. To see the complete outline of what is covered, go to www.finra.org/sites/default/files/Series_7_Content_Outline.pdfand www.finra.org/sites/default/files/Series_86-87_Content_Outline.pdf.

Series 99: Operations Professional Exam

Persons who have a Series 99 license have proved that they have the knowledge needed to perform the critical functions of an operations professional. As such, their functions include client on-boarding (welcoming new clients, addressing client concerns, making sure clients understand services available to them, and so on), receipt and delivery of securities and funds, account transfers, reinvestment and disbursement of funds, and so on. To see the complete outline of what is covered, go to www.finra.org/sites/default/files/Series_99_Content_Outline.pdf.

Signing Up

One of the things I really like about the SIE exam is that you don't need to be sponsored in order to take the exam (most of the other securities exams require sponsorship by a firm, bank, insurance company, and so on). This allows you to get a leg up on the competition and also shows your future employer that you're not fooling around.

Filling out an application to enroll

Although the enrollment process to take the SIE exam has not been hashed out at the time of this writing, by the time this exam goes live, you'll be able to find information and a link to the application at www.finra.org/industry/enroll-series-exam. You can also contact the test center at www.prometric.com/en-us/contact-us/Pages/default.aspx.

It's a date! Scheduling your exam

After you file your application and receive your enrollment notification, you can schedule an appointment to take the exam by contacting the Prometric Testing Center. Locate the test center nearest you by either calling the Prometric center (800-578-6273) during business hours or visiting www.prometric.com/FINRAto schedule online.

Like other securities exam enrollment, your SIE exam enrollment is valid for 120 days — you have to take the exam within this time frame. When scheduling your exam appointment, be ready to provide the exam administrators with

>> Your name and Social Security number

>> The name of the securities exam you're registering to take

>> Your desired test date

Getting an appointment usually takes about one to two weeks, depending on the time of year (you may wait longer in the summer than around Christmastime). Prometric will confirm your appointment on the phone or via email.

I suggest putting pressure on yourself and scheduling the exam a little sooner than you think you may be ready to take it; you can always move the test date back (there will be a charge if you cancel within ten business days of your test date). You know yourself best, but I think most students study better when they have a target test date.

You have a choice of locations to take the exam. If you're a travelin' man (or woman), you may want to schedule your exam at a location far away (maybe even in a different state) to get the test date that you want.

After you have your test date set, you may find that you're ready sooner or will be ready later than your scheduled appointment. The exam center administrators are usually pretty accommodating about changing appointments and/or locations as long as you call before noon at least two business days before your test date, but there may be a fee involved.

You can get an extension from the 120-day enrollment only if you call within ten days of your enrollment expiration and if no earlier test dates are available.

Planning ahead for special accommodations

If you require special accommodations when taking your securities exam, you can't schedule your exam online. You have to contact the FINRA Special Conditions Team at 800-999-6647 or fill out the special-accommodations form at www.finra.org/sites/default/files/SA-Eligibility-Questionairre.pdf. Read on for info on what the test administrators can do if you have a disability or if English isn't your first language.

Depending on your testing center, you may have to receive authorization to bring medical devices and supplies — such as insulin pumps, eyedrops, and inhalers — into the testing room. If you need authorization, call your local Prometric testing center, and a staff member will be able to guide you on the approval process.

Americans with Disabilities Act (ADA) candidates

If you're disabled or learning impaired, the FINRA provides testing modifications and aids in compliance with the provisions of the Americans with Disabilities Act (ADA). To qualify for ADA provisions, your disabilities have to permanently limit a major life activity, such as learning, speech, hearing, or vision.

TEST CENTER AMENITIES

The test centers are required to comply with FINRA site guidelines; however, some of the older centers may not have the amenities that the newer ones do (such as lockers and earplugs). To protect yourself from a whole variety of unpleasant, unexpected site surprises on exam day, the FINRA website (www.finra.org) offers general information, including test center security guidelines (including candidate ID requirements, personal items allowed, and provided aids), test center rules of conduct, and so on. For more site-specific questions, like whether a cafeteria, vending machines, or lockers are on site, ask the center's administrator when you schedule your test date.

To apply for special accommodations, you need to submit documentation from your physician or licensed healthcare professional to the FINRA, requesting the special arrangements. Additionally, you have to submit the FINRA Special Accommodations Eligibility Questionnaire and Special Accommodations Verification Request Form for all special arrangement requests (you can find links to the forms at www.finra.org/industry/special-accommodations).

You may request the accommodations you want approved; possible aids include

» Extra time

» A written exam (pencil and paper)

» A reader, writer, or recorder

» A sign language interpreter

» A large-print exam booklet

» Wheelchair-accessible locations

The FINRA reserves the right to make all final decisions about accommodations on a case-by-case basis.

English as a second language (ESL) candidates

If English is your second language, you can request additional time to take the exam when you schedule your SIE test date. If the FINRA approves, you receive a little extra time to complete the exam. In general, FINRA gives an extra 30 minutes for exams less than two hours and an extra hour for exams over two hours.

To qualify for extra time due to English being your second language (LEP — Limited English Proficiency), fill out the form at www.finra.org/sites/default/files/LEP-request-form.pdf.

Just in case: Cancelling as an option

If something comes up or if you feel you're just not ready, you can cancel your appointment to take the SIE exam without penalty if you do so at least ten business days before the exam date. If a holiday falls within the cancellation period, you have to cancel an additional business day earlier. For example, if you're scheduled to take the exam on a Wednesday, you have to cancel on Tuesday two weeks before your exam date. If a holiday falls between those dates, you have to cancel on Monday two weeks before your exam date. For more information, visit www.finra.org/industry/reschedule-or-cancel-your-appointment.

WARNING

If you cancel after the proscribed deadline, if you don't show up to take the exam, or if you show up too late to take the exam, you will be charged a cancellation fee equal to the cost of the exam fee paid. Don't try the old "I forgot" excuse, because not only is it ineffective, but I'm somewhat sure that it's illegal in all 50 states, Canada, and the U.S. territories.

Taking a Peek at the Tested Topics

As a practical exam, the SIE requires you to master vocabulary, handle customer accounts, understand the rules and regulations that govern the securities industry, and yes, work with some math formulas (although very few). For ease of use (and because humans have a limited life span), this book focuses on the information needed to pass the SIE exam. Here's an overview of what to expect:

- » The underwriting process (how new securities come to market) (Chapter 5)
- » Common and preferred stock (Chapter 6)
- » Corporate bonds and U.S. government securities (Chapter 7)
- » Securities issued by local governments (municipal bonds) (Chapter 8)
- » Investment companies (including mutual and closed-end funds) (Chapter 9)
- » Direct participation programs (limited partnerships) (Chapter 10)
- » Options (Chapter 11)
- » Customer accounts (Chapter 12)
- » Analyzing the benefits and risks associated with investments; making appropriate recommendations to customers (Chapter 13)
- » Following how new securities are brought to the market and how existing securities are traded in the market (Chapter 14)
- » Risk considerations and income-tax implications that stock market investors face (Chapter 15)
- » Rules and regulations governing the purchase and sale of securities and the registered representative's responsibility for maintaining accurate recordkeeping (Chapter 16)

The FINRA has released a listing of the distribution of questions on the SIE exam. See Table 1-1 for the number of questions devoted to each topic as it applies to a registered rep's performance.

TABLE 1-1 | **Distribution of SIE Exam Questions**

Topic	Number of Questions	Percent of Exam
Knowledge of capital markets	12	16%
Understanding products and their risks	33	44%
Understanding trading, customer accounts, and prohibited activities	23	31%
Overview of regulatory framework	7	9%
Total	**75**	**100%**

Each of these topics falls under multiple areas of study. For example, to correctly answer questions that address the topic of handling customer accounts, you have to know enough about different types of stocks, bonds, and so on to be able to guide your customers, including which investments are more beneficial to retirees and which work better for investors who are just entering the workforce.

Although Table 1-1 shows the outline of the exam, I (and most other study material providers) break the chapters down by similar content to keep you from having to jump back and forth through your study material.

Understanding the Exam Format and Other Exam Details

To make sure you don't walk into the testing center, take one look at the computer screen, go into shock, and start drooling on the keyboard, I use the next few sections to cover some of the testing details for the SIE exam.

Reviewing the exam basics

The SIE exam is a computerized, closed book (in other words, no book), one-hour and 45-minute exam. The exam consists of 85 multiple-choice questions (although only 75 of them count toward your score — see the next section).

TIP

You can take bathroom breaks at any time, but the clock continues to tick away, so you may want to reconsider drinking a mega-jumbo iced latte in the morning before you arrive at the exam center.

For information on the types of questions to expect, see Chapter 3. Flip to Chapter 4 for an overview of how your exam day may progress.

Practicing on ten additional trial questions

To ensure that new questions to be introduced in future exams meet acceptable standards prior to inclusion, you answer 10 additional, unidentified questions that don't count toward your score. In other words, you get 85 questions to answer, but only 75 are scored.

Note: If you see a question on the SIE that doesn't seem even remotely similar to anything that you've studied (or even heard about), it may very likely be an experimental question.

Mastering the computerized format and features

Although you don't need any previous computer experience to do well on the exam, you don't want your first encounter with a computerized exam to be on the date of the SIE exam. Being familiar with the way the questions and answer choices will appear on the screen is essential. Figure 1-1 can help you prepare for exam day.

A friendly exam-center employee will give you an introductory lesson to familiarize you with how to operate the computer before the exam session begins. Although the computer randomly selects the specific questions from each category, the operating system tracks the difficulty of each question and controls the selection criteria to ensure that your exam isn't ridiculously easier or harder than anyone else's.

The following list describes some important computer exam features:

>> Scroll bars for moving the questions on the screen

>> A clock to help you track how much time you have left during each part (if the clock is driving you batty, you can hide it with a click of the mouse)

FIGURE 1-1:
The PROCTOR computer system lets you select answers and mark them for review.

2006 National Association of Securities Dealers, Inc. Reprinted with permission from NASD (now known as FINRA).

>> A confirmation box that requires you to approve your answer choice before the computer proceeds to the next question

>> An indication of which question you're currently on

>> A choice of answering the questions by

   • Typing in the letter for the correct answer on the keyboard

   • Using the mouse to point and click on the correct answer

   • At some test centers, using a computer with a touch screen that lets you select the answer by pressing lightly against the monitor with your fingertip

>> The capability of changing your answers or marking questions that you're unsure of for later review, which allows you to go back and answer them at any time during that particular part

REMEMBER

You can mark answers for review or change responses only for the part of the test you're currently taking. In other words, after you begin the second part, you can't go back and change answers from the first part.

TIP

Although you can review and change all your answers at the end of your test, don't. Your brain is going to feel like it went through a blender by the time you get there. Review only your *marked* questions and change the answers only if you're 100 percent sure that you made a mistake. As an instructor, I know that people change a right answer to a wrong one five times more often than they change a wrong one to a right one.

Instant gratification: Receiving and evaluating your score

Remember having to wait weeks for a standardized test score, hovering somewhere between eagerness and dread? Those days are gone. At the end of the SIE exam, the system calculates your score and displays a grade result on the computer screen. Although the wait for your grade to pop up may feel like an eternity, it really takes only a few seconds to see your grade. When you sign out, the test center administrator will tackle you (well, approach you) and give you a printed exam report with your grade and the diagnostic score results with your performance in the specific topics tested on your exam.

Each question on the SIE exam is worth an average of 1⅓ points (some are worth more and some are worth less depending on the FINRA's feeling of how difficult a question is), and candidates need a score of 70 or better to achieve a passing grade. This percentage translates to 53 questions out of 75 that you have to answer correctly. The scores are rounded down, so a grade of 69.33 is scored as 69 on the SIE. When I took the Series 7 exam, back when the passing grade was 70, one of the other students from my class got a 69.6 (which was rounded down to a 69), and he had the NASD (now called the FINRA) review his exam to try and get him the extra point. Needless to say, FINRA ruled against him and he had to take the exam again.

You passed! Now what?

After you pass the SIE, Series 7, Series 63, and/or Series 66 exam, the FINRA will provide confirmation that you passed. At that point, you can now find a broker-dealer, bank, insurance company, or the like who wants you. Once you're hired, your employer will let you know which other exams you have to take and schedule them accordingly.

A LITTLE TESTING INFO FROM THE FINRA

The FINRA website (www.finra.org) is certainly worth checking out. It contains all the nitty-gritty details about the SIE and related exams. Use this website for the following:

- **FINRA Current Uniform Registration Forms for Electronic Filing in WEB CRD:** This page includes the registration forms and a link to the Uniform Forms Reference Guide, with contact numbers and other explanatory information for filers.

- **FINRA Test Center Rules of Conduct:** Just in case you're unable to distinguish the test center from that third-period algebra class you had back in high school, the FINRA gives you the rules and regulations for taking the SIE (do not hide a list of equations under the brim of your baseball cap, do not roam the halls during your restroom break, and do not pass notes, no matter how bored you are).

- **FINRA Registration and Exam Requirements:** This section gives a comprehensive list of the categories of securities representatives and the exam requirements.

- **FINRA Appointments and Enrollment:** Here you find FINRA tips for scheduling appointments to take securities exams, info about obtaining extensions, and the exam cancellation policy.

- **FINRA Registration Exam Fee Schedule:** Check out this page to see the fees for registering for different securities exams.

To continue working in the securities field, you'll need to fulfill the FINRA's continuing education requirements. Within 120 days after your second anniversary, and every three years thereafter, you have to take a computer-based exam covering regulatory elements such as compliance, regulatory, ethical, and sales practice standards at the Prometric exam center. In addition, there is a requirement (called a brokerage firm element) that requires broker-dealers to keep their registered representatives updated on job and product-related topics.

So you need a do-over: Retaking the exam

Sorry to end this chapter on a negative note, but the SIE is a relatively difficult exam, and certainly some people need a do-over.

If you fail the SIE, you'll have to request a new test date and pay to retake the test. You should reapply immediately, though you have to schedule the new test date for at least 30 days after the day you failed (that's 30 days of prime studying time!). If you fail the exam three times, you're required to wait six months before you can retake the exam.

Use the time between exams to understand what went wrong and fix it. Here are some of the reasons people fail their securities exams and some of the steps you can take to be successful:

>> **Lack of preparation:** You have to follow, and stick to, a well-constructed plan of study. You have your diagnostic printout after you take the exam, and you can use that to focus on the areas of study where you fell short.

Prep courses can help you identify and focus on the most commonly tested topics and provide valuable tips for mastering difficult math problems. Also consider tutoring sessions tailored to accommodate your busy schedule and pinpoint the areas of study where you need the most help.

>> **Nerves won out:** Some people are just very nervous test takers, and they need to go through the process to get comfortable in unfamiliar situations. Next time around, they know what to expect and pass with flying colors.

The people who are the most nervous about taking the exam tend to be the ones who haven't prepared properly. Make sure that you're passing practice exams on a consistent basis with grades in at least the high 70s before you attempt to take the real exam.

>> **Insufficient practice exams:** You need to take enough practice exams before you take the real test. I think getting used to the question formats and figuring out how to work through them is as important as learning the material to begin with.

Check out Chapter 2 for info on setting up a study schedule and making the most of your practice exams.

Chapter **2**

Preparing for the SIE Exam

When you're preparing for the SIE exam, a good cup of java and an all-nighter just aren't gonna cut it. Neither will a frantic two-week study session like the ones that used to work miracles when you were taking college finals. The SIE is not to be taken lightly, so you need to train for it both mentally and physically.

In this chapter, I discuss your options for studying to take the SIE exam. If you plan to enroll in an SIE exam prep course, I cover what to look for when selecting a course. I also help you organize your study time efficiently and effectively — even when your preparation time is limited.

Courses and Training Materials: Determining the Best Way to Study

When deciding how to go about studying for the SIE exam, your first mission is to identify the training mode that best suits your needs. If you're likely to benefit from a structured environment, you may be better off in a classroom setting. A prep course can also give you emotional guidance and support from your instructors and others in your class who are forging through this stressful ordeal with you. On the other hand, if you're the type of person who can initiate and follow a committed study schedule on your own every day, you may be able to pass the SIE exam without a prep course, and you can save the money you would have spent for classes. The following sections help you evaluate these options in more detail.

Back to school: Attending a prep course

People who learn best by listening to an instructor and interacting with other students benefit from attending prep courses. Unfortunately, not all SIE exam prep courses and training materials are created equally. Unlike high-school or college courses, the content of SIE prep courses and the qualifications of the instructors who teach them aren't regulated by your state's Department of Education, the Securities and Exchange Commission (SEC), the Financial Industry Regulatory

Authority (FINRA), or any other government agency. Do some research to locate the SIE training course that works best for you.

The following sections explain some things to consider and questions to ask before enrolling. Take a look at the info you gather and trust your gut. Is the primary function of the prep course to train students to be successful on the SIE exam, as it should be? Or do you suspect it's the brain-child of a broker-dealer who's looking for extra revenue to supplement her failing stockbroker business? (Run away!)

Training school background

To find information about a program you're considering, browse the training school's website or contact the school's offices. Find out how many years the training school has been in business and check with the Better Business Bureau or the Department of Consumer Affairs to see whether anyone has filed any complaints. Look for a school that has stayed in business at least five years. This staying power is generally a sign that the school is getting referral business from students who took the course and passed their securities exams such as the SIE, Series 7, Series 6, and so on.

Try to get recommendations from others who took the course. Word of mouth is an essential source of referrals for most businesses, and stockbroker training schools are no different. The stockbroker firm or financial institution you're affiliated with (or will be affiliated with) should be able to recommend training schools.

Courses offered through a local high school's continuing education program can be just as effective as those offered through an accredited university or a company that focuses solely on test prep, as long as the right instructors are teaching them. Read on.

Qualifications of the course instructor(s)

The instructor's qualifications and teaching style are even more important than the history of the company running the course (see the preceding section). An instructor should be not only knowledgeable but also energetic and entertaining enough to keep you awake during the not-so-exciting (all right, *boring*) parts.

When looking for a course, find out whether the teacher has taken — and passed — various securities exams. If so, the instructor probably knows the kinds of questions you'll be asked and can help you focus on the relevant exam material. The instructor is also likely to have developed good test-taking skills that she can share with her students.

Whether the instructor is a part-timer or full-timer may be important. For example, a full-time instructor who teaches 30 classes a year probably has a better grasp on the material than a part-time instructor who teaches four classes a year. By the same token, an instructor who owns the school that offers the course probably has greater interest in the success of the students than someone who's paid to teach the class by the hour. Use your best judgment.

Before you register, ask whether you can monitor a securities class for an hour or so with the instructor who would be training you. If the company says no, I suggest finding another course because that course provider may have something to hide. While you're at it, make sure the classroom is comfortable, clean, and conducive to learning.

Texts, course content, and extra help

To really benefit from a course, you need good resources — in terms of not only the actual training material but also the people in the classroom. These elements affect how the class shapes up and what you actually learn:

>> **Training material:** Will you have a textbook to study from or just some handouts? The instructor should provide you with textbooks that include sample exams, and a prep course should be loaded with in-class questions for you to work on. The course should also provide you with chapter exams that you can work on at night before the next session (yes, homework is a good thing). Remember, the more questions you see and answer, the better.

>> **In-class practice tests:** You want a prep course that includes test sessions where the instructor grades your exams, identifies incorrect answers, and reviews the correct answers.

>> **Instructor availability:** Ask whether the course instructors will be available to answer your questions after the class is over — not only at the end of the day but also during the weeks after you've completed the course and are preparing for the SIE exam.

The practical details

The perfect course can't do you any good if you never show up for class. Here are some issues to consider about the course offering:

>> **Days and times:** Make sure the class fits your schedule. If getting there on time is too stressful or you can't attend often enough to justify the expense, you won't benefit from registering to take the course.

>> **Class size:** If more than 30 to 35 people are in the class, the instructor may not be able to give you the individual attention you need.

>> **Cost:** Obviously, cost is a major concern, but it definitely shouldn't be your only consideration. Choosing a course because it's the least expensive one you can find may be a costly mistake if the course doesn't properly prepare you. You end up wasting your time and spending more money to retake the exam. You can expect to pay anywhere from $150 to $400 for a standard SIE prep course, including training materials (textbooks and final exams).

Quite a few people don't pass the first time around, so find out whether the school charges a fee for retaking the prep course. You may even decide to take the prep course again if you feel that you're not quite ready to take the test.

Selecting prep material to study on your own

If you're the type of person who can follow a committed study schedule on your own every day, you may be able to pass the SIE exam without a prep course. Many different types of study aids are available to help you prepare.

REMEMBER

No matter what your learning style is, I'm a firm believer in using a textbook as a primary training aid. You can use online courses, online testing programs, CDs, apps, and flash cards as supplements to your textbook, but give your textbook the starring role. By virtue of its portability and ease of use (you don't have to turn it on, plug it in, or have access to the Internet, and it can never, ever run out of batteries), the textbook is simply the most efficient and effective choice.

TAKING A COURSE ONLINE

Remember that not all classes take place in brick-and-mortar buildings. For people who want to take a course but have scheduling constraints or lack a vehicle for commuting, instructor-led virtual classrooms may be an option. Students interact through online chats, email, message boards, and/or phone conferences. Classes may be scheduled at specific times, or you may work on your own time at your own pace. Before purchasing an online course, find out whether you can monitor one for an hour or so to see whether it meets your needs.

Note: Some so-called "online courses" may consist solely of a packet of study materials without any outside instruction. Make sure the course you sign up for has the features you want.

My personal favorite is the Empire Stockbroker Training Institute's *SIE Course Textbook* (`http://www.empirestockbroker.com`). The textbook focuses on the relevant exam topics, is easy to read and understand, and includes plenty of practice questions and detailed explanations. Securities Training Corporation (`http://www.stcusa.com`) and Kaplan Financial (`http://www.kaplanfinancial.com`) also publish quality SIE books. A lot of the better SIE course textbooks are available online rather than in book stores. In addition to *Securities Industries Essential Exam For Dummies* and a textbook, consider investing in one or more of the following popular study aids:

>> **Online testing:** I'm all for online testing. Certainly, the more exams you take, the better. If the practice exam simulates the real test, it's even more valuable. With this study aid, you have access 24 hours a day, 7 days a week, and can pace yourself to take the exams at your leisure. Select a program (for example, `www.empirestockbroker.com` always has the most current, updated simulated exams) with several hundreds of questions or more, along with answers and explanations.

>> **Audio CDs:** You may be able to find audio CDs to help you prepare for the SIE exam, although audio CDs are becoming rarer. This form of training can be beneficial as a review for people who already have a decent understanding of the course material. You can listen to taped material while on the go or in your home.

TIP

Personally, I think recording your own notes — especially on topics you're having trouble with — is a better use of your time. Putting the info in your own words, saying ideas out loud, and listening to the recordings can really help reinforce the concepts.

>> **Flash cards:** For those who already have a grasp on the subject matter, flash cards are good because you can tuck 'em in your pocket and look at 'em anytime you want. Commercial cards may be confusing and long-winded. You're better off making cards that focus on the areas that are most problematic for you.

Managing Your Study Time Wisely

Unless you're a direct descendent of Albert Einstein, you probably need to allow yourself as much time as possible to prepare for the SIE. Even though the SIE exam is only 75 questions, the amount of material you have to study to be prepared to answer those 75 questions out of their universe of questions is quite extensive.

Get your affairs in order. Go to the dentist and get that sore tooth filled, pay your bills, get your flu shot, visit your friends and relatives, finish any critical home improvement projects — basically, clear the decks as best you can so you can concentrate on your studies. The following sections can help you establish a study plan.

22 PART 1 **Getting Started with the SIE Exam**

Blocking out some time to study

You have to use your time efficiently, and to accomplish this, you need to grab every spare moment and channel it into study time. If you're attending an SIE prep course, your instructors should help you (and your classmates) set up a study schedule for before, during, and after you complete the course.

If you're in charge of carving out your study time, then plan your study regime as if it were a full-time, 40-hour-per-week job and allot approximately 100–150 hours over a two- to four-week period for studying. If you don't have a job (other than studying), I suggest that you put in at least 5 or 6 hours a day. (For advice on how to study well, please look at "Exploring Study Strategies"; the following section discusses setting up an actual schedule.)

Especially for those of you who continue to work at your full-time job, now may be the time to have a heart-to-heart with your boss to negotiate some extra study time. After all, you need to work this out only for the next few weeks. Can you take vacation time? Will your boss allow you flex time (where you agree to work two hours later each day for four days and have the fifth day off)? Can you arrange a quiet place at work to study during breaks and lunch time?

TIP

Set aside a consistent time to study on a daily basis. If possible, schedule your study time around your internal clock. For example, if you're the type who needs a brass band to wake you up and get your mind functioning first thing in the morning but you're wide awake and ready to go at midnight, you may be better off with a study schedule that begins later in the day and lasts into the night. By contrast, if you're leaping out of bed like a jack-in-the-box at the crack of dawn but are dead on your feet by 10 p.m., a morning study schedule would be more favorable.

TIP

You never know when extra time to study will present itself, so carry your textbooks or some flash cards with you whenever you leave home. You can read or drill yourself whenever you find some spare time — on the train, waiting in line, and yes, even during your trips to the restroom.

It's a plan: Getting into a study routine

Establishing and sticking to a study routine is essential. Many people find the SIE exam to be difficult because they have to absorb so much material in a relatively short time span. Furthermore, most of the information on the test is easy to forget because it's not info you use every day. Therefore, you have to reinforce your knowledge on a daily basis by constantly reviewing and revisiting the old information while learning new material. You'll continue to follow this routine over and over and over again.

Organizing yourself to cover all the topics you'll be tested on is crucial. If you're taking a prep course or home study course, a huge benefit is that during the course, the time necessary to learn and review all the subject matter will be allotted for you.

TIP

If you're trying to study on your own, get yourself a course textbook and divide the pages by the number of days you have available for studying. Be sure to allow yourself an extra week or two for practice exams. Review each chapter and complete each chapter exam until you have a firm grasp on a majority of the information. Take notes, highlight, and review the material you're having problems with until you feel comfortable with the concepts. Initially, you'll spend a majority of your time on new material; after that, you'll spend your time reviewing and taking chapter quizzes.

During the last week or so leading up to the exam, take as many practice exams as possible. Remember to review each exam thoroughly before moving onto the next one. For more helpful tips, check out the section "Exploring Study Strategies" later in this chapter.

When you're first learning new material, set yourself up in a place where you have as few distractions as possible — the local library, a separate room, even the bathtub. One of my students used to retreat to his car in the driveway after dinner while his wife put their young kids to bed.

The exam room, with its small cubicles, places you in proximity with other people who are taking the exam at the same time. If clicks of the mouse, taps on the keyboard, the scratch of pencil on paper, and the frustrated sighs of less-prepared test takers are likely to distract you, you may want to use earplugs, which are available at most exam centers. If, however, you don't want to use earplugs, you can prepare for the worst by subjecting yourself to a somewhat noisy study environment somewhere along the line. (When I was taking one of my securities exams before earplugs were permitted, construction crews were working in the next room. Luckily, I'd studied in noisy settings; otherwise, the sound of screw guns and workmen talking would have driven me to distraction!) Go to a coffee shop (or any populated establishment) during lunch hour, or turn on a fan or a radio to familiarize yourself with background noise while you're taking your practice exams.

Give it a rest: Taking short breaks

If you find yourself reading the same words over and over and wondering what the heck you just read, it's probably time to take a break. Taking short (five- to ten-minute) breaks can help you process and absorb information without confusing new ideas with the old.

When you reach your saturation point and really start zoning out, you can practice a bit of productive procrastination — walk the dog, shower, do some sit-ups and/or push-ups, grab a meal or a snack, or do anything else that lets you move around or take care of the little things that have to get done. A little human contact can go a long way too, provided you have the discipline to hit the books again.

Sometimes, taking a break from one study method can be as good as taking a break from studying altogether. Use multiple types of study material (textbooks, class notes, flash cards, and so on). If, for example, you get sick of looking at a textbook, try reviewing your notes, flipping through or creating some flash cards, or taking some online practice exams.

Staying focused from day to day

Passing the SIE exam is a rite of passage. It's your ticket to wealth, fame, and fortune (or at least a decent job). If you put the time and effort into studying for the SIE, you'll be rewarded. If not, you'll have to relive the nightmare over and over again until you reach your objective. To reap your reward as quickly as possible, make a resolution: Until you pass the SIE, commit to limiting your social life and devoting most of your waking hours to one purpose — studying for the exam. Repeat after me: "This is my life for now."

If you find that you really need to take a mental health day off at some point, make sure that you don't separate yourself from your textbooks for more than one day — jump right back into the SIE fire the next day.

WARNING

Under no circumstances (except in the case of a family emergency) should you stop studying for more than one day within a two-week period. I've had students who were doing quite well come back to take another prep class because their test dates were too far off and they'd put the books down for a while. The next thing they knew, they'd forgotten half of what they'd learned. Fortunately, the information comes back faster the second time around.

TIP

To keep focused on your studies without permanently forgetting about otherwise important life activities, prepare a file folder labeled "To do after I pass the SIE." If anything comes up while you're studying, instead of interrupting your study time or stressing about things that need to be done, write down the task or event on a piece of paper, place it in your to-do file, and put it out of your mind.

Devoting time to practice tests

Certainly, when you're first going over new material, you should spend most of your time learning the information and taking chapter quizzes. After you feel like you have a good handle on the material, you should start taking full practice exams to see where you stand. (This book includes some questions throughout Parts 2–4, followed by two 75-question practice exams with answers and explanations in Part 5.) The last week or two before the exam should be almost entirely devoted to taking practice exams and reviewing them.

After you move into the practice-test phase, continue to use your textbook not only to reference material you don't understand, but also to ensure you don't forget what you've learned. Too many people rely solely on the tests and forget to read their textbook now and then. Figure on rereading one to two chapters per day. After taking a practice exam, always completely review it before you move on to the next one. And don't listen to the people who say you have to take three or four practice exams a day; you're better off taking one exam per day and spending twice as long reviewing it as you spent taking it. This method helps ensure that you know the subject matter and that you won't make the same mistakes twice.

Practice exams can help you gauge whether you're ready for the real SIE. See "Knowing When You're Ready" at the end of this chapter for details.

TIP

If you run out of exams to take, it's better to purchase more or see whether someone else in your firm has a different book with tests you can borrow than to take the same exams over and over again.

Avoiding study groups

Unless your study group includes your instructor, I recommend that you avoid a study group like the plague. The problem with study groups is that everyone wants to study the information that she's having problems with, and chances are not everyone is struggling with the same thing. And if everyone *is* having the same problem, who can help you? I strongly feel that your time is better spent studying on your own.

TIP

If you really feel you'd benefit from studying with someone else, try to arrange a tutoring session with an SIE instructor.

Staying in shape

Ignoring the importance of physical fitness when you prepare to take the SIE exam is a big mistake. The exam itself (and the prep time you put into your study schedule) is not only mentally exhausting but physically demanding as well. You have to be able to stay alert and concentrate on difficult questions for an hour and 45 minutes. In the weeks leading up to the test, any exercise you can do to keep yourself physically fit — including cardiovascular exercise such as jogging or bike riding — can help out. A workout also gives you a great reason to take a study break.

Exploring Study Strategies

TIP

The more ways you work with a piece of information, the better able you'll be to recall it. Here are some study strategies to supplement your routine of reading your textbook and taking practice exams:

>> **Aim to understand concepts and relationships, not just formulas and definitions.** Having a good grasp of how ideas are related can provide a safety net for when rote memory fails; you may be able to make educated guesses, re-create formulas, or come up with something to jog your memory. When you see an equation, try to figure out where the numbers come from and what the formula really tells you.

>> **Create an outline of your notes or write flash cards.** Using your own words, try to put the more difficult areas of study into an outline or on flash cards. The whole process of condensing large mountains of information into your own abbreviated outline helps you process and absorb difficult concepts.

>> **Mark up your textbook.** You don't have to return your textbook to the library, so use the margins to rephrase ideas, draw diagrams, repeat formulas or equations, and highlight unfamiliar words.

>> **Tape yourself reading your notes and then play back the tape at night while you're falling sleep or when you're driving.** Although the play-it-at-night technique has been known to give some people nightmares, this temporary condition usually clears up after the exam. I've also heard some people proclaim the nighttime playback is "as soothing as Sominex." (If it prevents you from falling asleep, turn off the tape and opt for getting some rest.)

   Note: While you're sleeping, the brain may process ideas you learned during your waking hours; however, you generally have to be paying attention to remember something new. The main benefit comes from making the initial recording and letting study material be the last thing you hear before you fall asleep.

>> **Use sticky notes to flag difficult topics or concepts.** As you study, put a sticky note on a section or page in the book where you need more work. After you've filled your book(s) with stickies, concentrate your study on those difficult areas (where the stickies are). After you feel that you have a good grasp on this information, remove the note from the book. As you learn more and more, you'll whittle down the number of pages with stickies until you've removed them all from the textbook.

Developing Solid Test-Taking Skills

To be successful on the SIE exam, developing your test-taking skills is just as important as mastering the concepts that form the basis of the questions. The best way to develop test-taking skills is to take practice tests, such as the ones in this book. Following are some tips that can also help you polish your skills.

Read the question carefully

Don't be fooled. Exam creators love to trip you up by making you jump ahead and answer the question — incorrectly — before you read the entire problem. Often one of the last words in the call (specific inquiry) of the question is worded in the negative, like "all of the following are true *except*," or "which of the following is the *least* likely to," and so on. When reviewing the answers to a practice test, these questions cause some students to groan or slap themselves in the head when they realize their mistake. Don't worry — this common reaction usually goes away after you start getting better at taking exams.

Look for phrases that lead to the topic tested

Try to identify the specific category that the question is testing you on. If you study for the number of hours that I recommend (see "Blocking out some time to study"), you'll most likely cover the material the question references at some point, and you'll be able to identify the topic that the question applies to. After you know the topic, your brain can retrieve the information you need from its mental file cabinet, making it easier for you to focus on the applicable rule, equation, or concept so you can answer the question correctly.

Work with what you have

If possible, work with the facts — and only the facts — in the question. Too often, students add their own interpretation to the question and turn a straightforward problem into a mess. Use the facts that are given, dump the garbage information that isn't necessary to answer the question, and don't make the question more difficult or assume that there's more to the question than what appears.

Adding irrelevant information into a question seems to be a very common practice for students (for example, they ask, "Yeah, but what if she were married?"). My standard answer is, "Did it say that in the question?" to which the response is *no*. Don't make your life more difficult by adding your own speculations into the question; just answer the question that's given to you.

Don't obsess; mark for review

If you experience brain freeze while taking the exam, don't panic or waste valuable time on one question. Eliminate any answer(s) you know must be wrong (if any), take your best guess, and *mark the question for review* so you can easily return to it later. The question may even resolve itself. For example, another question may trigger your memory as you continue to take the exam, and the correct answer to the earlier question may become clear.

Keep track of time

Time yourself so you're always aware of how much time you have left to complete the exam. One way to do so is to figure out which question you need to be up to at the end of each 15 minutes; use that as a benchmark to keep track of your progress. You have one hour and 45 minutes to complete the exam. You have to answer 85 questions (10 don't count toward your score). This gives you roughly 1.23 minutes (or 1 minute and 13.8 seconds) to answer each question.

Translating these numbers to half-hour benchmarks gets you the results shown in the following table.

Time	Number of Questions Completed
15 minutes	12
30 minutes	24
45 minutes	36
1 hour	48
1 hour and 15 minutes	61
1 hour and 30 minutes	73
1 hour and 45 minutes	85

TIP

Memorize these benchmarks, write them on your scrap paper (or dry erase board) as soon as the exam administrators allow you to begin, and keep referring to your watch or the clock on the computer screen to track your progress in relation to the benchmark. If you find yourself falling behind, pick up your pace. If you're really falling behind, mark the lengthier, more difficult questions for review and spend your time answering the easier questions. Why waste two minutes on one long question for 1⅓ points when you could answer two shorter questions in that time and earn twice as many points?

Most students don't have a problem finishing the SIE exam on time. If you easily and consistently finish 85-question SIE practice exams in less than 1¾ hours, you should be okay on the real SIE exam.

TIP

When you are taking the SIE exam at the test center, if you find yourself obsessing over the clock on the computer to the point that you can't concentrate on the question in front of you, hide it by clicking on the lower left-hand corner of the computer screen. (Check out Figure 1-1 in Chapter 1.)

Master the process of elimination

The SIE exam is a standardized exam. This format makes it similar to other practical exams of this type: The best way to find the correct answer may be to eliminate the incorrect answers one at a time. I help you develop this crucial skill as you tackle the topic-specific questions throughout this book.

Maintain your concentration

To maintain your concentration, read the *stem* of the question (the last sentence before the answer choices) first to keep yourself focused on what the question is asking. Next, read through the entire problem (including the stem) to get a grip on the facts you have to consider to select the correct answer. You can then anticipate the correct answer and read all the answer choices to see whether your anticipated answer is there. If you don't see your answer and none of the other choices seems to fit, reread the stem to see whether you missed an important fact. Check out Chapter 3 for more detailed test-taking tips.

You can also take care to keep yourself physically alert. The last half hour or so is usually the most difficult. I recommend eating a small protein bar prior to starting the test to help keep your levels of energy and concentration high. Forget high-sugar/high-carb foods; leave them for after the exam. These foods boost your sugar level temporarily, but when the level drops, your energy and concentration levels sink like a lead balloon.

Low energy levels can lead to sloppy mistakes. If you feel yourself fading, do whatever it takes to stay alert and focused: Get up and get a drink of water, splash some water on your face, stretch, or dig your fingernails into the palms of your hands.

Think carefully before changing your answers

In general, if you select an answer and you can't really explain why, maybe it was just a *gut* answer. You're five times more likely to change to a wrong answer than to the right one, so change your answer only if

>> You didn't read the question correctly the first time and missed a major point that changes the answer choice (for example, you didn't see the word *except* at the end of the question).

>> You're absolutely sure you made a mistake.

Use the scrap paper wisely

In the testing room, you receive a few pages of letter-sized scrap paper (or a dry erase board), all of which will be collected — so restrain yourself from writing any obscenities about the exam or its creators. Here are some more productive ways to use this valuable resource:

>> **Mark dubious questions for review.** You have to answer each question before you can go to the next, so if you're not sure of the correct answer, eliminate the wrong answers, take your best guess, and mark the question for review later. On your scrap paper, write down the numbers of any questions you want to check before the end of the session.

>> **Eliminate wrong answers.** You can't write on the computer screen, so for each question, you may find it helpful to write A, B, C, and D on your scrap paper (in a column) as they appear on the screen and eliminate answers directly on your paper.

>> **Do a brain dump.** After the exam begins and before your brain gets cluttered with SIE exam questions, use your scrap paper or dry erase board to jot down the topic matters that tend to give you problems so that you can refresh your memory during the exam.

TIP

When doing a brain dump, write only the things that you're really having problems with. You know — the ones that you still feel the need to study the morning of the test. Don't worry about cataloguing things you already know and feel comfortable with, because it's a waste of your time (and paper). Those items should come to the surface of your brain as soon as you need them.

>> **Time yourself.** Write down your 15-minute benchmarks (prepared for you in the "Keep track of time" section earlier in this chapter) on your scrap paper and check periodically to make sure you stay on track.

Knowing When You're Ready

Your goal is to consistently score 80 to 85 percent on the sample tests that you take to ensure that you're ready for the real exam.

REMEMBER

To determine your readiness, consider your scores on the practice exams the *first time* you take them. In other words, don't convince yourself that you're ready if you score 85 percent on an exam that you've already taken three times. If you take a practice exam more than once, you may just be remembering the answers. I'm not against taking the same exams more than once, but don't use exams you've taken before to gauge how prepared you are.

Chapter **3**

Examining and Mastering Question Types

Yes, I know, I know: "Why can't they just ask regular questions?" This problem has perplexed test takers throughout the ages (all right, maybe not, but it does bug me). The test designers have riddled the old pick-the-best-answer questions with all kinds of pitfalls. The people in charge want you to choose combinations of correct answers and pick out exceptions; and, as if you don't have enough to worry about, they even give you extraneous information to try to trip you up. Sheesh!

In this chapter, I introduce you to the types of questions to expect on the SIE exam, and I show you how to analyze the facts in the questions and identify what the examiners are *really* testing you on. I also show you how to use the process of elimination to find the right answer and, if all else fails, how to logically guess the best answer.

TIP

You should also be aware that in its effort to make the SIE more fair to all test takers, FINRA has decided to weight the questions according to levels of difficulty. What this means to you is that for the most part easier questions (or what FINRA deems to be easier questions) will be worth less than the average question and more difficult ones will be worth more than average.

Familiarizing Yourself with Question Formats

Because of the number of questions that could be asked, the SIE exam is a beast of a test that poses questions in many different ways. You have to deal with multitiered Roman numeral nightmares, open- and closed-ended sentences, and killers like *except* and *not*. In this section, I show you how the examiners phrase the questions and how they can trip you up if you aren't careful.

Working with the straight shooters: The straightforward types

Straightforward question types include a group of sentences with the facts followed by a question or incomplete sentence; you then get four answer choices, one of which correctly answers the question or completes the idea.

Closed-stem questions

You'll find more closed-stem questions than any other question type on the SIE and co-requisite exams, so you'd better get a handle on answering these babies, for sure. Thankfully, closed-stem questions are fairly run-of-the-mill. They begin with one or more sentences containing information and end with a question (and, appropriately enough, a question mark). The question mark is what makes closed-stem questions different from open-stem questions, which I discuss in the next section. Your answer choices, lettered (A) through (D), may be complete or incomplete sentences. Here's a basic closed-stem question.

EXAMPLE

Mr. Bearishnikoff is a conservative investor. Which of the following investments would you recommend to him?

(A) Buying put options

(B) Buying long-term income adjustment bonds

(C) Buying common stock of an aggressive growth company

(D) Buying Treasury notes

The right answer is Choice (D). The first sentence tells you that Mr. Bearishnikoff is a conservative investor. This detail is all the information you need to answer the question correctly, because you know that conservative investors aren't looking to take a lot of investment risks and that U.S. government securities such as Treasury notes (T-notes) are considered the safest of all securities — they're backed by the fact that the government can always print more money to pay off the securities that it issues.

Of course, sometimes the phrasing of the answer choices can help you immediately cut down the number of feasible answer choices. For instance, Mr. Bearishnikoff would probably balk at investing in an *aggressive growth* company, which certainly doesn't sound stable or safe. Check out the section titled "Picking up clues when you're virtually clueless: The process of elimination" for details on raising your odds of answering questions correctly.

By the way, the *you* in the question refers to you on your good days, when you're considerate and rational and have had a sufficient amount of sleep. Mr. Bearishnikoff probably wouldn't appreciate any rogue-elephant investing, even if you think he should be more daring. The question also assumes normal market conditions, so don't recommend a different investment because you think the government is going to collapse and T-notes are going to take a dive. Just accept the conditions the problem presents to you.

TIP

Be careful to focus only on the information you need to answer the question. The securities exam creators have an annoying tendency to include extra details in the question (such as the maturity date, coupon rate, investor's age, and so on) that you may not need. See "Focusing on key information," later in this chapter, for some tips on zeroing in on the necessary info.

Open-stem questions

An open-stem question poses the problem as an incomplete sentence, and your mission, should you choose to accept it, is to complete the sentence with the correct answer. The following example shows how you can skillfully finish other people's thoughts.

EXAMPLE

The initial maturity on a standard option is

(A) three months

(B) six months

(C) nine months

(D) one year

The answer you want is Choice (C). *Options* give the purchaser the right to buy or sell securities at a fixed price (see Chapter 12). Options are considered *derivatives* (securities that derive their value from another security) because they're linked to an underlying security. Standard options have an initial maturity of nine months. On the other hand, Long-Term Equity AnticiPation Securities (LEAPS) may have initial maturities of one, two, or three years. But this example question asks about a standard option; therefore, you don't assume that it's a LEAP.

The preceding example is quite easy. Anyone who has been studying for the SIE or Series 7 exam should know the answer. However, what makes securities exams so difficult is that the exams are loaded with so many date-oriented details. Not only do you have to memorize the initial maturities of all the different securities, but unfortunately (and believe me, I feel your pain), you also have to remember a truckload of time frames (for example, accounts are frozen for 90 days, new securities can't be purchased on margin for 30 days, an options account agreement must be returned within 15 days after the account is approved, and so on).

TIP

Date-oriented details are excellent material to include in your flash cards. See Chapter 2 for more study suggestions.

Encountering quirky questions with qualifiers

To answer questions with qualifiers, you have to find the best answer to the question. The qualifier keeps all answer choices from being correct because only one answer rises above the rest.

Working with extremes: Most, least, best

Recognizing the qualifier in the question stem and carefully reading every single answer choice are very important. Check out the following example.

EXAMPLE

Which of the following companies would be MOST affected by interest rate fluctuations?

(A) SKNK Perfume Corp.

(B) Bulb Utility Co.

(C) Crapco Vitamin Supplements, Inc.

(D) LQD Water Bottling Co.

The answer is Choice (B). Although all companies may be somewhat affected by interest rate fluctuations, the question uses the word *most*. If interest rates increase, companies have to issue bonds with higher coupon (interest) rates. This higher rate, in turn, greatly affects the companies' bottom lines. Therefore, you're looking for a company that issues a lot of bonds. Utility companies are most affected by interest rate fluctuations because they're *highly leveraged* (issue a lot of bonds).

Making exceptions: Except or not

When a question includes the word *except* or *not*, you're looking for the answer that's *the exception* to the rule stated in the stem of the question. In other words, the correct answer is always the *false* answer. The question can be open (as it is in the next example) or closed.

WARNING

Right off the bat, look for an *except* or *not* in the stem of every question on the SIE exam. Many students who really know their material accidentally pick the wrong answer on a few questions because they carelessly miss the *except* or *not*.

Take a look at the following exception problem.

EXAMPLE

A stockholder owns 800 shares of WHY common stock. WHY stockholders were given cumulative voting rights. If there are three vacancies on the board of directors, stockholders can cast any of the following votes EXCEPT

(A) 800 for one candidate

(B) 800 for each candidate

(C) 2,400 for one candidate

(D) 900 for each candidate

The answer you're looking for is Choice (D). Cumulative voting rights give smaller stockholders (not height-wise, but in terms of the number of shares they own) an easier chance to gain representation on the board of directors because a stockholder may combine his total voting rights and vote the cumulative total in any way he wants. Here, the stockholder has a total of 2,400 votes to cast (800 shares × 3 vacancies = 2,400 votes).

In this example, you may be tempted to select Choices (A), (B), or (C), any of which would be correct if you were asked for the number of votes this stockholder *could* cast. For example, the stockholder can use 800 shares to vote for only one candidate (Choice [A]) — he doesn't have to use all 2,400 votes. Choice (B) is another possible voting arrangement because nobody said the stockholder has to use all his votes for one candidate. Choice (C) is an option because the stockholder has a total of 2,400 votes to cast. In this question, however, you're looking for the number of votes the stockholder *can't* cast because the word *except* in the question stem requires you to find a false answer. Therefore, Choice (D) is the correct answer because in order to cast 900 votes for each candidate, the stockholder would need a total of 2,700 votes (900 × 3).

REMEMBER

If you're one of the unlucky people who gets an "all of the following are false except" question, you have to find the *true* answer. Don't forget, two negatives in a sentence make a positive statement. You may want to try rephrasing the question so you know whether you're looking for a true or false answer.

Roman hell: Complex multiple choice

Yes, the SIE exam creators even sneak complex (two-tiered) Roman numeral questions in on you. They can pose the question by asking you to put something in order, or they can ask you to find the best combination in a series of answer choices. To make things even more enjoyable, sometimes they even add *except* and *not* to the question (see the preceding section).

Imposing order: Ranking questions

To answer a ranking question, you have to choose the answer that places the information in the correct order — for example, first to last, last to first, highest to lowest, lowest to highest, and so on. Check out the following example.

In which order, from first to last, are the following actions taken when opening a new options account?

I. Send the customer an ODD.

II. Have the ROP approve the account.

III. Execute the transaction.

IV. Have the customer send in an OAA.

(A) I, II, III, IV

(B) II, I, IV, III

(C) III, I, II, IV

(D) I, III, II, IV

The correct answer is Choice (A). Wasn't it nice of me to arrange all the answers in order for you? Because option transactions are so risky, the customer has to receive an options risk disclosure document (ODD) prior to opening the account. Statement I has to come first, so you can immediately eliminate Choices (B) and (C), giving you a 50 percent chance of answering correctly. After the client receives the ODD, the registered options principal (ROP) needs to approve the account before any transactions can be executed; II has to come before III, so you can finish the problem here — the answer is Choice (A). Last but not least, the customer signs and returns an options account agreement (OAA) within 15 days after the account is approved by the ROP.

Taking two at a time

The Roman numeral format also appears on the SIE with questions that offer two answer choices as the correct response. In these types of questions, you choose the responses that best answer the question.

Which TWO of the following are the minimum requirements for an investor to be considered accredited?

I. An individual with a net worth of $500,000

II. An individual with a net worth of $1,000,000

III. An individual who earned $200,000 per year in the most recent two years and has a reasonable expectation of reaching that same level in the current year

IV. An individual who earned $300,000 per year in the most recent 3 years and has a reasonable expectation of reaching that same level in the current year

(A) I and III

(B) I and IV

(C) II and III

(D) II and IV

The correct answer is Choice (C). Statements I and II both deal with net worth; III and IV deal with earnings. Therefore, you're dealing with two questions in one; to be accredited, the answer to at least one of these two questions must be satisfactory:

>> What is the individual's minimum net worth?

>> What is the individual's minimum income?

To be considered an accredited (sophisticated) investor, the minimum requirement is a net worth of $1,000,000 and/or a yearly income of $200,000 in the most recent two years, with a reasonable expectation of reaching that same level in the current year. If the word *minimum* were not used in the question, answer IV would also be correct.

A little mystery: Dealing with an unknown number of correct statements

In the preceding section, the question states that only two responses can be correct. The following question may have one, three, or four correct answers. You can recognize this type of question simply by glancing at your answer choices. To make the problem more difficult (don't hate me, now), I add an *except* because I'm feeling really good about you, and I just know you're up to it.

EXAMPLE

All of the following are true about open-end funds EXCEPT

I. they issue common stock

II. they issue preferred stock

III. they issue debt securities

IV. shares can be purchased in the market

(A) I only

(B) II only

(C) II, III, and IV only

(D) I, II, III, and IV

The correct answer is Choice (C).

Open-end funds are mutual funds. Mutual funds are constantly issuing new shares (thus the open-end name). Since mutual funds only issue common stock and can only be purchased directly from the issuer, the only true answer is I. However, since we are looking for the exception(s), answers II, III, and IV are the correct ones. (Chapter 13 covers the information you need to know about open- and closed-end funds). Had the question asked which is true regarding closed-end funds, the answer would've been Choice (D).

Looking at exhibits: Diagram questions

The SIE exam will not likely give you more than a couple of exhibit questions, if any. However, even if you don't get an exhibit question on the SIE exam, you can use the following information to help you on one of the companion exams that you're going to have to take. Exhibit questions may include newspaper clippings, option prices, bond prices, trading patterns, income statements, balance sheets, and so on. Out of the exhibit questions you get, some of them just require you to find the correct information; others require a little calculating. I wouldn't be too concerned about them if I were you, because most of them are quite easy.

Take a look at the following problem.

GHI Corporation Balance Sheet at 12-31-XX
(In Thousands)

Assets		Liabilities	
Cash and cash equivalents	$8,000	Accounts payable	$1,000
Receivables (net)	$1,000	Wages payable	$800
Inventory	+$3,000	Taxes payable	$700
Total current assets	**$12,000**	Interest payable	+ $500
		Total current liabilities	**$3,000**
Notes receivable due after one year	$1,000	Long-term debt 8%	+$4,000
		Total liabilities	**$7,000**
Property, plant, and equipment (net)	$4,000		
Goodwill	+$1,000	**Stockholder's Equity**	
Total long-term assets	**$6,000**	Preferred stock $100 par 9%	$2,000
		Common stock $1 par	$2,000
Total assets	**$18,000**	Paid-in capital	$4,000
		Retained earnings	+$3,000
		Total stockholder's equity	**$11,000**
		Total liabilities and stockholder's equity	**$18,000**

EXAMPLE

What is the value placed on the reputation of GHHI Corporation?

(A) $1,000

(B) $1,000,000

(C) $6,000

(D) $6,000,000

The answer you're looking for is Choice (B). This example accurately portrays the difficulty level of most of the exhibit questions on the SIE exam. In this case, you had to remember what "Goodwill" means. You can find out more balance sheet information by looking at Chapter 13. "Goodwill," as you may have surmised by now, means a value placed on the reputation of a company. For example, the name Dunkin' is worth more than Bring Me My Donuts and Step on It, which is why people are willing to pay for Dunkin' franchises. So, all you really have to do is look for "Goodwill" on the balance sheet exhibit. You can see that "Goodwill" is listed at $1,000, but you have to take into consideration the top of the balance sheet where it says "in Thousands." This means that you have to take that number and multiply it by a thousand to get your answer. So, $1,000 × 1,000 = $1,000,000.

WARNING

When you answer exhibit questions, take care not to miss labels like "in thousands" in headings or scales on a graph that would change your answer. Almost nothing is worse than missing a question that you know because you carelessly overlook something right in front of you.

Shredding the Questions: Tips and Tricks

In Chapter 2, I give you general exam proficiency tips. In this section, I show you how to improve your analysis of topic-specific SIE questions. I also provide you with more sample exam questions to further demonstrate the art of choosing the correct answers.

Focusing on key information

The SIE and co-requisite exam questions can be particularly difficult if you rush through the exam and miss details that change the meaning of the question.

TIP

When you first start taking practice exams, read through the question to determine what's being asked; then go back to the beginning of the problem to identify the key facts and underline and/or highlight them. Marking the questions may seem time-consuming when you first begin to study, but if you get into the habit of picking out key words in each question, zoning in on the important information should be second nature by the time you take the test. Of course, you can't underline items on the computer screen at the testing center (the test center administrators may get upset if you write on the computer screen). So instead, if you find yourself getting distracted by useless information, use the scrap paper or dry erase board to write down the information you do need.

This example zeroes in on the essential information.

EXAMPLE

A 55-year-old investor purchases a <u>6 percent</u> DEF convertible mortgage bond at 90 with 10 years until maturity. If the bond is currently trading at <u>97</u>, what is the <u>current yield</u>?

(A) 5.72%

(B) 6.00%

(C) 6.19%

(D) 6.67%

The correct answer is Choice (C). When determining the current yield of a bond, all you need is the market price of the bond and the coupon (interest) rate (see Chapter 7). The fact that the investor is 55 years old or that the bond is a convertible mortgage bond that was purchased at $900 (90 percent of $1,000 par) with 10 years until maturity means nothing in terms of determining the answer. Underline or highlight what you do need (6 percent, 97, current yield) so you don't get distracted.

To determine the current yield, divide the annual interest by the market price. The annual interest is $60 (6 percent of $1,000 par) and the market price is $970 (97 percent of $1,000 par):

$$\text{current yield} = \frac{\text{annual interest}}{\text{market price}} = \frac{\$60}{\$970} = 6.19\%$$

TIP

To avoid confusion when faced with a math problem (and there's not much on the SIE), read the stem of the question to determine what's being asked; before you consider the rest of the question, jot down the formula you need to calculate your answer.

Answer me this: Picking the correct answer

The SIE exam is a practical, multiple-choice exam. The correct answer has to be one of the choices. This setup means you don't have to *provide* the correct answer; you just have to *recognize* it when you see it.

Picking up clues when you're virtually clueless: The process of elimination

When you don't straight-out know an answer, your approach can definitely make the difference between passing and failing the exam. Your best strategy may be eliminating the wrong answers. In theory, you should be able to eliminate, one by one, three incorrect answers for each question.

Even if you can't eliminate three incorrect answers, you'll certainly be able to eliminate one or two answers that are definitely wrong. Don't try to guess the right answer until you've axed as many wrong answers as you can. Obviously, if you can get the choices down to two potential answers, you have a 50-50 chance of answering correctly.

REMEMBER For an answer choice to be correct, every aspect has to be correct, and the selection has to specifically answer the question that's asked. As a rule of thumb on the SIE exam, a more-precise answer is correct more often than a less-precise answer, and a longer answer usually (but not always) prevails over a short answer.

If a response is potentially correct, write T for *true* next to the answer in your practice exam, and if a response is wrong, eliminate it by writing F for *false* next to the answer. If you do this step correctly, you should end up with three Fs and one T, with T indicating the correct answer. Or, if the question is looking for a false answer, you should end up with three Ts and one F (see the earlier section "Making exceptions: Except or not" for more info on this scenario). On the actual test, you can write the letters A through D on your scrap paper or dry erase board and mark the answer choices appropriately.

TIP Always look to eliminate any wrong answers that you can. Pay attention to the wording, and get rid of choices that simply sound wrong or make statements that are too broad or absolute. If you're still undecided, use your scrap paper or dry erase board to write down the question number and the answer choices that remain. Take your best guess and mark the answer for review. When you review, look at your scrap paper or dry erase board to help you zone in on your potential answers. Change your answer only if you're sure you made a mistake.

Stop opposing me: Dealing with opposite answers

If you see two opposing answer choices, only one can be right. Traditionally, in practical exams like the SIE, when you see two answer choices that are complete opposites, the exam creators are trying to test your knowledge of the correct rule, procedure, or law, so one of those opposing choices is most likely the correct answer. Take a look at the following example.

EXAMPLE Which of the following is TRUE of UGMA accounts?

(A) There can be only one minor and one custodian per account.

(B) There can be more than one minor and one custodian per account.

(C) Securities can only be purchased on margin.

(D) They must be set up for children who have reached the age of majority.

The answer you want is Choice (A). Notice that Choices (A) and (B) oppose each other. If you have two opposing answers, in almost all cases, one of them is the right answer. Therefore, you can ignore Choices (C) and (D), which gives you a 50-percent chance of getting the answer right. Uniform Gifts to Minors Act (UGMA) accounts are set up for minors who are too young to have their own accounts. Each account is limited to one minor and one custodian. (See Chapter 12 for details on custodial accounts.)

Facing Roman numerals: Not as hard as you think

Complex (two-tiered) multiple-choice questions, with both Roman numerals and letters, can be really frustrating because they usually signal the test taker (you) that you need more than one correct answer. Well, today's your lucky day, because I show you a shortcut that can help you blow these questions right out of the water.

Traditionally, the first tier of these types of questions gives you several statements preceded by Roman numerals; the second tier (preceded by letters) provides you with choices about which of those statements are correct. Fifteen different combinations of I, II, III, and IV are possible (16 if you count "none of the above," which is almost never correct), but each problem can list only four of them in the answer choices. Because of the limited answer choices, you may not have to evaluate every statement — certain combinations of Roman numerals may be logically impossible.

TIP

Read the question carefully, and then mark T for *true* or F for *false* next to the Roman numerals to indicate whether they're correct answers to the question. If a Roman-numeral statement is correct, circle that number in the choices that follow the letters in the second tier. If the Roman-numeral statement is false, all the letter answers that include that numeral must also be false, and you can cross them out. If you're really lucky, three of the Roman numerals can be eliminated right away, leaving you with one answer choice.

Look over this Roman numeral question.

EXAMPLE

Which of the following is TRUE of the 5% Markup Policy?

   I. It covers commissions charged to customers when executing trades on an agency basis.

   II. It covers markups on stock sold to customers from inventory.

   III. It covers markdowns on stock purchased from customers for inventory.

   IV. Riskless and simultaneous transactions are covered.

(A) I and IV only

(B) IV only

(C) II and III only

(D) I, II, III, and IV

The correct answer is Choice (D). The 5% Markup Policy applies to nonexempt securities sold to or purchased from customers. This situation is one where you should look at the Roman-numeral statements and pick out those that you know answer the question. For example, if you know Statement I is right (which it is), put a T (for true) next to it. Next, look at Choices (A), (B), (C), and (D) and eliminate Choices (B) and (C), because neither one includes the Roman numeral I. Because both answers that remain, (A) and (D), include the Roman numerals I and IV, you don't even have to bother reading statement IV — it's in both remaining answers, so you know it has to be true. Write T next to the Roman numeral IV. If you know that either statement II or III is correct (which they both are), the answer has to be Choice (D) because it's the only one that lists all the correct choices.

GETTING DOWN WITH NUMBERS: ELIMINATING SOME MATH

The process of elimination can get you out of some messy calculations. When dealing with math, look at the answer choices before you begin working out the problem. You may be able to get the answer without doing any calculations at all. For instance, if you have a forward stock split, you know that the number of shares has to increase and that the price of the stock has to decrease (see Chapter 6). If three of the answers fail to meet these conditions, you have your answer right off the bat.

Don't make the same mistake twice

TIP

When studying for the SIE exam, the practice exams can help you pinpoint your weaker areas of knowledge. The questions you answer incorrectly can be your best learning tools if you thoroughly review the explanations for each wrong answer. You may be tempted to jump from one practice exam to the next without taking adequate time to review your wrong answers. Don't do it! If you put the effort into finding out why your choices are wrong when you're practicing, you're less likely to repeat the same mistake on the SIE exam, when it really counts.

Chapter **4**

Surviving Test Day

You've done your homework, taken practice exams, and completed your prep course, and now the day of reckoning is upon you. You're ready to exchange the gazillion hours of study and hard work for your SIE license. The last hurdle awaits you at the test center.

In this chapter, I give you a snapshot of the SIE exam experience so you know the procedure before, during, and after you take the exam and can hit the ground running.

Composing Yourself the Day Before

On the day before the exam, review the information that you're still having problems with until noon; then call it a day. Get away from the books, go out to dinner (maybe skip the spicy foods and alcohol), go to a movie. Rest your mind. If you've put the required time and effort into studying up to now, you'll benefit more from a good night's rest than anything you can learn in the final hours the night before your exam. Taking the evening off can help prevent brain fatigue and make zoning into exam mode easier tomorrow, when it counts most.

REMEMBER

Before you go to sleep, gather the items you need to take with you to the exam. If you prepare yourself the night before, you'll be more relaxed on exam day. Here are some activities to complete the night before the exam to finalize your preparations for the big day:

» Make sure you have the proper government-issued ID bearing your name, signature, and a recent photo. The name on your ID must identically match the name on the Web CRD registration form. An expired ID won't be accepted. Official (primary) identification can be in the form of a valid passport, a driver's license, or a military ID card. A current (unexpired) State ID is acceptable in lieu of a driver's license, as long as it includes the person's full name as it appears on the Web CRD registration form, an expiration date, the student's signature, and a current photograph.

If you use a military ID that doesn't have a signature, you need to bring a secondary form of ID with a signature. Secondary ID can be a valid credit card, a bank automatic-teller machine (ATM) card, a library card, a U.S. Social Security card, an employee ID/work badge, or a school ID.

DOING TEST RUNS IN THE FINAL WEEKS

TIP

Getting too little sleep (you'll be a nervous wreck) or too much sleep (you'll be in a stupor) the night before the exam can be a disaster. For the week before the exam (if possible), follow the routine you'll be following on the day of your exam. Set your alarm at the same time you'll wake up on exam day, take a complete practice exam for the hour and 45-minute interval at the same time as you'll be taking the real exam, and so on.

Also, the day of the exam is not the time to find out that a big construction project is underway on the exact route you're taking to get to the test center, the traffic is backed up for miles, and you'll be at least an hour late. The last thing you need to worry about on exam day is getting to the test center late and having to reschedule your exam.

To help avoid this disaster, do a test run sometime before the test date. Travel the route you'll take at the same time (and, if possible, on the same day of the week) as your exam date to get a preview of what you can expect. You may even be able to check your local newspaper for details on upcoming construction or repairs that may affect roadways and public transportation. Having an alternate route established in advance is also a good idea in case your route of choice isn't the best option on exam day.

>> Pack earplugs (if allowed — ask when you schedule your exam).

>> Put your lunch and/or a snack with the rest of your stuff.

>> Bring study materials — including the topics and/or math formulas you're having trouble with — for a final review before you enter the test center.

>> Have your watch ready to make sure you're on time.

>> Lay out your clothes (dress in layers in case the test center feels like either your refrigerator or your oven).

>> Review the directions to the exam site. Make sure you have a charged cellphone and the test center number in case you get lost.

Additionally, you have to bring at least one finger with you, preferably yours, so that the exam administrators can take a fingerprint (though you probably have that packed already).

REMEMBER

You can't bring study material, textbooks, briefcases, purses, electronic devices, cellphones, notes of any kind, or your really smart friend with you into the testing room. Calculators, pencils, and scrap paper or a dry erase board will be provided for you at the exam center, and the exam administrators will collect the calculators, pencils, and all scrap paper (used and unused) or dry erase board at the end of each session.

Making the Most of the Morning

Now the big day is here. Certainly, you don't have to dress up for the pictures the SIE administrator takes, but you should at least do what you need to do to feel awake and alive and good about yourself (do some push-ups, take a shower, shave, whatever).

Be sure to eat at least a light breakfast. You may feel like you're too nervous to eat, but if you're hungry when you take the exam, you won't be able to concentrate. And if you overeat, you'll be wasting valuable energy (and blood flow!) digesting the meal — energy your brain needs to sustain you. To avoid an energy crash, I suggest a protein bar, fruit, and/or veggies rather than sugar or carbs.

Grab everything you packed up the night before (see the preceding section) and head out the door.

Leave your home in time to arrive at the test center at least 30 minutes before your scheduled exam so you have time to check in. I recommend that you arrive at the test center 1½ hours before the exam so you have 1 hour to review the topics and/or math formulas that give you the most trouble and a half-hour to check in.

Arriving on the Scene

The SIE exam and other Securities exams are administered by Prometric, and you can contact the center for additional information. In this section, I cover the steps to take upon your arrival at the exam center.

In Chapter 1, I discuss the availability of special accommodations if you're disabled or learning impaired or if English is your second language. If you require special accommodations, contact the FINRA Special Conditions Team at (800) 999-6647 for information about registration and for instructions about arriving at the exam center.

Taking advantage of one last chance to cram

The information you review just before the exam will be on the surface of your mind. When you arrive at the exam center (or even during your commute if you take public transportation), do some last-minute cramming. Review the topics and/or math formulas you're having trouble with.

Each SIE exam center is set up differently; you may find areas in the building where you can study, or you may have to study outside in your car, on a bench, or at a nearby coffee shop. When you're ready to enter the exam center (30 minutes before the exam), you can leave your books in your vehicle if the exam center doesn't have lockers (see the section "Getting seated").

Signing in

To enter the exam center, you have to provide the administrators with valid ID. (See "Composing Yourself the Day Before" for what constitutes "valid.") After you're inside the test center, you have to sign in and get photographed and fingerprinted. In addition, before you begin the exam, you have to read a form called the Rules of Conduct and agree to the terms. A preview of the Rules of Conduct is available on the FINRA website (www.finra.org/industry/test-center-rules-conduct).

Getting seated

Basically, the only things you may bring into the testing room are your own sweet self and possibly a set of earplugs. You can store all other personal property in a locker at the exam center. (All new testing sites are supposed to have lockers, but some older sites may have been grandfathered without them. You can ask when you make your appointment.) For a list of the (mostly) medical items you can bring into the exam room, including which ones need inspection or preauthorization, please call your testing center.

Some exam centers have cafeterias and/or vending machines with snacks and drinks, but you can't even bring chewing gum into the exam room. I don't know why — maybe because of the noise, or maybe so the exam staff doesn't have to scrape gum wads off computer screens.

The exam administrators escort you to the exam room. In the testing room, you receive scrap paper (or a dry erase board), a pencil, and a basic calculator. You'll have to return the paper, pencil, and calculator to the exam center administrators at the end of the session (yes, even the unused scrap paper). You can't bring anything else into the cubicle where you take the exam.

Tackling the SIE

Take a deep breath, crack your knuckles, and get ready to make things count — this SIE exam is the genuine article. The exam is one hour and 45 minutes in duration, and you're graded on a total of 75 questions. The test designers have even prepared a bonus for you: To ensure that new questions to be introduced in future exams meet acceptable standards, you also answer 10 additional, unidentified questions that don't count toward your score. Lucky you! This means that you answer 85 questions, but only 75 really count toward your score.

REMEMBER

Most test centers offer the inspirational creature comforts of the office: You take your SIE in a cubicle (approximately 4 feet wide) with a computer and a small desk area. You may leave your cubicle for restroom breaks at any time, if necessary. The clock continues to run, however, so try to limit your intake of fluids before each session.

Just before you begin your exam, a member of the test center staff will walk you through the steps of how to use the computerized system. Don't worry — you don't need any previous computer experience to understand the way the computer operates (it's that easy). If you do have any tech problems during the test, you can use the help button or summon the exam administrators. A picture of how a question appears on the computer screen is in Chapter 1.

As the test begins, you're ready to put all those test-taking skills to use (check out Chapter 2 for a rundown of what those skills are). Right off the bat, write down everything you think you're likely to forget. Keep track of time. Mark questions for review. Concentrate on the facts in question and look for key words that can give you clues. Use your amazing powers of elimination to identify wrong answer choices. Work your magic with specific question types (see Chapter 3). You've done your homework, so be confident.

REMEMBER

Before your session ends, double-check the questions you marked for review. Don't change any answers unless you're certain your initial answer is wrong.

TIP

If you're one of those speed demons (and I hope you're not) who finishes the test in an hour and are tempted to review all your answers, don't do it. Go over only the questions you marked for review. If you try to review all the questions, not only will you drive yourself bonkers, but you'll also do more harm than good by second-guessing your right answers.

STAYING RELAXED, FOCUSED, AND CONSCIOUS

Here are some ways to keep stress at bay and make sure you're giving the test the attention it deserves:

- If you feel tense, take a few slow, deep breaths and give yourself a mini-massage.

- If you find yourself growing tired, stretch, sit up straight, or go to the restroom just for a chance to walk around.

- Give your eyes a rest from the computer screen by looking away from the computer every so often.

  Avoid looking at someone else's computer screen — it's not only frowned upon, it will get you ejected.

- If you have trouble focusing, write down significant details from the question. If you're stuck on a multipart question, break down the question into segments. Try drawing diagrams. If you're still having trouble, choose a tentative answer and mark the question for review.

- Don't lose track of your mission here — now is not the time to let up. Visualize success and hang in there!

Getting the Results: Drum Roll, Please . . .

You've completed many hours of studying. You've deprived yourself of weekend parties and long afternoons of leisure. Your social life has been almost nonexistent, and if you're the type who becomes unpleasant when in a stressful state of being, you may have alienated the people who used to hang out with you.

After surviving an hour and 45 minutes of mental abuse from taking the SIE exam, you're ready to push the button that reveals your score and can change your life.

The time may seem much longer, but in reality, you have to wait only a little while before your score is revealed. Your grade and the word *passed* or *failed* appear on the computer screen. If your grade is 70 or better, you pass the exam. (Please remember that you're now a professional and refrain from doing a victory dance in the middle of the test center.) If your score is less than 70, you don't pass the exam. Don't call your friends and tell them you've decided to become an astronaut or firefighter instead. You can retake the test, so you may still have a future on Wall Street. See Chapter 1 for what to do next.

Regardless of whether you pass or fail the exam, you receive a printout of your grade and the breakdown of your performance on the SIE exam topics, which is unfortunately pretty vague. Employers receive a copy of the results in the mail, or, if tied into the FINRA computer system, they can get results online.

2

Mastering Basic Security Investments

Chapter **5**

Underwriting Securities

All issuers of securities need a starting point, just as all securities need a birth date (just not the kind that's celebrated with funny-looking hats and a cake). Most securities go through a registration procedure before the public can buy them. The SIE exam tests your ability to recognize the players and institutions involved in the registration process.

In this chapter, I cover topics related to bringing new issues (securities) to market. You find out about key players, types of security offerings, kinds of securities that don't need to be registered, and other details about the underwriting process.

Bringing New Issues to the Market

A lot of things need to happen before securities hit the market. Not only do the securities have to be registered, but the issuer has to find a broker–dealer (like your firm) to sell the securities to the public. The SIE exam tests your expertise in answering questions about this process.

Starting out: What the issuer does

For an entity to become a corporation, the founders must file a document called a *corporate charter* (bylaws) in the home state of their business. Included in the corporate charter are the names of the founders, the type of business, the place of business, the number of shares that can be issued, and so on. If a corporation wants to sell securities to the public, it has to register with states and the Securities and Exchange Commission (SEC). Read on for info on how the registration process works.

Registering securities with the SEC

Unless the securities are exempt from registration (see "Exempt securities" later in this chapter), when a company wants to go public (sell stock to public investors), it has to file a registration statement and a prospectus (see "Getting the skinny on the issue and issuer: The prospectus" later in this chapter) with the SEC.

THE SECURITIES ACTS

Registration helps ensure that securities issued to the public adhere to certain regulations (though anti-fraud rules also apply to exempt securities). The following acts are designed to protect investors from unscrupulous issuers, firms, and salespeople (see Chapter 16 for details on other rules and regulations).

The Securities Act of 1933: This act — also called the Truth in Securities Act, the Paper Act, the Full Disclosure Act, the Prospectus Act, and the New Issues Act — regulates new issues of corporate securities. An issuer of corporate securities must provide full and fair disclosure about itself and the offering. Included in this act are rules to prevent fraud and deception.

The Securities Exchange Act of 1934: The Act of 1934, which established the SEC, was enacted to protect investors by regulating the over-the-counter (OTC) market and exchanges, such as the New York Stock Exchange (NYSE). (Chapter 14 can tell you more about markets.) In addition, the Act of 1934 regulates

- The extension of credit in margin accounts (see Chapter 12)
- Transactions by insiders
- Customer accounts
- Trading activities

The Trust Indenture Act of 1939: This act prohibits bond issues valued at over $5 million from being offered to investors without an indenture. The trust indenture is a written agreement that protects investors by disclosing the particulars of the issue (coupon rate, maturity date, any collateral backing the bond, and so on). As part of the Trust Indenture Act of 1939, all companies must hire a trustee who's responsible for protecting the rights of bondholders.

The *registration statement* includes

- >> The issuer's name, address, and description of its business
- >> The company's articles of incorporation (unless previously supplied)
- >> The names and addresses of the underwriter(s) and all commissions or discounts they will receive either directly or indirectly from the sale
- >> The price at which the security shall be offered to the public
- >> The names and addresses of all the company's control persons, such as officers, directors, and anyone owning more than 10 percent of the corporation's securities and how much they hold of the corporation's securities
- >> The estimated net proceeds of the sale from the security to be issued and what the proceeds will be used for, including property (if any), good will (if any), or other businesses to be purchased (if any)
- >> The company's capitalization (authorized and outstanding stock; par value of its stock, if any; voting rights; exchange rights; and so on)
- >> Complete financial statements (including balance sheets and income statements)
- >> Any legal proceedings against the corporation that may have an impact on it
- >> Any net proceeds derived from any security sold by the issuer in the previous two years along with the underwriter's particulars

>> The names and addresses of the counsel who have passed on the legality of the issue and a copy of their opinion or opinions with regard to legality of the issue

>> Any agreements or indentures which might affect the securities being offered

REMEMBER

The information above regarding the Registration Statement is known as *Schedule A* and it typically applies to corporations issuing new securities. There is also a *Schedule B,* which applies to local government issues (typically municipal bonds). The information required when a local government issues securities is, as you can imagine, geared toward what a local government would have to supply in its registration statement. Most of the information required is very similar; in fact, you can substitute the word "municipality" for "company" for most of the items required. You need to know the name of the borrowing government or subdivision, what it is raising the money for, the amount of funded debt and the amount of floating debt there will be after the new security is issued, whether the issuer has defaulted on debt in the last 20 years, the names of all people involved (in other words, counsel, underwriter(s), and so on), commission to be paid to the underwriters, a copy of the agreement(s) made with the underwriter(s), a legal opinion made by the counsel with regard to the legality and possible tax-free nature of the issue, and so on.

Shelving the issue: Shelf registration

Because the registration process to sell securities is a somewhat daunting and costly process for issuers, they may register more securities than they may need to sell now. Shelf registration (SEC Rule 415) allows issuers to sell securities that were previously registered with the SEC without needing additional permission. Shelf registration allows issuers up to two to three years (depending on their status) to sell previously registered shares.

Cooling-off period

After the issuer files a registration statement (the filing date) with the SEC, a 20-day cooling-off period begins. During the 20-day (and often longer) cooling-off period, the good old SEC reviews the registration statement. At the end of the cooling-off period, the issue will (hopefully) be cleared for sale to the public (the effective date of registration). In the event that the SEC sees that the registration statement needs to be amended or additional information is needed, it will issue a deficiency letter and halt the registration process until it receives the information required. If the SEC (the Commission) finds that the registration statement is misleading because the issuer included untrue statements of material fact or omits a material fact, it issues a *stop order,* which suspends the effectiveness of the registration statement. At this point, the issuer will be required to amend the registration statement and answer any questions posed by the Commission in order to continue the registration process.

REMEMBER

Neither the SEC nor any self-regulatory organization approves an issue. The SEC just clears the issue for sale. The SEC also is not responsible for making sure that the information included on the registration statement is true and accurate. As a matter of fact, it is unlawful to in any way represent that the SEC approved of an issue or issuer.

During the cooling-off period, the underwriter (or underwriters) can obtain indications of interest from investors who may want to purchase the issue. Agents scramble to get indications of interest from prospective purchasers of the securities.

REMEMBER

Indications of interest aren't binding on customers or underwriters. A customer always has the prerogative to change his mind, and underwriters may not have enough shares available to meet everyone's needs.

A *tombstone ad* — a newspaper ad that's shaped like a, well, tombstone (it's rectangular with black borders) — is simply an announcement (but not an offer) of a new security for sale. It's the only advertisement allowed during the cooling-off period. These ads contain just a simple statement of facts about the new issue (for example, the issuer, type of security, number of shares or bonds available, underwriter's name, and so on). In addition, tombstone ads often provide investors with information about how to obtain a prospectus. Tombstone ads are optional.

Underwriters and selling group members use the preliminary prospectus to obtain indications of interest from prospective customers. The preliminary prospectus must be made available to all customers who are interested in the new issue during the cooling-off period. I talk more about what that prospectus has to include in the section "Getting the skinny on the issue and issuer: The prospectus" a little later in this chapter.

Due diligence meeting

Toward the end of the cooling-off period, the underwriter holds a due diligence meeting. During this meeting, the underwriter provides information about the issue and what the issuer will use the proceeds of the sale for. This meeting is designed to provide such information to syndicate members, selling groups, brokers, analysts, institutions, and so on.

REMEMBER

The last time syndicate members can back out of an underwriting agreement is toward the end of the cooling-off period (around the time of the due diligence meeting). You can assume that if syndicate members are backing out, it's most likely due to negative market conditions.

Blue skies: Registering with the states

All *blue sky laws*, or state laws that apply to security offerings and sales, say that in order to sell a security to a customer, the broker-dealer (brokerage firm), the registered representative, and the security must be registered in the customer's home state. The issuer is responsible for registering the security not only with the U.S. Securities and Exchange Commission (the SEC) but also with the State Administrator in each state in which the securities are to be sold.

Here are the methods of state security registration:

>> **Notification (registration by filing):** Notification is the simplest form of registration for established companies. Companies that have previously sold securities in a state can renew their previous application.

>> **Coordination:** This method involves registering with the SEC and states at the same time. The SEC helps companies meet the blue sky laws by notifying all states in which the securities are to be sold.

>> **Qualification:** Companies use this registration method for securities that are exempt from registration with the SEC but require registration with the state.

Role call: Introducing the team players

The following list explains who's involved in the securities registration and selling process. Registered reps can work for any of these firms:

>> **Investment banking firm:** An *investment banking firm* is an institution (a broker-dealer) that's in the business of helping issuers raise money. You can think of investment bankers as the brains of the operation, because they help the issuer decide what securities to issue, how much to issue, the selling price, and so on. Not only do investment bankers advise issuers, but they usually underwrite the issue and may also become the managing underwriter in the offering of new securities.

>> **Underwriter:** The *underwriter* is a broker-dealer that helps the issuer bring new securities to the public. Underwriters purchase the securities from the issuer and sell them to the public for a nice profit (yippee!).

>> **Syndicate:** When an issue is too large for one firm to handle, the syndicate manager (managing underwriter) forms a syndicate to help sell the securities and relieve some of the financial burden on the managing underwriter. Each syndicate member is responsible for selling a portion of the securities to the public.

>> **Managing (lead) underwriter:** The managing underwriter (syndicate manager) is the head firm that's responsible for putting together a syndicate and dealing directly with the issuer. The managing underwriter receives financial compensation (buckets-o-bucks) for each and every share sold.

>> **Selling group:** In the event that the syndicate members feel they need more help selling the securities, they can recruit selling group members. These members are brokerage firms that aren't part of the syndicate. Selling group members help distribute shares to the public but don't make a financial commitment (that is, they don't purchase shares from the issuer) and therefore receive less money per share when selling shares to the public.

Although corporations could use a bidding process to pick the underwriter for new issues, they typically choose the underwriter directly. This type of offering is called a *negotiated offering*. However, because Municipal GO (general obligation) bonds are backed by the taxes of the people living in the community, they will most likely choose a *competitive offering* (bidding process) to insure that they are getting the best deal for taxpayers. (This topic is covered in more detail in Chapter 8.)

Agreement among underwriters

When an issuer hires a(n) underwriter(s) (dealer[s]) to help sell its securities to the public, the parties must sign an underwriting agreement, which is also known as an agreement among underwriters. The underwriting agreement will outline, among other things, the method of distribution (firm commitment, best efforts, or standby).

The Underwriting Agreement is a contract between the issuer of the securities and the managing or lead underwriter. It must be agreed upon and signed prior to any securities can be sold to the public. Now, for SIE purposes, you don't need to know all the details about the Underwriting Agreement, but you should have a basic understanding of the types of underwritings: firm commitment and best efforts.

Firm commitment

In a firm commitment underwriting, the lead underwriter and syndicate members (other underwriters who may be helping in the sale of the securities) agree to purchase all the securities that remain unsold after the offering. In this case, the underwriter(s) assume(s) all the financial risk.

Another type of firm commitment offering is a standby. A stand-by underwriter signs an agreement with the issuer to purchase any stock not purchased by the public if/when an issuer has a rights offering (Chapter 10).

Best efforts

In a best efforts underwriting, the underwriter(s) is/are agreeing to make their best effort(s) to sell all the securities to the public (hey, that's how they make money). If, however, they cannot sell all the securities to the public, the issuer has the right to either cancel the offering or take back some of the unsold securities depending on whether it is an All or None offering or a Mini-Max offering:

>> **All or None (AON):** If the offering is set up as an AON agreement, all the securities must be sold by the deadline or the deal is canceled.

>> **Mini-Max:** A mini-max offering is one in which a specified minimum number of securities must be sold in order for the deal not to be canceled. If that minimum threshold is reached, the issuer will take back any securities that remain unsold.

You should be aware that if securities are sold on a best efforts basis, purchasers and potential purchasers must be made aware that the offering could be canceled. Purchasers' money is held in an escrow account until the terms are met or the deal is canceled. Once the specified number of securities are sold, the underwriter(s) release(s) the securities to the purchasers. If, however, the underwriters do not sell enough of the securities by the deadline, the purchasers receive their money back.

REMEMBER

According to FINRA, "A member, in the conduct of its business, shall observe high standards of commercial honor and just and equitable principles of trade." So regardless of whether the securities offered during an IPO are sold on a firm commitment or best efforts underwriting, it must be a *bona fide offering* of the securities at the public offering price. Firms cannot hold back securities for themselves, associated persons and their immediate family, industry insiders, portfolio managers, and so on.

Getting the skinny on the issue and issuer: The prospectus

The issuer prepares a preliminary prospectus (sometimes with the help of the underwriter) that's sent in with the registration statement. The preliminary prospectus must be available for potential purchasers when the issue is in registration (during the cooling-off period) with the SEC. The preliminary prospectus is abbreviated, but it contains all the essential facts about the issuer and issue except for the final offering price (public offering price, or POP) and the *effective date* (the date that the issue will first be sold).

A preliminary prospectus is sometimes called a *red herring*, not because it smells fishy (or is totally misleading and irrelevant) but because a statement in red lettering on the cover of the preliminary prospectus declares that it's not the final version and that some items may change in the meantime.

The *final prospectus*, which is prepared toward the end of the cooling-off period, is a legal document that the issuer prepares; it contains material information about the issuer and new issue of securities. The final prospectus has to be available to all potential purchasers of the issue. It includes

>> The final offering price

>> The underwriters' spread (the profit the underwriters make per share)

>> The delivery date (when the securities will be available)

Note: Because all mutual (open-end) funds constantly issue new securities, they must always have a prospectus available. In addition, many mutual funds also provide a *statement of additional information (SAI),* which provides more detailed information about the fund's operation that may be useful to some investors. A statement of additional information is also known as "Part B" of a fund's registration statement.

Counting the securities along the way

When a company issues securities and they're traded in the market, someone has to be responsible for keeping track of the owners of the securities, and someone has to make sure that the number of securities in the market isn't greater than it's supposed to be. These jobs are assigned to a registrar and a transfer agent:

» **Registrar:** The *registrar* is an independent entity that works along with a company's transfer agent to maintain a record of stock and bond owners. The main function of a registrar is to make sure that the outstanding shares don't exceed the amount of stock the issuer authorizes under its corporate *charter* (or *bylaws,* rules the company lives by).

» **Transfer agent:** The *transfer agent* maintains records of a corporation's stock and bond owners (much like a registrar) but also mails and cancels stock certificates as necessary.

TIP

An easy way to keep these folks straight is to remember that a registrar is responsible for counting things and a transfer agent is responsible for transferring or sending things.

Getting Up to Speed on the Types of Securities Offerings

Table 5-1 deals with the different types of offerings that you (as a mega-broker) should be familiar with. The offerings that follow usually require the services of an underwriter or underwriting syndicate to sell the securities to the public.

TABLE 5-1   Types of Securities Offerings

Type	Description	Who Profits
Initial public offering (IPO)	The first time an issuer sells stock to the public to raise capital; issuers usually hold back some stock for future primary offerings.	The bulk of the moolah raised goes to the issuer, and the rest goes to the underwriters.
Primary offering	An offering of new securities from an issuer that has previously issued securities; a company can have an initial public offering and several primary offerings if it wants to.	The proceeds of sale go to the issuer and underwriters.
Secondary offerings	A sale of a large block of outstanding (stockholder-owned) securities or previously outstanding securities (treasury stock, or stock the issuer has repurchased); typically, one or more major stockholders of a corporation are the ones who make the secondary offerings; new investors are essentially buying used, so the number of shares outstanding doesn't change.	The sales proceeds don't go to the issuer (except with treasury stock); they go to the big shots selling the securities.
Split (combined) offering	A combination of a primary and secondary offerings, with both new and outstanding securities.	A portion of the sales proceeds goes to the issuer, and a portion goes to the selling stockholders.

For initial public offerings (IPOs), a final prospectus needs to be available to all purchasers of the IPO for 90 days after the *effective date* (the first day the security starts trading).

With primary, secondary, or combined offerings, a final prospectus has to be available to all purchasers of the primary offering for 25 days after the effective date for all issuers whose securities are already listed on an exchange or NASDAQ. If an issuer has already issued securities but not on an exchange or NASDAQ, the final prospectus has to be available for 40 days after the effective date.

In the event that a member is acting as a dealer or has some other financial interest in recommending a security other than the commission received from the buyer, it must be disclosed in writing to the client at or before the completion of the transaction. So, in that regard, all buyers must be notified in writing if your firm is involved in a primary or secondary distribution of securities.

Reviewing Exemptions

Certain securities are exempt from registration because of either the type of security or the type of transaction involved. You may find that securities that are exempt because of who's issuing them are a bit easier to recognize. You'll probably have to spend a little more time on the securities that are exempt from registration because of the type of transaction.

Exempt securities

Certain securities are exempt from the registration requirements under the Securities Act of 1933. Either these securities come from issuers that have a high level of creditworthiness, or another government regulatory agency has some sort of jurisdiction over the issuer of the securities. These types of securities include

>> Securities issued by the U.S. government or federal agencies

>> Municipal bonds (local government bonds)

>> Securities issued by banks, savings institutions, and credit unions

>> Public utility stocks or bonds

>> Securities issued by religious, educational, or nonprofit organizations

>> Notes, bills of exchange, bankers' acceptances, and commercial paper with an initial maturity of 270 days or less

>> Insurance policies and fixed annuities

Fixed annuities are exempt from SEC registration because the issuing insurance company guarantees the payout. However, variable annuities require registration because the payout varies depending on the performance of the securities held in the separate account. For more info on annuities and other packaged securities, see Chapter 9.

Exempt transactions

Some securities that corporations offer may be exempt from the full registration requirements of the Securities Act of 1933 due to the nature of the sale. The following list shows you these exemptions:

WARNING

>> **Intrastate offerings (Section 3[a][11] and Rule 147):** An intrastate offering is, naturally, an offering of securities within one state. For such an offering to be exempt from SEC registration, the company must be incorporated in the state in which it's selling securities, 80 percent of its business has to be within the state, and it may sell securities only to residents of the state. The securities still require registration at the state level.

Don't confuse *intra*state offerings (securities sold in one state) with *inter*state offerings (securities sold in many states). *Inter*state offerings do need SEC registration. To help you remember, think of an interstate roadway, which continues from one state to the next.

>> **Regulation A (Reg A) offerings:** An offering of securities worth $5 million or less within a 12-month period is Regulation A. Although this company may seem large to you, it's relatively small in market terms. Regulation A offerings are exempt from the full registration requirements, but the issuer still has to file a simplified registration or abbreviated registration statement.

>> **Regulation D (Reg D) offerings:** Also known as a *private placement* (private securities offering), a Regulation D offering is an offering to no more than 35 unaccredited investors per year. Companies that issue securities through private placement are allowed to raise an unlimited amount of money but are limited in terms of the number of unaccredited investors. Sales of Reg D securities are subject to the sales limitations set forth under Rule 144.

An *accredited investor* is one with a net worth of $1 million or more or an investor who has had a yearly income of at least $200,000 (for an individual investor) or $300,000 (for joint income with spouse) for the previous two years and is expected to earn at least that much in the current year.

>> **Rule 144:** This rule covers the sale of restricted, unregistered, and control securities (stock owned by directors, officers, or persons owning 10 percent or more of the issuer's voting stock). According to Rule 144, sellers of these securities must wait anywhere from six months to a year, depending on whether the corporation that issued the securities is subject to the reporting requirements of the Securities Exchange Act of 1934 prior to selling the securities to the public. Additionally, the most an investor can sell at one time is 1 percent of the outstanding shares or the average weekly trading volume for the previous four weeks, whichever is greater.

The following example tests your ability to answer restricted-stock questions.

EXAMPLE

John Bullini is a control person who purchased shares of restricted stock and wants to sell under Rule 144. John has fully paid for the shares and has held them for over one year. There are 1,500,000 shares outstanding. Form 144 is filed on Monday, May 28, and the weekly trading volume for the restricted stock is as follows:

Week Ending	Trading Volume
May 25	16,000 shares
May 18	15,000 shares
May 11	17,000 shares
May 4	15,000 shares
April 27	18,000 shares

What is the maximum number of shares John can sell with this filing?

(A) 15,000

(B) 15,750

(C) 16,200

(D) 16,250

The right answer is Choice (B). The test writers often try to trick you on the SIE exam by giving you at least one week more than you need to answer the question. Because John has held his restricted stock for over a year, he can sell 1 percent of the outstanding shares or the averaged weekly trading volume for the previous four weeks, whichever is greater:

$$1\% \times 1,500,000 \text{ shares outstanding} = 15,000 \text{ shares}$$

$$\frac{16,000 + 15,000 + 17,000 + 15,000}{4 \text{ weeks}} = \frac{63,000}{4 \text{ weeks}} = 15,750 \text{ shares}$$

In this case, the previous four weeks are the top four in the list, but be careful; the examiners are just as likely to use the bottom four to give the table a different look.

Figure out 1 percent of the outstanding shares by multiplying the outstanding shares by 1 percent (easy, right?). In this case, you come up with an answer of 15,000 shares. That's one possible answer. The other possible answer is the average weekly trading volume for the previous four weeks. Add the trading volume for the previous four weeks (the top four in the chart) and divide by 4 to get an answer of 15,750 shares. Because you're looking for the greater number, the answer is Choice (B).

Even securities exempt from registration are subject to antifraud rules. All securities are subject to antifraud provisions of the Securities Act of 1933, which requires issuers to provide accurate information regarding any securities offered to the public.

Chapter **6**

Corporate Ownership: Equity Securities

quity securities — such as common and preferred stock — represent ownership interest in the issuing company. All publicly held corporations issue equity securities to investors. Investors love these securities because they've historically outperformed most other investments, so an average (or above-average, in your case) stockbroker sells more of these types of securities than any other kind.

The SIE exam tests you on your ability to recognize the types of equity securities and on some other basic information. Although you may find that the SIE doesn't test you heavily on the info provided here, this chapter forms a strong foundation for many other chapters in the book. I think that you'll find it difficult (if not impossible) to understand what an option or mutual fund is if you don't know what a stock is. Needless to say, even though this chapter is small, don't ignore it or it may come back to bite you.

Beginning with the Basics: Common Stock

Corporations issue common stock (as well as other securities) to raise business capital. As an equity security, common stock represents ownership of the issuing corporation. If a corporation issues 1 million shares of stock, each share represents one-millionth ownership of the issuing corporation. Read on for the ins and outs of common stock.

Stockholders have *limited liability*. Stockholders' liability is limited to the amount invested. In other words, if a corporation that you invested in goes belly up, you lose only what you invested and nobody will come knocking on your door for additional bucks. If a corporation goes bankrupt, it must distribute any remaining assets in the following way (also known as the *order of liquidation*):

1. **Unpaid workers**

2. **The IRS**

3. **Secured creditors**

   Secured creditors have issued loans that are secured with collateral, bonds, and so forth.

4. **General creditors**

   General creditors have issued unsecured loans, which are not secured with collateral (bank loans, accounts payable, and so on).

5. **Subordinated debentures**

   Subordinated debentures are junior, unsecured bonds and holders of subordinated debentures are the last *creditors* to be paid in the event of corporate bankruptcy.

6. **Preferred stockholders**

7. **Common stockholders**

REMEMBER

Common stockholders have what are known as *residual rights*, which means they are the last to get paid in the event of corporate bankruptcy. Bonds and preferred stock are considered *senior securities* in relationship to common stock.

Understanding a stockholder's voting rights

One of the most basic rights that most common stockholders receive is voting rights — although rarely corporations issue *nonvoting common stock*. Nonvoting stock may be issued by corporations to protect their board of directors, but it's not as attractive to investors who like to have some control over who's running the company. Most preferred stock is nonvoting.

When investors have voting rights, every so often a corporation may have those investors vote to change members on the board of directors. Although investors may be able to vote on other issues (like stock splits — see "Splitting common stock" later in this chapter), the SIE focuses on voting to change board members.

Because having all stockholders actually attend the annual corporate meeting to vote would be difficult, stockholders usually vote by *proxy*, or absentee ballot.

Statutory (regular) voting

Statutory, or regular, voting is the most common type of voting that corporations offer to their shareholders. This type of voting is quite straightforward. Investors receive one vote for every share that they own multiplied by the number of positions to be filled on the board of directors (or issues to be decided). However, investors have to *split the votes evenly* for each item on the ballot.

For example, if an investor owns 500 shares and there are four positions to be filled on the board of directors, the investor has a total of 2,000 votes (500×4), which the investor must split evenly among all open positions (500 each). The investor votes yes or no for each candidate.

Cumulative voting

Cumulative voting is a little different from statutory voting (see the preceding section). Although the investor still gets the same number of overall votes as if the corporation were offering statutory voting, the stockholder can vote the shares in any way she sees fit. Cumulative voting gives smaller shareholders (in terms of shares) an easier chance to gain representation on the board of directors.

For example, if an investor owns 1,000 shares and three positions on the board of directors are open, the investor has a total of 3,000 votes (1,000 shares × 3 candidates), which the investor can use to vote for any candidate(s) in any way she sees fit.

REMEMBER

Cumulative voting doesn't give an investor more voting power, just more voting flexibility. The only way to get more voting power is to buy more shares.

Proxies: Voting by mail

Regardless of whether a corporation offers statutory or cumulative voting, when a corporation requires a vote on certain issues — such as splitting its stock, voting for members on the board of directors, and so on — shareholders (since they are owners) are allowed to vote unless the corporation issued non-voting stock (Class B shares). Certainly, the more shares you own, the more voting power you have. Now, suppose you live in New York City and the vote is taking place in Los Angeles . . . what do you do? Well, short of taking a trip across the country, you can vote by proxy (basically an absentee ballot). So, what happens is the issuer will send you a proxy, which will describe the issue(s) to be voted on. You can check the box describing how you want to vote and mail it back. By doing that, you are actually authorizing (giving a limited power of attorney to) another person to vote according to your wishes. A *transfer agent* is responsible for sending out proxies.

Proxy contests

A *proxy fight* or *proxy battle* is an unfriendly event that occurs when a group of stockholders of a corporation decide to vote together to help gain control of the corporation. This usually happens when the stockholders are not happy with the way the corporation is being run. They are typically trying to replace members of the board of directors or individuals in management positions.

Categorizing shares corporations can sell

All publicly held corporations have a certain quantity of shares that they can sell based on their corporate charter. These shares are broken down into a few categories depending on whether the issuer or investors hold the shares:

>> **Authorized shares:** Authorized shares are the number of shares of stock that a corporation can issue. The issuer's bylaws or *corporate charter* (a document filed with the state that identifies the names of the founders of the corporation, the company's objectives, and so on) states the number of shares the company is authorized to sell. However, the issuer usually holds back a large percentage of the authorized stock (which it can sell later through a primary offering — see Chapter 5 for details on offerings).

>> **Issued shares:** Issued shares are the portion of authorized shares that the issuer has sold to the public to raise money.

>> **Outstanding shares:** Outstanding shares are the number of shares that are in investors' hands. This quantity may or may not be the same number as the issued shares. At times, an issuer may decide to repurchase its stock in the market to either help increase the demand (and the price) of the stock trading in the market or to avoid a *hostile takeover* (when another company is trying to gain control of the issuer). Stock that the issuer repurchases is called *treasury stock.*

The standard formula for outstanding shares follows:

outstanding = issued − treasury

Considering the par value of common stock

Par value for common stock is not as important to investors as it is to bondholders and preferred stockholders (see the later section "Considering characteristics of preferred stock"). *Par value* for common stock is more or less a bookkeeping value for the issuer. Although issuers may set the par value at $1 (or $5, $10, or whatever), the selling price is usually much more. A stock's par value has no relation to the market price of the stock.

REMEMBER

The amount over par value that an issuer receives for selling stock is called *paid-in capital, paid-in surplus,* or *capital surplus.*

The *stated par value* is printed on the stock certificate; it may change as the result of corporate actions such as a stock split (see "Splitting common stock" later in this chapter). An issuer can also issue *no par value stock* (stock issued without a stated par value); in this case, the stock has a stated value that the corporation uses for bookkeeping purposes. A lack of par value doesn't affect investors.

Corporate actions

Besides just attempting to build their business, corporations may take other actions that will affect the price of their securities. They can split their stock (see the next section, "Splitting common stock"), reverse split their stock (see the section "Reverse splits"), or engage in buybacks, tender offers, exchange offers, rights offerings (see the later section "Rights: The right to buy new shares at a discount"), mergers, or acquisitions.

» **Buybacks:** This happens when a cash-rich corporation repurchases some of its own shares in the market. Buybacks typically increase the market value of the underlying security. After a successful buyback, fewer shares will be outstanding.

» **Tender offers:** This is when a corporation, person, or group attempts to gain control (make a *takeover bid*) of a corporation (the *target corporation*). A tender offer is typically announced in financial publications, and the offer will be at a premium to the market value of the securities. Tender offers are only for a specified period of time, and the purchaser will require a minimum number of shareholders (in other words, holders of over 50 percent of the outstanding shares of the target corporation) to agree or the offer is canceled. Tender offers increase the market price of the securities being targeted.

» **Exchange offers:** Sometimes a corporation may decide to exchange some of its securities for other ones. For example, a corporation may offer its bondholders the right to exchange certain debt securities for stock to reduce the corporation's debt. Or, the corporation may offer to exchange 4 percent bonds due to mature in 2 years with 5 percent bonds due to mature in 20 years, thus extending the amount of time the corporation has to pay back its debt.

» **Mergers:** Two existing corporations may decide to merge (combine) their two companies into one larger one. This is often done to gain market share, expand a corporation's reach, or possibly to expand into new segments. Mergers typically have a positive impact on investors.

» **Acquisitions:** As compared to mergers, where two corporations are working together to make one big corporation, an acquisition happens when a larger corporation takes control of a smaller one or a portion of another corporation. For one corporation to acquire another, it must obtain a majority ownership of the target corporation.

As you can imagine, in the event of a corporate action such as a stock split, a merger, an acquisition, and so on, investors of the securities must be notified. For public companies listed on an exchange such as the New York Stock Exchange, the exchanges handle the notification of their clients as well as make the information available online. If the securities trade over-the-counter (OTC), FINRA (the Financial Industry Regulatory Authority) is responsible for handing the announcement.

Splitting common stock

You may ask yourself, "Why would a company split its stock?" The obvious answer is that the company wants to make the market price of the security more attractive. The normal unit of trading is 100 shares of stock (*a round lot*) and if the price of a security gets too high, the number of investors who can purchase it becomes limited. If Microsoft had never split its stock (which it has already done nine times), a round lot would cost investors about $750,000 at the time of this writing. Know a lot of investors who could afford that?

Companies may alternatively use a reverse split, consolidating shares so they can raise the price of the stock and perhaps boost investor confidence. The next couple of sections take you through splits so you know them forward and backward.

Stockholders can vote on stock splits (please see "Understanding a stockholder's voting rights" earlier in the chapter for info on types of voting). Be aware that after a stock split, investors may have more or fewer votes, but they still hold the same percentage of votes. When a company splits its stock, the number of authorized shares needs to be changed on the *corporate charter* (see the earlier section "Categorizing shares corporations can sell").

Forward splits

During a *forward stock split*, the number of shares increases and the price decreases without affecting the total market value of the outstanding shares. After a company forward splits its stock, investors receive additional shares, but the market price (and par value) per share drops. A forward split may be *even* such as a 2-for-1, 3-for-1, 4-for-1 and so on, or *uneven* such as a 3-for-2, 5-for-3, 5-for-2 and so on. You will find that regardless of whether the forward split is even or uneven, the same formula works. Check out the following equations where *A* represents the first number and *B* represents the second number.

Use the following calculations to figure out an investor's position after an *A*-for-*B* split:

$$\text{shares after a split} = \text{shares} \times \frac{A}{B}$$

$$\text{price after a split} = \text{stock price} \times \frac{B}{A}$$

The following question tests your ability to answer a stock split question.

Bob Billingham owns 1,200 shares of DEF common stock at a current market price of $90 per share. If DEF splits its stock 3-for-1, what would Bob's position be after the split?

(A) 400 shares at $270 per share

(B) 400 shares at $90 per share

(C) 3,600 shares at $33.33 per share

(D) 3,600 shares at $30 per share

The answer you're looking for is Choice (D). A forward stock split, like a 3-for-1, increases the number of shares and decreases the price of the stock, so you can immediately cross off Choices (A) and (B). Now check your work:

$$1,200 \text{ shares} \times \frac{3}{1} = 3,600 \text{ shares}$$

$$\$90 \times \frac{1}{3} = \$30$$

TIP

A good way to double-check your work is to make sure that the overall value of the investment doesn't change after the split. Using the example, Bob had $108,000 worth of DEF (1,200 shares × $90) before the split, and after the split he has $108,000 worth of DEF (3,600 shares × $30).

Reverse splits

A reverse stock split has the opposite effect on a security than a forward split does; with a reverse split, the market price of the security increases and the number of shares decreases. As with forward stock splits, the overall market value of the securities doesn't change. A company may reverse split its stock if the market price gets too low, whereby potential investors may think the company has a problem.

In the event of a reverse split, investors usually have to send in their old shares to the transfer agent to receive the new shares. If a company were executing a 1-for-3 reverse split, investors would receive one new share for every three they sent in.

TIP

You can use the same formula to determine an investor's position after a reverse split that you use for forward splits.

The following question tests your ability to answer a reverse stock split question.

EXAMPLE

Betty Billings owns 3,600 shares of GHI common stock at a current market price of $2 per share. If GHI reverse splits its stock 1-for-5, what would Betty's position be after the split?

(A) 600 shares at $10 per share

(B) 720 shares at $10 per share

(C) 18,000 shares at $0.40 per share

(D) 18,000 shares at $10 per share

The correct answer is Choice (B). With a reverse split, the number of shares has to decrease and the price has to increase, so you can immediately eliminate Choices (C) and (D). Check your work:

$$3,600 \text{ shares} \times \frac{1}{5} = 720 \text{ shares}$$

$$\$2 \times \frac{5}{1} = \$10$$

Sharing corporate profits through dividends

If a corporation is profitable (and the board of directors is in a good mood), the board of directors may decide to issue a dividend to investors. If and/or when the corporation declares a dividend, each shareholder is entitled to a *pro rata* share of dividends, meaning that every shareholder receives an equal proportion for each share that she owns. The SIE exam expects you to know the forms of dividends an investor can receive and how the dividends affect both the market price of the stock and an investor's position. Although the investor can receive dividends in cash, stock, or *property forms* (stock of a subsidiary company or sample products made by the issuer), I focus on cash and stock dividends because those scenarios are more likely.

REMEMBER

Investors can't vote on dividends; instead, the board of directors decides dividend payouts. You can imagine that if this decision were left in the investors' hands, they'd vote for dividends weekly! For more info on voting, see "Understanding a stockholder's voting rights," earlier in this chapter.

Cash dividends

Cash dividends are a way for a corporation to share its profits with shareholders. When an investor receives cash dividends, it's a taxable event. Corporations aren't required to pay dividends; however, dividends provide a good incentive for investors to hold onto stock that isn't experiencing much growth. Although cash dividends are nice, the market price of the stock falls on the *ex-dividend date* (the first day the stock trades without a dividend) to reflect the dividend paid:

stock price – dividend = price on ex-dividend date

Try your hand at answering a cash dividend question.

EXAMPLE

ABC stock is trading for $49.50 on the day prior to the ex-dividend date. If ABC previously announced a $0.75 dividend, what will be the next day's opening price?

(A) $48.25

(B) $48.75

(C) $49.50

(D) $50.25

The correct answer is Choice (B). Check your work:

$49.50 – $0.75 = $48.75

The math's as simple as that. Because stocks are now trading in pennies instead of eighths like they used to, calculating the price on the ex-dividend date is a snap.

Stock dividends

Stock dividends are just like forward stock splits in that the investor receives more shares of stock (see the earlier section "Splitting common stock"), only the corporation gives a percentage dividend (5 percent, 10 percent, and so on) instead of splitting the stock 2-for-1, 3-for-1, or whatever. Unlike cash dividends, stock dividends aren't taxable to the stockholder because the investor's overall value of investment doesn't change.

The primary reason for a company to give investors a stock dividend is to make the market price more attractive to investors (if the market price gets too high, it limits the number of investors who can purchase the stock), thus adding *liquidity* (ease of trading) to the stock.

The following question tests your expertise in answering stock dividend questions.

EXAMPLE

Terry Trader owns 400 shares of OXX common stock at $33 per share. OXX previously declared a 10 percent stock dividend. Assuming no change in the market price of OXX prior to the dividend, what is Terry's position after the dividend?

(A) 400 shares at $30

(B) 440 shares at $33

(C) 400 shares at $36.30

(D) 440 shares at $30

The answer you want is Choice (D). In this case, you can find the answer without doing any math. Because the number of shares increases, the price of the stock has to decrease. Therefore, the only answer that works is Choice (D). I can't guarantee that you'll get a question where you don't have to do the math, but don't rule it out; scan the answer choices before pulling out your calculator.

Anyway, here's how the numbers work. You have to remember that the investor's overall value of investment doesn't change. Terry gets a 10 percent stock dividend, so she receives 10 percent more shares. Now Terry has 440 shares of OXX (400 shares + 40 shares [10 percent of 400]). Next, you need to determine her overall value of investment:

$$400 \text{ shares} \times \$33 = \$13{,}200$$

Because the overall value of investment doesn't change, Terry needs to have $13,200 worth of OXX after the dividend:

$$\frac{\$13{,}200}{440 \text{ shares}} = \$30 \text{ per share}$$

Terry's position after the split is 440 shares at $30 per share.

REMEMBER

When you or one of your clients owns securities subject to corporate actions such as splits, stock dividends, mergers, and so on, the securities are going to change. In some cases, such as forward stock splits and stock dividends, you or your client will receive more shares at a lower cost basis and the cost basis of the shares held will be lowered accordingly. The adjustment to the cost basis is important for tax purposes.

For argument's sake, say that you purchased 1,000 shares of UPPP Corporation at $40 per share. In this case, you have stock with a cost basis of $40,000 (1,000 shares at $40 per share). If the stock splits 2 for 1, you will have 2 shares for every 1 purchased. The corporation is not just giving you another $40,000 worth of stock, it cut the price in half to adjust for the split. So, as your market price gets cut in half, so does the cost basis per share. In the example, you would now have 2,000 shares with a cost basis of $20 per share ($40,000 cost basis) even if the market value is $55,000. In the event of a split, the issuer would mail new securities at a lower par value and give you a sticker to place on the old securities to lower the par value. In the event of an exchange offer, merger, or acquisition, the security that you're holding would likely change. In this case (assuming you were physically holding the security), the issuer would be responsible for mailing the new security. Whether the securities are physically held or in book-entry form, the issuer must update its books for any changes.

Getting Preferential Treatment: Preferred Stock

Equity securities represent shares of ownership in a company, and debt securities, well, represent debt (see Chapters 7 and 8 for info on debt securities). Although preferred stock has some characteristics of both equity and debt securities, preferred stock is an equity security because it represents ownership of the issuing corporation the same way that common stock does.

Considering characteristics of preferred stock

One advantage of purchasing preferred stock over common stock is that preferred shareholders receive money back (if there's any left) before common stockholders do if the issuer declares bankruptcy. However, the main difference between preferred stock and common stock has to do with dividends. Issuers of common stock pay a cash dividend only if the company's in a position to share corporate profits. By contrast, issuers of preferred stock are required to pay consistent cash dividends. Preferred stock generally has a par value of $100 per share and tends to trade in the market somewhere close to that par value.

Some of the drawbacks of investing in preferred stock over common stock are the lack of voting rights, the higher cost per share (usually), and limited growth. You can assume for SIE exam purposes that preferred stockholders don't receive voting rights unless they fail to receive their expected dividends (a few other exceptions exist, but you don't need to worry about them now). Also, because the price of preferred stock remains relatively stable, preferred stockholders may miss out on potential gains that common stockholders may realize.

REMEMBER

If the issuer can't make a payment because earnings are low, then in the case that the preferred stock is *cumulative* (see the next section, "Getting familiar with types of preferred stock"), owners are still owed the missing dividend payment(s). The dividend (sharing of profits) that preferred stockholders receive is based on par value. Thus, although par value may be nothing more than a bookkeeping value when you're dealing with common stock, par value is definitely important to preferred stockholders.

To calculate the annual dividend, multiply the percentage of the dividend by the par value. For instance, if a customer owns a preferred stock that pays an 8 percent dividend and the par value is $100, you set up the following equation:

8% preferred stock × $100 par = $8 per year in dividends

If the issuer were to pay this dividend quarterly (once every three months), an investor would receive $2 every three months.

REMEMBER

When working on a dividend question on preferred stock, you need to look for the par value in the problem. It's normally $100, but it could be $25, $50, and so on.

Getting familiar with types of preferred stock

You need to be aware of several types of preferred stock for the Series 7. This section gives you a brief explanation of the types and some of their characteristics. Some preferred stock may be a combination of the different types, as in cumulative convertible preferred stock. Here are the distinctions between noncumulative and cumulative preferred stock:

>> **Noncumulative (straight) preferred:** This type of preferred stock is rare. The main feature of preferred stock is that investors receive a consistent cash dividend. In the event that the issuer doesn't pay the dividend, the company usually still owes it to investors. This isn't the case for noncumulative preferred stock. If the preferred stock is noncumulative and the issuer fails to pay a dividend, the issuer doesn't owe it to investors. An investor may choose noncumulative preferred stock over common stock because the company is still supposed to pay a consistent cash dividend.

>> **Cumulative preferred:** Cumulative preferred stock is more common. If an investor owns cumulative preferred stock and doesn't receive an expected dividend, the issuer still owes that dividend. If the issuer declares a common dividend, the issuer first has to make up all delinquent payments to cumulative preferred stockholders.

The following question tests your understanding of cumulative preferred stock.

EXAMPLE

An ABC investor owns 8 percent cumulative preferred stock ($100 par). In the first year, ABC paid $6 in dividends. In the second year, it paid $4 in dividends. If a common dividend is declared the following year, how much must the preferred shareholders receive?

(A) $6

(B) $8

(C) $12

(D) $14

The right answer is Choice (D). Because ABC is cumulative preferred stock, issuers have to catch up preferred stockholders on all outstanding dividends before common shareholders receive a dividend. In this example, the investor is supposed to receive $8 per year in dividends (8% × $100 par). In the first year, the issuer shorted the investor $2; in the second year, $4. The investor hasn't yet received payment for the following year, so she is owed $8. Add up these debts:

$$(\$8 - \$6) + (\$8 - \$4) + \$8 = \$2 + \$4 + \$8 = \$14$$

All preferred stock has to be either cumulative or noncumulative. Both types may have other features, including the ability to turn into other kinds of stock, offerings of extra dividends, and other VIP treatment. I run through some of these traits in the list that follows:

>> **Convertible preferred:** Convertible preferred stock allows investors to trade their preferred stock for common stock of the same company at any time. Because the issuers are providing investors with another way to make money, investors usually receive a lower dividend payment than with regular preferred stock.

The *conversion price* is the dollar price at which a convertible preferred stock par value can be exchanged into a share of common stock. When the convertible preferred stock is first issued, the conversion price is specified and is based on par value. The *conversion ratio* tells you the number of shares of common stock that an investor receives for converting one share of preferred stock.

You can use the following conversion ratio formula for convertible preferred stock and also for convertible bonds (see Chapter 7 for info on convertible bonds):

$$\text{conversion ratio} = \frac{\text{par value}}{\text{conversion price}}$$

REMEMBER

The conversion ratio helps you determine a *parity price* where the convertible preferred stock and common stock would be trading equally. For example, say you have a convertible preferred stock that's exchangeable for four shares of common stock. If the convertible preferred stock is trading at $100 and the common stock is trading at $25, they're on parity because four shares of stock at $25 equal $100. However, if there's a disparity in the exchange values, converting may be profitable. If the convertible preferred stock is trading at $100 and the common stock is trading at $28, the common stock is trading above parity; converting makes sense because investors are exchanging $100 worth of securities for $112 worth of securities ($28 × 4).

>> **Callable preferred:** Callable preferred stock allows the issuer to buy back the preferred stock at any time at a price on the certificate. This stock is a little riskier for investors because they don't have control over how long they can hold the stock, so corporations usually pay a higher dividend on callable preferred stock than on regular preferred stock.

- **Participating preferred:** Although rarely issued, participating preferred stock allows the investors to receive common dividends in addition to the usual preferred dividends.

- **Prior (senior) preferred:** Preferred stockholders receive compensation before common stockholders in the event of corporate bankruptcy. In this case, senior preferred stockholders receive compensation even before other preferred stockholders. Because of the extra safety factor, senior preferred stock pays a slightly lower dividend than other preferred stock from the same issuer.

- **Adjustable (floating rate) preferred:** Holders of adjustable preferred stock receive a dividend that's reset every six months to match movements in the prevailing interest rates. Because the dividend adjusts to changing interest rates, the stock price remains more stable.

Securities with a Twist

Some securities fall outside the boundaries of the more normal common and preferred stock, but I still include them in this equities chapter because they involve ownership in a company or the opportunity to get it. This section gives you an overview of those special securities.

Opening national borders: ADRs

American Depositary Receipts (ADRs) are receipts for foreign securities traded in the United States. ADRs are negotiable certificates (they can be sold or transferred to another party) that represent a specific number of shares (usually one to ten) of a foreign stock. ADR investors may or may not have voting privileges. U.S. banks issue them; therefore, investors receive dividends in U.S. dollars. The stock certificates are held in a foreign branch of a U.S. bank (the custodian bank) and, to exchange their ADRs for the actual shares, investors return the ADRs to the bank that's holding the shares. In addition to the risks associated with stock ownership in general, ADR owners are subject to currency risk (the risk that the value of the security may decline because the value of the currency of the issuing corporation may fall in relation to the U.S. dollar). For information on how the strength of the dollar affects the relative prices of goods in the international market, flip to Chapter 13.

Rights: The right to buy new shares at a discount

Corporations offer rights (subscription or preemptive rights) to their common stockholders. To maintain their proportionate ownership of the corporation, *rights* allow existing stockholders to purchase new shares of the corporation at a discount directly from the issuer, before the shares are offered to the public. Stockholders receive one right for each share owned. The rights are short-term (usually 30 to 45 days). The rights are marketable and may be sold by the stockholders to other investors. If existing stockholders don't purchase all the shares, the issuer offers any unsold shares to a standby underwriter. A *standby underwriter* is a broker-dealer that purchases any stock that wasn't sold in the rights offering and then resells the shares to other investors.

TIP

For the SIE exam, you can assume that common stockholders automatically receive rights.

Warrants: The right to buy stock at a fixed price

Warrants are certificates that entitle the holder to buy a specific amount of stock at a fixed price; they're usually issued along with a new bond or stock offering. Warrant holders have no voting rights and receive no dividends. Bundled bonds and warrants or bundled stock and warrants are called *units*. They are long term and sometimes perpetual (without an expiration date). Warrants are *sweeteners* because they're something that the issuer throws into the new offering to make the deal more appealing; however, warrants can also be sold separately on the market. When warrants are originally issued, the warrant's exercise price is set well above the underlying stock's market price.

For example, suppose QRS warrants give investors the right to buy QRS common stock at $20 per share when QRS common stock is trading at $12. Certainly, exercising their warrants to purchase QRS stock at $20 wouldn't make sense for investors when they can buy QRS stock in the market at $12. However, if QRS rises above $20 per share, holders of warrants can exercise their warrants and purchase the stock from the issuer at $20 per share.

IN THIS CHAPTER

» Understanding the specifics on
  bonds

» Examining securities issued by the
  U.S. government

» Looking at short-term bonds

Chapter **7**

Debt Securities: Corporate and U.S. Government Loans

I nstead of giving up a portion of their company (via stock certificates), corporations can borrow money from investors by selling bonds. Local governments (through municipal bonds) and the U.S. government also issue bonds. For SIE exam purposes, most bonds are considered safer than stocks.

Bondholders aren't owners of a company like stockholders are; they're creditors. Bondholders lend money to an institution for a fixed period of time and receive interest for doing so. This arrangement allows the institution to borrow money on its terms (with its chosen maturity date, scheduled interest payments, interest rate, and so on), which it can't do by borrowing from a lending institution.

The SIE exam tests you on your ability to understand the different types of bonds issued, terminology, and yes, some math. This chapter has you covered in topics relating to corporate and U.S. government debt securities.

Tackling Bond Terms, Types, and Traits

Before you delve deeper into bonds, make sure you have a good handle on the basics. Understanding the bond basics is a building block that can make all the rest of the bond stuff easier. In this section, I first review basic bond terminology and then move on to some bond characteristics.

Remembering bond terminology

The SIE exam designers expect you to know general bond terminology. (And I give it to you here — that's why I get paid the big bucks!) In this section, I help you reinforce the information you may have already learned from a prep course or study material (or are in the process of learning). This stuff is basic, but the SIE exam does test it:

REMEMBER

>> **Maturity date:** All issued bonds have a stated maturity date (for example, 20 years, 30 years, and so on). The maturity date is the year bondholders get paid back for the loans they made. At maturity, bondholders receive par value (see the next bullet).

>> **Par value:** Par value is the face value of the bond. Although par value isn't significant to common stockholders (whose issuers use it solely for bookkeeping purposes), it's important to bondholders. For SIE exam purposes, you can assume that the par value for each bond is $1,000 unless otherwise stated in the question.

Bond prices are quoted as a percentage of par value, often without the percent sign. A bond trading at 100 is trading at 100 percent of $1,000 par. Regardless of whether investors purchase a bond for $850 (85), $1,000 (100), or $1,050 (105), they'll receive par value at the maturity date of the bond, usually with interest payments along the way. Corporate bonds are usually quoted in increments of 1/8 percent (1/8% = 0.00125 or $1.25), so a corporate bond quoted at 99⅜ (99.375 percent) would be trading at $993.75.

>> **Coupon rate:** Of course, investors aren't lending money to issuers for nothing; investors receive interest for providing loans to the issuer. The coupon rate on the bond tells the investors how much annual interest they'll receive.

The coupon rate is expressed as a percentage of par value. For example, a bond with a coupon rate of 6 percent would pay annual interest of $60 (6% × $1,000 par value). You can assume that bonds pay interest semiannually unless otherwise stated. So in this example, the investor would receive $30 every six months.

REMEMBER

Bondholders receive *interest* (payment for the use of the money loaned), and stockholders receive *dividends* (see Chapter 6).

>> **The bond indenture:** The *indenture* (also known as *deed of trust*) is the legal agreement between the issuer and the investor. It's printed on or attached to the bond certificate. All indentures contain basic terms:

- The maturity date

- The par value

- The coupon rate (interest rate) and interest payment dates

- Any collateral securing the bond (see "Comparing secured and unsecured bonds" later in this chapter)

- Any callable or convertible features (check out "Contrasting callable and put bonds" and "Popping the top on convertible bonds" later in this chapter)

The bond indenture also includes the name of a trustee. A *trustee* is an organization that administers a bond issue for an institution. It ensures that the bond issuer meets all the terms and conditions associated with the borrowing. Essentially, the trustee tries to make sure that the issuer does the right thing.

The following question tests your knowledge of bond interest.

EXAMPLE

Jane Q. Investor purchased 100 AA rated bonds issued by COW Corp. Jane purchased the bonds at 105 percent of par value, and they are currently trading in the market at 104. If the coupon rate is 7½ percent, how much annual interest does Jane receive?

(A) $37.50

(B) $75.00

(C) $3,750.00

(D) $7,500.00

The correct answer is Choice (D). This is a nice, easy question after you wade through the information that you don't need. You need only the number of bonds and the coupon rate to figure out the answer. Don't let yourself get distracted by the rating, purchase price, or market price. That information is there to confuse you.

Jane purchased 100 bonds at $1,000 par (remember you can assume $1,000 par) with a coupon rate of 7½ percent, so do the math:

$$100 \text{ bonds} \times \$1,000 \text{ par} \times 7\ 1/2\% = \$7,500.00$$

Choice (C) would have been correct if the question had asked for the semiannual interest.

Following bond issue and maturity schedules

Not only can bond certificates be in different forms, but they can also be scheduled with different types of maturities. Maturity schedules depend on the issuer's needs. The following list presents an explanation of the types of bond issues and maturity schedules:

>> **Term bonds:** Term bonds are all issued at the same time and have the same maturity date. For example, if a company issues 20 million dollars' worth of term bonds, they may all mature in 20 years. Because of the large payment that's due at maturity, most corporations issuing this type of bond have a sinking fund. Most corporations issue term bonds because they lock in a coupon rate for a long period of time.

A corporation creates a *sinking fund* when it sets aside money over time in order to retire its debt. Investors like to see that a sinking fund is in place because it lowers the likelihood of *default* (the risk that the issuer can't pay interest or par value back at maturity).

>> **Series bonds:** These bonds are issued in successive years but have only one maturity date. Issuers of series bonds pay interest only on the bonds that they've issued so far. Construction companies that are building developments in several phases issue this type of bond.

>> **Serial bonds:** In this type of bond issue, a portion of the outstanding bonds mature at regular intervals (for example, 10 percent of the entire issue matures yearly). Serial bonds are usually issued by corporations and municipalities to fund projects that provide regular income streams. Most municipal (local government) bonds are issued with serial maturity.

A serial bond that has more bonds maturing on the final maturity date is called a *balloon issue.*

TIP

The SIE exam focuses mainly on term and serial bonds. A typical SIE exam question may ask, "Which of the following types of bonds is most likely to have a sinking fund?" Answer: Term bonds.

Comparing secured and unsecured bonds

The assets of the issuer may or may not back bonds. For test purposes, assume that bonds backed by *collateral* (assets that the issuer owns) are considered safer for the investor. *Secured bonds,* or bonds backed by collateral, involve a pledge from the issuer that a specific asset (for instance, property) will be sold to pay off the outstanding debt in the event of default. Obviously, with all else being equal, secured bonds normally have a lower yield than unsecured bonds.

The SIE exam tests your knowledge of several types of secured bonds:

>> **Mortgage bonds:** These bonds are backed by property that the issuer owns. In the event of default or bankruptcy, the issuer must liquidate the property to pay off the outstanding bonds.

» **Equipment trusts:** This type of bond is mainly issued by transportation companies and is backed by equipment they own (for instance, airplanes or trucks). If the company defaults on its bonds, it sells the assets backing the bonds to satisfy the debt.

» **Collateral trusts:** These bonds are backed by financial assets (stocks and bonds) that the issuer owns. A *trustee* (a financial institution the issuer hires) holds the assets and sells them to pay off the bonds in the event of default.

» **Guaranteed bonds:** Guaranteed bonds are backed by a firm other than the original issuer, usually a parent company. If the issuer defaults, the parent company pays off the bonds. As such, the rating of the bonds is tied to the rating of the guarantor.

Unsecured bonds are the opposite of secured bonds: These bonds are not backed by any assets whatsoever, only by the good faith and credit of the issuer. If a reputable company that has been around for a long time issues the bonds, the bonds aren't considered too risky. If they're issued by a relatively new company or one with a bad credit rating, hold onto your seat! Again, for SIE exam purposes, assume that unsecured bonds are riskier than secured bonds. Here's the lineup of unsecured bonds:

» **Debentures:** These bonds are backed only by the issuer's good word and written agreement (the indenture) stating that the issuer will pay the investor interest when due (usually semiannually) and par value at maturity.

» **Income bonds:** These bonds are the riskiest of all. The issuer promises to pay par value back at maturity and will make interest payments only if earnings are high enough. Companies in the process of reorganization usually issue these bonds at a deep discount (for example, the bonds sell for $500 and mature at par, or $1,000). For test purposes (and real-world purposes), you shouldn't recommend these bonds to investors who can't afford to take a lot of risk.

REMEMBER

Because secured bonds are considered safer than unsecured bonds, secured bonds normally have lower coupon rates. You can assume that for the SIE, the more risk an investor takes, the more reward he will receive. Remember the saying "more risk equals more reward." More reward may be in the form of a higher coupon rate or a lower purchase price. Either one — or both — lead to a higher yield for the investor.

Check out the following question for an example of how the SIE may test your knowledge of the types of bonds.

EXAMPLE

Jon Bearishnikoff is a 62-year-old investor who has 50 percent of his portfolio invested in common stock of up-and-coming companies. The other 50 percent of his portfolio is invested in a variety of stocks of more secure companies. Jon would like to start investing in bonds. If Jon's main concern is the safety of his investment, which of the following bonds would you LEAST likely recommend?

(A) Collateral trust bonds

(B) Mortgage bonds

(C) Equipment trust bonds

(D) Income bonds

The answer you're looking for is Choice (D). This problem includes a lot of garbage information that you don't need to answer the question. One of your jobs (should you decide to accept it) is to dance your way through the question and cherry-pick the information that you do need. The last sentence is usually the most important one when answering a question. Jon is looking for safety; therefore, you'd least likely recommend income bonds because they're usually issued by companies in the process of reorganizing. As a side note, if you become Jon's broker, he shouldn't have 100 percent of his investments in stock. At his age, Jon should have a decent amount of his portfolio invested in fixed-income securities.

REMEMBER

When comparing short-term versus long-term debt securities, short-term bonds from the same issuer are considered safer because the investor is not tying up his money for as long a period of time. Because of the extra risk long-term bondholders are taking for tying up their money for a longer period of time, long-term bondholders generally (except in rare cases) receive a higher coupon (interest rate) for taking that additional risk.

Making Basic Bond Price and Yield Calculations

Although there's not a lot of math on the SIE exam, it does test your knowledge of bond prices, bond yields, and how to calculate them. In this section, I review the relationship between bond prices and bond yields. I also show you how accrued interest can affect how much customers have to pay for the bond. Outstanding bond prices typically don't remain static. As you can imagine, they too are affected by things like supply and demand, corporate rating change (see "Determining the Best Investment: Comparing Bonds" later in this chapter), interest rate changes, whether the bond was purchased at a discount (below par value) or a premium (above par value), and so on.

REMEMBER

The relationship between outstanding bond prices and yields is an inverse one. You can assume for SIE exam purposes that if interest rates decrease, outstanding bond prices increase and vice versa. Say, for example, that a company issues bonds with a 7 percent coupon rate for $1,000. After the bonds are on the market, interest rates decrease. The company can now issue bonds with a 6 percent coupon rate. Investors with the 7 percent bonds are then in a very good position and can demand a premium for their bonds.

Rates down ⇓ = Prices up ⇑

Rates up ⇑ = Prices down ⇓

Finding bond yields

The following sections review the types of bond yields and how the SIE exam tests this topic.

Nominal yield (coupon rate)

The *nominal yield* (NY) is the easiest yield to understand because it's the coupon rate on the face of the bonds. For exam purposes, you can assume that the coupon rate will remain fixed for the life of a bond. If you have a 7 percent bond, the bond will pay $70 per year interest (7% × $1,000 par value) for the life of the bond. When a problem states that a security is a 7 percent (or 6 percent or whatever) bond, it's giving the nominal yield.

Current yield

The *current yield* (CY) is the annual rate of return on a security. The CY of a bond changes when the market price changes; you can determine the CY by dividing the annual interest by the market price:

$$\text{Current yield (CY)} = \frac{\text{annual interest}}{\text{market price}}$$

The following question involves bond yields.

Monique Moneybags purchased one XYZ convertible mortgage bond at 105. Two years later, the bond is trading at 98. If the coupon rate of the bond is 6%, what is the current yield of the bond?

(A) 5.7%

(B) 6.0%

(C) 6.1%

(D) Cannot be determined

The correct answer is Choice (C). Yes, I'm giving you a question with a lot of unnecessary information. All I can tell you is that, unfortunately, you'll have to get used to it. The securities exam creators are notorious for inserting useless (and sometimes misleading) information into the questions to daze and confuse you. In this case, you need only the annual interest and the market price to calculate the answer. Use the following formula to get your answer:

$$CY = \frac{\text{annual interest}}{\text{market price}} = \frac{\$60}{\$980} = 6.1\%$$

The annual interest is $60 (6% coupon rate × $1,000 par value), and the current market price is $980 (98% of $1,000 par). The facts that the bond is convertible (bondholders can trade it for common stock — see "Popping the top on convertible bonds" later in this chapter) or a mortgage bond (backed by the issuer's property) and that it was purchased at 105 ($1,050) are irrelevant.

"Cannot be determined," as tempting as it may be, is almost never the correct answer on the SIE exam.

Yield to maturity (basis)

The *yield to maturity* (YTM) is the yield an investor can expect if holding the bond until maturity. The YTM takes into account not only the market price but also par value, the coupon rate, and the amount of time until maturity. When someone yells to you, "Hey, what's that bond yielding?" (all right, maybe I run in a different circle of friends), he's asking for the YTM. The formula for YTM is as follows:

$$YTM = \frac{\text{annual interest} + \text{annual accretion or} - \text{annual amortization}}{(\text{market price} + \text{par value}) / 2}$$

$$\text{annual accretion} = \frac{\text{par value} - \text{market price}}{\text{years until maturity}}$$

$$\text{annual amortization} = \frac{\text{market price} - \text{par value}}{\text{years until maturity}}$$

I wouldn't worry about committing the preceding equations to memory. The amount of math you will need on the SIE exam is pretty small. However, it is important that you understand the concepts of measurement and what things like yield to maturity, yield to call, total return, yield to worst, and so on mean.

Accretion and amortization (the adjustment of the bond price toward par over the amount of time until the bond matures), such as in the earlier equation, will not be tested on the SIE exam. However, you will need to be able to calculate them on some of the co-requisite exams. So, the preceding equation should help you visualize how yield-to-maturity works.

Yield to call

The *yield to call* (YTC) is the amount that the investor receives if the bond is called prior to maturity. The calculations are similar to those for the YTM (see the preceding section), but you substitute the call price for the par value. The chances of needing it on the SIE exam are even more remote than needing the YTM calculations.

Yield to worst

To determine the *yield to worst* (YTW), you have to calculate the yield to maturity and yield to call for all the call dates (if there's more than one) and choose the lowest. If you get a question on yield to worst, knowing the definition should be enough to get you by.

Total return

The *total return* calculates the full return on a particular investment over a given period of time. As with the other yields noted, you will likely not need to calculate it but rather to understand it. The total return will provide you with a percentage of gain or loss of an investment. To determine the total return, you need to use the following steps:

1. **Determine the initial cost of the investment.**

2. **Calculate the total amount of interest or dividends received over the time of investment.**

3. **Add the interest or dividends to the selling price.**

4. **Take that number and divide it by the initial cost of the investment and subtract 1.**

Basis point

A *basis point* is actually one of the easier calculations. Basis points are typically used in the bond market, mutual funds, and exchange-traded funds (ETFs). Basis points are simply 1/100th of a percent. For example, if the yield on a T-Bond lowers 1.2 percent to 1.1 percent, it is said to have moved ten basis points. Also, when comparing expenses on a fund, people often refer to the fund expenses by basis points. For example, if you are comparing two comparable funds, one fund's expenses might be 0.15 percent and the other's 0.13 percent for a difference of 0.02 percent or two basis points.

Determining the Best Investment: Comparing Bonds

As you grind your way through SIE exam questions, you may be asked to determine the best investment for a particular investor. You need to carefully look at the question for clues to help you choose the correct answer. (For instance, is the investor looking for safety? Is the investor close to retirement?) Consider several factors, including credit rating, callable and put features, and convertible features.

Considering bond credit ratings

The institutions that rate bonds are most interested in the likelihood of *default* (the likelihood that the interest and principal won't be paid when due). For the exam, you can assume that the higher the credit rating, the safer the bond and, therefore, the lower the yield.

The two main bond credit rating companies are Moody's and Standard & Poor's (S&P). S&P ratings of BB and lower and Moody's ratings of Ba and lower are considered *junk bonds* or *high-yield bonds*, which have a high likelihood of default, as Table 7-1 explains. (Another credit rating service, called Fitch, uses the same rating symbols as Standard & Poor's.) *Note:* Different sources may show some slight variations in how S&P and Moody's ratings compare; however, the relationships here are the most common.

TABLE 7-1 ## Bond Credit Ratings (by Quality)

Quality	S&P (Standard & Poor's)	Moody's
Highest	AAA	Aaa
High	AA	Aa
Upper medium	A	A
Lower medium	BBB	Baa
Speculative (junk)	BB	Ba
Speculative (junk): Interest or principal payments missed	B	B
Speculative (junk): No interest being paid	C	Caa
In default	D	D

As if these categories aren't enough, S&P can break down each category even further by adding either a plus (+) or minus (−) sign after the letter category. The plus sign represents the high end of the category, and the minus sign designates the lower end of the category. If you see no plus or minus sign, the bond is in the middle of the category. Moody's can further break down a category by adding a 1, 2, or 3. The number 1 is the highest ranking, 2 represents the middle, and 3 is the lowest. The top four ratings are considered *investment grade,* and the letters below that are considered *junk bonds* or *high-yield bonds.*

TIP

The rating company with the capital letters (S&P) uses all capital letters (AAA, AA, and so on). Additionally, S&P has an ampersand (&) between the "S" and the "P" in its name. Think of the ampersand as being like a plus sign to help you remember that S&P uses pluses and minuses within its categories.

Here's a typical bond-ratings question.

EXAMPLE

Place the following Standard & Poor's bond ratings in order from highest to lowest.

 I. A+

 II. AA

 III. A−

 IV. BBB+

 (A) I, II, III, IV

 (B) I, III, II, IV

 (C) IV, I, II, III

 (D) II, I, III, IV

The correct answer is Choice (D). When answering this type of question, always look at the letters first. The only time pluses or minuses come into play is when two answers have the same letters, as in Statements I and III. The highest choice is AA, followed by A+ because it's higher than A−, which is even higher than BBB+.

Contrasting callable and put bonds

Your mission for the SIE exam is to know which bonds are better for investors and when bonds are likely to be called or put. As you may know, bonds can be issued in callable and put forms:

>> **Callable bonds:** A *callable bond* is a bond that the issuer has the right to buy back from investors at the price stated on the indenture (deed of trust). Callable bonds are riskier for investors because investors can't control how long they can hold onto the bonds. To compensate for this risk, they're usually issued with a higher coupon rate (more risk = more reward).

Most callable bonds are issued with call protection. *Call protection* is the amount of time (usually several years) that an issuer has to wait before calling its bonds. Some callable bonds also have a *call premium,* which is an amount over par value that an issuer has to pay if calling its bonds in the year or years immediately following the expiration of the call protection.

If there is a *make whole call provision*, it allows the issuer to call the bonds providing that the issuer makes a lump sum payment to investors that not only includes payment for the bond but also the present value of any future interest payments investors will miss because of the call.

Another type of bond that can be callable is a *step coupon bond*. Also known as stepped coupon bonds or step-up coupon securities, step coupon bonds typically start at a low coupon rate, but the coupon rate increases at predetermined intervals, such as every five years. The issuer typically has the right to call the bonds at par value at the time the coupon rate is due to increase.

>> **Put bonds:** *Put bonds* are better for investors. Put bonds allow the investor to "put" the bonds back (redeem them) to the issuer at any time at the price stated on the indenture. Because the investors have the control, put bonds are (of course) rarely issued. Because these bonds provide more flexibility to investors (who have an interest in the bond and stock prices), put bonds usually have a lower coupon rate.

Remember, there's a direct correlation between interest rates and when bonds are called or put. Issuers call bonds when interest rates decrease; investors put bonds when interest rates increase. Check out the following question to see how this works.

EXAMPLE

Issuers would call their bonds when interest rates

(A) increase

(B) decrease

(C) stay the same

(D) are fluctuating

The correct answer is Choice (B). Being adaptable when taking the SIE exam can certainly help your cause. In this question, you have to look from the issuer's point of view, not the investor's. An issuer would call bonds when interest rates decrease because he could then redeem the bonds with the higher coupon payments and issue bonds with lower coupon payments to save money. Conversely, investors would put their bonds back to the issuer when interest rates increase so they could invest their money at a higher interest rate.

REMEMBER

You can assume for SIE exam purposes that if interest rates increase, bond yields increase.

Popping the top on convertible bonds

Bonds that are convertible into common stock are called *convertible bonds*. Convertible bonds are attractive to investors because investors have an interest in the bond price as well as the price of the underlying stock. *Parity* occurs when a convertible bond and its underlying stock (the stock it's convertible into) are trading equally (that is, when a bond trading for $1,100 is convertible into $1,100 worth of stock).

TIP

If a convertible bond is trading below parity (below the value of the underlying shares it covers), it would make sense for an investor to convert. It costs the investor nothing to convert her bonds into the underlying stock.

In the event that you have to answer a question about convertible bonds to determine whether they're worth converting to the underlying stock, you can use the following formula:

$$\text{conversion ratio} = \frac{\text{par value}}{\text{conversion price}}$$

You can then use the conversion ratio to calculate the parity price:

$$\text{parity price of the bond} = \text{market price of the stock} \times \text{conversion ratio}$$

Exploring U.S. Government Securities

On the SIE and companion exams, you need to know the basic types of U.S. government securities, their initial maturities, and certain characteristics.

As you may already know, the U.S. government also issues bonds. U.S. government bonds are considered the safest of all securities. Yes, you did read that correctly: the *safest of all securities*. I feel it's worth repeating. How can U.S. government securities be so safe when we're running such a large deficit? Guess what — I don't know, and you don't need to know, either. I can only assume that the U.S. government can always print more currency to make payments on its securities if needed. However, even U.S. government securities are subject to certain risks such as interest risk, reinvestment risk, purchasing power risk, and so forth (see Chapter 13).

U.S. government securities are now all issued and held in electronic (book-entry) form. However, because Treasury bonds have maturities of up to 30 years, some are still out there in paper form.

TIP

With government bonds, you use some of the same types of calculations you use for corporate bonds.

Understanding the types and characteristics of U.S. government securities

Table 7-2 gives you an overview of different types of U.S. government securities and their specifics. Memorize all the information in the following chart so you can ace U.S. government securities questions on the SIE exam.

TABLE 7-2 **U.S. Government Securities and Time until Maturity**

Security	Initial Maturity	Characteristics
T-bills (Treasury bills)	4, 13, 26, and 52 weeks. Considered short-term U.S. debt securities.	Issued at a discount and mature at par. The difference between the purchase price and par is considered interest even though no interest payments were made.
T-notes (Treasury notes)	2, 3, 5, 7, and 10 years. Considered intermediate-term U.S. debt securities.	Pay interest every 6 months.
T-bonds (Treasury bonds)	30 years. Considered long-term U.S. debt securities.	Pay interest every 6 months.
T-STRIPS (Separate Trading of Registered Interest and Principal of Securities)	6 months to 30 years.	Issued at a discount and mature at par.
TIPS* (Treasury Inflation-Protected Securities)	5, 10, and 30 years.	Pay interest every 6 months; par value and interest payments adjust according to inflation or deflation.

* TIPS are tied to the Consumer Price Index (CPI), which measures inflation. The par value changes according to inflation. If inflation is high (prices of goods and services are increasing), the par value increases. If we're in a period of deflation (prices on goods and services are decreasing), the par value decreases. Because investors are getting a percentage of par value as their interest payments, the interest payments vary along with the par value.

REMEMBER

For the SIE exam, remember that the interest received on U.S. government securities is exempt from state and local taxes. The interest received on municipal bonds is exempt from federal taxes (although I get into that a little more in the next chapter). Chapter 15 gives you the scoop on taxes.

Agency Securities

Agency bonds are ones issued by a U.S. government–sponsored agency (GSEs — government-sponsored entities). The bonds are backed by the U.S. government, but not all are guaranteed by the full faith and credit of the U.S. government (except for GNMA — Government National Mortgage Association — which are directly backed). As such, agency bonds (although almost as safe) are considered riskier than U.S. government bonds and notes such as T-bonds, T-notes, T-bills, and so on.

GSEs include the following:

>> **GNMA** (Government National Mortgage Association — Ginnie Mae): GNMAs are the only agency securities backed by the full faith and credit of the U.S. government. GNMAs support the Department of Housing and Urban Development (HUD).

>> **FNMA** (Federal National Mortgage Association — Fannie Mae): FNMA is a publicly held corporation that is responsible for providing capital for certain mortgages. As such, FNMA may purchase conventional mortgages, VA mortgages, FHA mortgages, and so on. FNMA is privately owned and publicly held but is still government sponsored (a GSE).

>> **FHLMC** (Federal Home Loan Mortgage Corporation — Freddie Mac): As a public corporation, Freddie Mac was designed to create a secondary market for mortgages. Freddie Mac purchases residential mortgages from financial institutions and packages them into mortgage-backed securities that are sold to investors.

>> **FCS** (Farm Credit System): The FCS consists of lending institutions that provide financing and credit to farmers. It is a government-sponsored agency but is privately owned. The FCS sells securities to investors and in turn loans the funds raised to farmers. The FCS is overseen by The FCA (Farm Credit Administration).

>> **SLMA** (Student Loan Marketing Association): SLMA is not involved in providing mortgages but provides a secondary market for student loans. As such, SLMA purchases student loans and repackages them as short- and medium-term debt securities for sale to investors.

TIP

Certain mortgage-backed securities are susceptible to reinvestment risk because many home-owners refinance when interest rates fall (prepayment risk). In that case, holders of mortgage-backed securities get paid back sooner than expected and would be reinvesting at a lower interest rate. In addition, if interest rates stay the same or increase, homeowners will not refinance as often and holders of mortgage-backed securities may end up having to hold their investment for a longer period of time than expected (extension risk).

Playing It Safe: Short-Term Loans or Money Market Instruments

Your SIE exam will likely include a question or two on money market instruments. *Money market instruments* are relatively safe short-term loans that can be issued by corporations, banks, the U.S. government, and municipalities. Most have maturities of one year or less, and they're usually issued at a discount and mature at par value. The following list reviews some basic characteristics of money market instruments to help you earn an easy point or two on the SIE exam:

>> **Repurchase agreements:** Repurchase agreements (Repos) are a contract between a buyer and a seller. The seller of the securities (usually T-bills) agrees to buy them back at a previously determined price and time. Repos are short-term loans.

>> **Federal Funds:** Federal Funds are loans between banks to help meet reserve requirements. Federal Funds are usually overnight loans for which the rates change constantly depending on supply and demand.

REMEMBER

Reserve requirements are the percentage of deposits that member banks must hold each night. Banks that aren't able to meet their reserve requirements may borrow from other banks at the Fed Funds rate. For more info on the Fed Funds rate and other tools that the Federal Reserve Board uses to influence money supply, see Chapter 13.

>> **Corporate commercial paper:** Commercial paper is unsecured corporate debt. Commercial paper is issued at a discount and matures at par value. Commercial paper is issued with an initial maturity of 270 days or less and is exempt from SEC registration.

>> **Brokered (negotiable) certificates of deposit:** Brokered CDs are low-risk investments, which originate from a bank and are outsourced to broker-dealers to sell to investors. Unlike typical CDs, which are purchased directly from a bank, brokered CDs can be traded in the market. Negotiable certificates of deposit that require a minimum investment of $100,000 are often called *jumbo CDs*.

>> **Eurodollars:** Eurodollars are American dollars held by a foreign bank outside the U.S. This situation is usually the result of payments made to overseas companies. Eurodollars are not to be confused with Eurodollar bonds (dollar-denominated bonds issued and held overseas).

>> **Banker's acceptances:** A banker's acceptance (BA) is a time-draft (short-term credit invest-ment) created by a company whose payment is guaranteed by a bank. Companies use BAs for the importing and exporting of goods.

>> **T-bills:** The U.S. government issues T-bills at a discount, and they have initial maturities of 4, 13, 26, or 52 weeks. T-bills are somewhat unique in that they're sold and quoted on a discount-yield basis (YTM). U.S. government securities — and especially T-bills — are considered the safest of all securities.

Here's what a question on money market instruments may look like.

EXAMPLE

SNK Surfboard Company wants to import boogie boards from an Italian manufacturer in Sicily. SNK would use which of the following money market instruments to finance the importing of the boogie boards?

(A) T-bills

(B) Collateral trust bonds

(C) Repurchase agreements

(D) Banker's acceptances

The correct answer is Choice (D). You can eliminate Choice (B) right away because collateral trust bonds aren't money market instruments; they're secured long-term bonds. A banker's acceptance is like a post-dated check that's used specifically for importing and exporting goods.

TIP

Word association can help you here. If you see *importing*, *exporting*, or *time draft*, your answer is probably banker's acceptance (BA).

Chapter **8**

Municipal Bonds: Local Government Securities

M unicipal bonds are securities that state governments, local governments, or U.S. territories issue. The municipality uses the money it borrows from investors to fund and support projects, such as roads, sewer systems, hospitals, and so on.

Even though you're most likely going to spend a majority of your time selling equity securities (stocks), for some unknown reason, the SIE and some of the co-requisite exams such as the Series 7, test heavily on municipal securities. If you've flipped ahead, you may have noticed that this chapter isn't one of the biggest in the book. Why is that? Well, I cover a lot of the bond basics, such as par value, maturity, types of maturities (term, serial, and balloon), and so on, in Chapter 7. Also, you can find some of the underwriting information in Chapter 5.

In this chapter, I cover the SIE exam topics that are going to be tested relating to municipal bonds. This chapter and the real exam focus mainly on the differences between GO (general obligation) bonds and revenue bonds.

General Obligation Bonds: Backing Bonds with Taxes

Most SIE municipal test questions are on general obligation (GO) bonds. The following sections help you prepare.

General characteristics of GOs

REMEMBER

When you're preparing to take the SIE exam, you need to recognize and remember a few items that are specific to GO bonds:

>> **They fund nonrevenue-producing facilities.** GO bonds are not self-supporting because municipalities issue them to build or support projects that don't bring in enough (or any) money to help pay off the bonds. GOs fund schools, libraries, police departments, fire stations, and so on.

>> **They're backed by the full faith and credit (taxing power) of the municipality.** The taxes of the people living in the municipality back general obligation bonds.

>> **They require voter approval.** Because the generous taxes of the people living in the municipality back the bonds, those same people have the right to vote on the project.

The following question tests your knowledge of GO bonds.

EXAMPLE

Which of the following projects are MORE likely to be financed by general obligation bonds than revenue bonds (discussed later in this chapter)?

I. New municipal hospital

II. Public sports arena

III. New junior high school

IV. New library

(A) I and II only

(B) III and IV only

(C) I and III only

(D) I, III, and IV only

The correct answer is Choice (B). Remember that GO bonds are issued to fund nonrevenue-producing projects. A new municipal hospital and a public sports arena will produce income that can back revenue bonds. However, a new junior high school and a new library need the support of taxes to pay off the bonds and, therefore, are more likely to be financed by GO bonds.

Analyzing GO bonds

The SIE exam tests your ability to analyze different types of municipal securities and help a customer make a decision that best suits her needs. You should be able to analyze a GO bond like you'd analyze other investments; however, because they're backed by taxes rather than sales of goods and services (like most corporations are), GO bonds have different components to look at when analyzing the marketability and safety of the issue.

Ascertaining marketability

Many different items can affect the marketability of municipal bonds, including the characteristics of the issuer, factors affecting the issuer's ability to pay, and municipal debt ratios. You certainly want to steer investors away from municipal bonds that aren't very marketable, unless those investors are willing to take extra risk. Here's a list of some of the other items that can affect the bonds' marketability:

>> **Quality (rating):** The higher the credit rating, the safer the bond, and therefore the more marketable it is.

>> **Maturity:** The shorter the maturity, the more marketable the bond issue.

>> **Call features:** Callable bonds are less marketable than noncallable bonds.

>> **Interest (coupon) rate:** Everything else being somewhat equal, bonds with higher coupon (interest) rates are more marketable.

>> **Block size:** The larger the block size, the more marketable the bond usually is.

>> **Dollar price:** All else being equal, the lower the dollar price, the more marketable the bond is.

>> **Issuer's name (local or national reputation):** Bonds are more marketable when the issuer has a good reputation for paying off its bonds on time.

>> **Sinking fund:** If the issuer has put money aside to pay the bonds off at maturity, the bonds are more marketable because the default risk is lower.

>> **Insurance:** If the bonds are insured against default, they're considered very safe and are much more marketable. Bond insurance is considered a *credit enhancement.*

Dealing with debt

One factor that influences the safety of a GO bond is the municipality's ability to deal with debt. After you consider the issuer's name, you can look at previous issues that the municipality had and find out whether it was able to pay off the debt in a timely manner.

In addition to the municipality's name (and credit history), you want to look at its current debt (the debt the municipality owes directly) and its net overall debt (this includes the debt the issuer owes directly and overlapping debt). Overlapping debt is debt that an issuer owes for being part of a larger state and local government (in other words, a town is part of a county and in turn is part of a state).

Bringing in taxes, fees, and fines

Taxes — one of life's little certainties — are another factor that influence the safety of GO bonds. Property taxes (which local municipalities — not states — collect) and sales taxes are the driving force behind paying back investors. So, in general, the higher the property values and the larger the tax base, the safer the municipal bond issue. GOs are also backed by traffic fines, licensing fees, sales taxes, and so on.

REMEMBER

Municipal GO bonds are backed by the huge taxing power of a municipality, so GO bonds usually have higher ratings and lower yields than revenue bonds. Because investors aren't taking as much risk, they don't get as much reward, or *yield.*

Dealing with Revenue Bonds: Raising Money for Utilities and Such

Unlike the tax-backed GO bonds (see the preceding sections), *revenue bonds* are issued to fund municipal facilities that'll generate enough income to support the bonds. These bonds raise money for certain utilities, toll roads, airports, hospitals, student loans, and so on.

A municipality can also issue *industrial development revenue bonds* (IDRs) to finance the construction of a facility for a corporation that moves into that municipality. Remember that even though a municipality issues IDRs, they're actually backed by lease payments made by a corporation. Because the corporation is backing the bonds, the credit rating of the bonds is derived from the credit rating of the corporation.

Because IDRs are backed by a corporation rather than a municipality, IDRs are generally considered the riskiest municipal bonds. Additionally, because these bonds are issued for the benefit of a corporation and not the municipality, the interest income may not be federally tax-free to investors subject to the alternative minimum tax (AMT).

General characteristics of revenue bonds

Before taking the SIE exam, you need to recognize and remember a couple items that are specific to revenue bonds:

>> **They don't need voter approval.** Because revenue bonds fund a revenue-producing facility and therefore aren't backed by taxes, they don't require voter approval. The revenues that the facility generates should be sufficient to pay off the debt.

>> **They require a feasibility study.** Prior to issuing revenue bonds, the municipality hires consultants to prepare a feasibility study. The study basically answers the question, *Does this make sense?* The study includes estimates of revenues that the facility could generate, along with any economic, operating, or engineering aspects of the project that would be of interest to the municipality.

Analyzing revenue bonds

As with any investment, you need to check out the specifics of the security. For instance, when gauging the safety of a revenue bond, you want to see whether it has a credit enhancement (insurance), which provides a certain degree of safety. You also want to look at *call features* (whether the issuer has the right to force investors to redeem their bonds early). You can assume that if a bond is callable, it has a higher yield than a noncallable bond because the investor is taking more risk (the investor doesn't know how long she can hold onto the bond).

For SIE exam purposes (and if you ever sell one or more revenue bonds), you also need to be familiar with the revenue-bond-specific items in this section. For instance, municipal revenue bonds involve covenants, wonderful little promises that protect investors by holding the issuer legally accountable. Table 8-1 shows some of the promises that municipalities make on the municipal bond indenture.

TABLE 8-1 **Revenue Bond Covenants**

Type of Covenant	Promises That the Municipality Will . . .
Rate covenant	Charge sufficient fees to people using the facility to be able to pay expenses and the debt service (principal and interest on the bonds)
Maintenance covenant	Adequately take care of the facility and any equipment so the facility continues to earn revenue
Insurance covenant	Adequately insure the facility

If you see the word *covenant* on the SIE exam or any of the co-requisite exams, immediately think of revenue bonds.

Other factors that provide investors with a certain degree of comfort are that municipalities must provide *financial reports* and are subject to *outside audits* for all their revenue bond issues.

The Primary Market: Bringing New Municipal Bonds to Market

As you can imagine, like corporations and partnerships, municipalities need help selling their issues. To that end, they can choose their underwriter(s) directly (the way almost all corporations and DPPs do it) or through a competitive (bidding) process.

» **Negotiated offering:** This is the type of offering where the issuer chooses the underwriter(s) (a group of underwriters is called a *syndicate*) directly with no competition from other underwriters. Municipalities issuing revenue bonds or IDRs typically choose the underwriter(s) directly, although they have the option of taking bids. Like most corporations, quite often the municipality will already have a relationship with one or more underwriters that it is comfortable working with. Since revenue bonds are not backed by taxing power (like GOs), the issuers are not obligated to get the best price or coupon rate for their bond issue.

» **Competitive offering:** Because general obligation (GO) bonds are backed by the taxing power of the municipality, the municipal issuers are responsible for getting the best deal for the people living in their municipality. In order to insure the best deal, they will post an advertisement known as a *Notice of Sale* in the *Daily Bond Buyer* (the main source of information about new municipal bonds) saying that they are accepting bids on a new issue of bonds. At this point, interested underwriters will submit a good faith deposit (to prove their sincerity) and their bids to the issuer. As you may suspect, the winner of the bid will be the underwriter that presents the lowest cost to the taxpayers backing the bond. The lowest cost could be the result of issuing the bond with a lower coupon rate and/or agreeing to pay more to purchase the bonds. Don't be too concerned about the underwriters who don't win; they'll get their good faith deposit back.

REMEMBER

The Notice of Sale contains all bidding information about new municipal issues. Besides just saying that it is taking bids, the issuer also gives bidding details. It will tell potential underwriters where to submit bids, the amount of the good faith deposit, whether it is expecting bids on an NIC (net interest cost) or a TIC (true interest cost) basis, the amount of bonds to be issued, the maturity of bonds to be issued, and so on. It is the responsibility of the underwriters to determine the coupon rate (they'll determine this based on the credit history of the issuer, the amount of outstanding debt, the size of the issue, the tax base, and so on) and selling price of the issue. Remember, the underwriter(s) need to be able to sell the issue and still make a profit. So, the selling price and the coupon rate have to be attractive to investors. You should remember that the difference between the cost the issuer pays for the security and the amount it receives from investors is called the *spread*. For argument's sake, say that the underwriter(s) agrees(s) to purchase the bonds for $990 each from the issuer and then reoffer them to the public for $1,000 each; then the spread is $10 per bond. The underwriter(s)' profit lies within that spread.

MUNICIPAL ADVISORS

Municipal advisors are firms or professionals who provide professional advice on bond sales and other financial advice to state and local governments. They help the state or local government decide the timing, structure, terms, amount, coupon rate, maturity schedule, and so on regarding the borrowing of money (issuing debt securities).

Allocation of orders

Under Municipal Securities Rulemaking Board (MSRB) rules, all syndicates must establish an allocation of orders. The allocation of orders states which orders are to filled first — basically a priority provision. The allocation of orders must be supplied to customers who request it. The allocation of orders is in the syndicate agreement (agreement among underwriters) and must be signed by all syndicate members. The typical allocation of orders is as follows:

1. Presale orders

These are orders entered before the date the securities were officially available for sale.

2. Syndicate (group-net) orders

In this case, the syndicate member receiving the order will credit the sale to all of the syndicate members, so they all profit.

3. Designated orders

For designated orders, the buyer specifies which syndicate member is to profit from the sale.

4. Member orders

If there are any securities left after the presale, syndicate, and designated orders, syndicate members may purchase them for their own portfolios.

Definitions for new issues

The information contained in this section would be covered under the last section as MSRB Rule G-9. However, because the rule has to do with the underwriting of municipal securities, it certainly makes more sense to put it here.

>> **Date of sale:** The date of sale is the date that the bids are submitted to the issuer for competitive offerings. For negotiated offerings, it's the date that the final contract is signed by the syndicate. In both cases the syndicate manager will send a commitment wire to the other syndicate members on the date of sale.

>> **Pre-sale period:** The pre-sale period is the period preceding the date of sale.

>> **Order period:** The order period is the time established by the syndicate manager that allows the syndicate members to solicit customers.

>> **Underwriting period:** The underwriting period begins when the first order is submitted to the syndicate or when the securities are purchased from the issuer, whichever happens first. The underwriting period ends when the issuer delivers securities to the syndicate or the syndicate sells all the securities purchased from the issuer, whichever happens last.

Examining Other Types of Municipal Bonds on the Test

Along with standard revenue and GO bonds (see the earlier sections on these topics), you're required to know the specifics of the following bonds:

» **Special tax bonds:** These bonds are secured by one or more taxes other than ad valorem (property) taxes. The bonds may be backed by sales taxes on fuel, tobacco, alcohol, and so on.

» **Special assessment (special district) bonds:** These bonds are issued to fund the construction of sidewalks, streets, sewers, and so on. Special assessment bonds are backed by taxes only on the properties that benefit from the improvements. In other words, if people who live a few blocks away from you get all new sidewalks, they'll be taxed for it, not you.

» **Double-barreled bonds:** These bonds are basically a combination of revenue and GO bonds. Municipalities issue these bonds to fund revenue-producing facilities (toll bridges, water and sewer facilities, and so forth), but if the revenues taken in aren't enough to pay off the debt, tax revenues make up the deficiency.

» **Limited-tax general obligation bonds (LTGO):** These bonds are types of general obligation bonds for which the taxes backing the bonds are limited. Limited-tax general obligation bonds are secured by all revenues of the municipality that aren't used to back other bonds. However, the amount of property taxes municipalities can levy to back these bonds is limited.

» **Public housing authority bonds (PHAs):** These bonds are also called new housing authority (NHA) bonds and are issued by local housing authorities to build and improve low-income housing. These bonds are backed by U.S. government subsidies, and if the issuer can't pay off the debt, the U.S. government makes up any shortfalls.

TIP

Because PHAs are backed by the issuer and the U.S. government, they're considered among the safest municipal bonds.

» **Moral obligation bonds:** These bonds are issued by a municipality but backed by a pledge from the state government to pay off the debt if the municipality can't. Given this additional backing of the state, they're considered safe. Moral obligation bonds need legislative approval to be issued.

REMEMBER

Because they're called moral obligation bonds, the state has a *moral* responsibility — but not a legal obligation — to help pay off the debt if the municipality can't.

The following question tests your ability to answer questions about the safety of municipal bonds:

Rank the following municipal bonds in order from safest to riskiest.

  I. Revenue bonds

 II. Moral obligation bonds

III. Public housing authority bonds

IV. Industrial development revenue bonds

(A) I, II, III, IV

(B) III, II, I, IV

(C) II, III, IV, I

(D) II, IV, III, I

The correct answer is Choice (B). If you remember that public housing authority bonds are considered the safest of the municipal bonds because they're backed by U.S. government subsidies, this question's easy, because only one answer choice starts with III. Anyway, public housing authority bonds would be the safest; moral obligation bonds, which are also considered very safe because the state government has a moral obligation to help pay off the debt if needed, follow. Next come revenue bonds, which are backed by a revenue–producing facility. Remember that industrial development revenue bonds (IDRs) are considered the riskiest municipal bonds because although they're technically municipal bonds, they're backed only by lease payments made by a corporation.

Taxable Municipal Bonds

Although the interest on most municipal bonds is federally tax free and sometimes triple tax free (the interest is exempt from federal, state, and local taxes), you need to be aware that some bonds are taxable. These bonds are still issued and backed by a municipality but are still taxable. These bonds were created under the Economic Recovery and Reinvestment Act of 2009 and are called Build America Bonds (BABs). The idea behind the BABs is to help municipalities raise money for infrastructure projects such as tunnels, bridges, roads, and so on. These bonds have either a higher coupon rate than most other municipal bonds because the municipality receives tax credits from the federal government or are more attractive because the investors receive tax credits from the federal government. As such, these municipal bonds become more attractive to all investors, even ones with lower income tax rates. Even though the Build America Bond program expired in 2010, there are still plenty of these bonds out there, so you will be tested on them. The two types of Build America Bonds are as follows:

>> **Tax Credit BABs:** Investors of this type of Build America Bonds receive tax credits equal to 35 percent of the coupon rate.

>> **Direct Payment BABs:** When a municipality issues Direct Payment BABs, it receives reimbursements from the U.S. treasury equal to 35 percent of the coupon rate. As such, direct payment BABs tend to have a higher coupon rate than tax credit BABs.

Don't Forget Municipal Notes!

When municipalities need short-term (interim) financing, municipal notes come into play. These notes bring money into the municipality until other revenues are received. Municipal notes typically have maturities of one year or less (usually three to five months). Know the different types of municipal notes for the SIE exam:

>> **Tax anticipation notes (TANs):** These notes provide financing for current operations in anticipation of future taxes that the municipality will collect.

>> **Revenue anticipation notes (RANs):** These notes provide financing for current operations in anticipation of future revenues that the municipality will collect.

>> **Tax and revenue anticipation notes (TRANs):** These notes are a combination of TANs and RANs.

>> **Grant anticipation notes (GANs):** These notes provide interim financing for the municipality while it's waiting for a grant from the U.S. government. The notes are paid off from the grant funds once received.

>> **Bond anticipation notes (BANs):** These notes provide interim financing for the municipality while it's waiting for long-term bonds to be issued.

>> **Construction loan notes (CLNs):** These notes provide interim financing for the construction of multifamily apartment buildings.

>> **Project notes (PNs):** These notes provide interim financing for the building of subsidized housing for low-income families.

>> **Tax-exempt commercial paper:** These short-term notes are usually issued by organizations such as universities with permission of the government. This debt obligation usually lasts only a few months to help the organization cover its short-term liabilities.

AON (all or none) is an order qualifier (fill an entire order at a specific price or not at all) or type of underwriting; it is not a municipal note, no matter how much it looks like one.

Municipal notes are not rated the same as municipal or corporate bonds (AAA, AA, A, and so on). Municipal notes have ratings as follows (from best to worst):

>> **Moody's:** MIG 1, MIG 2, MIG 3, MIG 4

>> **Standard & Poor's:** SP-1, SP-2, SP-3

>> **Fitch:** F-1, F-2, F-3

Municipal Fund Securities

Municipal fund securities are similar to investment company securities (see Chapter 9) but are exempt from that definition under section 2(b) of the Investment Company Act of 1940. Municipal fund securities are established by municipal governments, municipal agencies, or educational institutions but do not represent loans to the government. Included in municipal fund securities are Section 529 plans, ABLE accounts, and Local Government Investment Pools.

Note: Rule G-45 requires dealers underwriting ABLE programs or 529 savings plans (not Local Government Investment Pools . . . LGIPs) to submit information such as plan descriptive information, assets, asset allocation information for each plan available, contributions, performance data, and so on semiannually and performance data annually through the Electronic Municipal Market Access (EMMA) system. MSRB's EMMA system is designed to provide market transparency to help protect market participants.

Section 529 Plans

529 plans are specialized educational savings accounts available to investors. These plans are also known as *qualified tuition plans* because they are designed to allow money to be saved for qualified expenses for higher education (colleges, postsecondary trade and vocational schools, postgraduate programs, and so on). As such, there is an owner (the one who sets up and contributes to the plan — typically a parent, but it doesn't have to be) and a beneficiary (the one who benefits from the plan — typically a child or relative of the person who set up the plan). The contribution allowance varies from state to state, and contributions are made from after-tax dollars. However, withdrawals of the amount invested plus interest received is tax free, meaning that the earnings grow on a tax-deferred basis and no tax is due if earnings are used for qualified educational expenses. Investors must receive an official statement or offering circular prior to opening the account. You should note the following:

>> Contribution levels may vary from one state to another.

>> No income limits are placed on the investors of a 529 plan.

>> Many investors contribute monthly, although this is not required.

>> Any account balances that are unused (if, for example, the beneficiary decides not to go to college or goes to a cheaper local college) can be transferred to another related beneficiary.

>> The assets in the account always remain under control of the owner (donor) even after the beneficiary becomes of legal age (18 in most states).

>> In some cases, plans can be set up as *prepaid tuition plans* (allowing investors to prepay college at a locked-in rate) or as a college savings plan, which allows owners to invest as they see fit (aggressively, moderately, or conservatively).

ABLE accounts

ABLE (Achieving a Better Life Experience) accounts are designed for individuals with provable disabilities and their families. Because of the extra needs and expenses (educational, housing, transportation, health, assistive technology, legal fees, and so on) incurred in taking care of individuals with disabilities, ABLE accounts allow people to invest after-tax dollars into an ABLE account. Any earnings or distributions are tax-free as long as they are used to pay for qualified disability expenses for the beneficiary.

ABLE accounts may be opened by the eligible individual, a parent or guardian, or a person granted power of attorney on behalf of the individual with the disability. However, once the account is opened, anyone can contribute. As with college savings plans (see the preceding section), the investments may be conservative, moderate, or aggressive. Many states have annual contribution caps and maximum account balances. ABLE accounts may be opened for the disabled person even if he or she is receiving other benefits such as social security disability, Medicaid, private insurance, and so on. In order to be eligible, the onset of the disability must have been discovered before the individual reached age 26.

Local Government Investment Pools

Local government investment pools (LGIPs) are established by states to provide other government entities (cities, counties, school districts, and so on) with a short-term investment vehicle for investing their funds. Since these are set up by state governments for state entities, LGIPs are exempt from SEC registration. As such, there is no prospectus requirement, but they do have disclosure documents to cover investment policies, operating procedures, and so on. Although they aren't money market funds, they are similar in the fact that many LGIPs operate similar to one. Like money market funds, the net asset value (NAV) is typically set at $1 and normally the money is invested safely, although it doesn't have to be. LGIPs may be sold directly to municipalities or through municipal advisors hired by the municipal issuers.

Understanding the Taxes on Municipal Bonds

Municipal bonds typically have lower yields than most other bonds. You may think that because U.S. government securities (T-bills, T-notes, T-bonds, and so on) are the safest of all securities, they should have the lowest yields. Not so, because municipal bonds have a tax advantage that U.S. government bonds don't have: The interest received on municipal bonds, with a few exceptions (see the earlier section "Taxable Municipal Bonds") is federally tax-free (the interest on most U.S. government securities is state tax free).

Comparing municipal and corporate bonds equally

The *taxable equivalent yield* (TEY) tells you what the interest rate of a municipal bond would be if it weren't federally tax-free. You need the following formula to compare municipal bonds and corporate bonds equally:

$$\text{taxable equivalent yield (TEY)} = \frac{\text{municipal yield}}{100\% - \text{investor's tax bracket}}$$

REMEMBER

Because the investor's tax bracket comes into play with municipal bonds, municipal bonds are better suited for investors in higher tax brackets.

The following question tests your ability to answer a TEY question.

EXAMPLE

Mrs. Stevenson is an investor who is in the 30-percent tax bracket. Which of the following securities would provide Mrs. Stevenson with the BEST after-tax yield?

(A) 5 percent GO bond

(B) 6 percent T-bond

(C) 7 percent equipment trust bond

(D) 7 percent mortgage bond

The right answer is Choice (A). If you were to look at this question straight up without considering any tax advantages, the answer would be either (C) or (D). However, you have to remember that the investor has to pay federal taxes on the interest received from the T-bond, equipment trust bond, and mortgage bond but doesn't have to pay federal taxes on the interest received from the GO municipal bond. So you need to set up the TEY equation to be able to compare all the bonds equally:

$$\text{taxable equivalent yield (TEY)} = \frac{\text{municipal yield}}{100\% - \text{investor's tax bracket}} = \frac{5\%}{100\% - 30\%} = \frac{5\%}{70\%} = 7.14\%$$

Looking into the SIE examiners' heads, you have to ask yourself, "Why would they be asking me this question?" Well, because they want to make sure that you know that the interest received on municipal bonds is federally tax-free. Therefore, if you somehow forget the formula, you're still likely to be right if you pick a municipal bond as the answer when you get a question like the preceding one.

Note: Although this situation is less likely, the SIE may ask you to determine the *municipal equivalent yield* (MEY), which is the yield on a taxable bond after paying taxes. Once you have that yield, you can compare it to a municipal bond to help determine the best investment for one of your customers. The formula for the municipal equivalent yield is as follows:

$$\text{MEY} = \text{municipal yield} \times (100\% - \text{investor's tax bracket})$$

Scot-free! Taking a look at triple tax-free municipal bonds

Bonds that U.S. territories (and federal districts) issue are triple tax-free (the interest is not taxed on the federal, state, or local level). These places include

» Puerto Rico

» Guam

>> U.S. Virgin Islands

>> American Samoa

>> Washington, D.C.

Additionally, in most cases (there are a few exceptions), if you buy a municipal bond issued within your own state, the interest will be triple tax-free.

TIP

Unless you see the U.S. territories or Washington, D.C., in a municipal bond question, don't assume that the bonds are triple tax-free. Even if the question states that the investor buys a municipal bond issued within her own state, don't assume that it's triple tax-free unless the question specifically states that it is.

REMEMBER

The tax advantage of municipal bonds applies only to interest received. If investors sell municipal bonds for more than their cost basis, the investors have to pay taxes on the capital gains.

Following Municipal Bond Rules

Yes, unfortunately, the SIE tests you on rules relating to municipal bonds. Rules are a part of life and a part of the SIE exam. This section covers just a few rules that are specific to municipal securities, but if you're itching for more regulations, don't worry — you can see plenty more rules in my favorite (and I use that term loosely) chapter: Chapter 16.

Confirmations

All confirmations of trades must be sent or given to customers at or before the completion of the transaction (settlement date). Municipal securities settle the regular way (two business days after the trade date — T+2). The following items are included on the confirmation:

>> The broker-dealer's name, address, and phone number

>> The capacity of the trade (whether the firm acted as a broker or dealer)

>> The dollar amount of the commission (if the firm's acting as a broker)

>> The customer's name

>> Any bond particulars, such as the issuer's name, interest rate, maturity, call features (if any), and so on

>> The trade date, time of execution, and the settlement date

>> Committee on Uniform Securities Identification Procedures (CUSIP) identification number (if there is one)

>> Bond yield and dollar price

>> Any accrued interest

>> The registration form (registered as to principal only, book entry, or fully registered)

>> Whether the bonds have been called or pre-refunded

>> Any unusual facts about the security

Each broker, dealer, or municipal securities dealer must report to the MSRB all transactions in municipal securities through the Real-Time Reporting System (RTRS). The RTRS will make public reports on market activity and prices. In addition, the MSRB will assess transaction fees to make sure that they are in line with MSRB rules. The information of a transaction must be reported promptly. Exempt from the reporting process are transactions in securities without a CUSIP number, transactions in municipal fund securities, and inter-dealer transactions.

Advertising and record keeping

A brokerage firm has to keep all advertising for a minimum of three years, and these ads must be easily accessible (not in a bus storage locker) for at least two years.

The MSRB requires a principal (manager) to approve all advertising material of the firm prior to its first use. The principal must ensure that the advertising is accurate and true.

REMEMBER

Advertising includes any material designed for use in the public media. Advertising includes offering circulars, market and form letters, summaries of official statements, and so on. However, preliminary and final official statements are not considered advertising because they're prepared by the issuer; therefore, they don't require approval from a principal.

Gifts

According to MSRB rules, municipal securities dealers can't give gifts valued at more than $100 per year to customers. (The board kind of has this thing against bribery.) Business expenses are exempt from the rule.

TIP

If you get a question on the SIE exam relating to what qualifies as a gift, remember that business expenses are exempt. Business expenses can be airline tickets (for the customer to meet with you, not for the customer to vacation in the Bahamas), hotel expenses (for the customer's lodging while she's meeting with you), business meals, and so on. You should note that FINRA gift rules fall directly in line with MSRB's gift rules.

Commissions

Although no particular guideline states what percentage broker-dealers can charge (as with the 5 percent markup policy — see Chapter 16), all commissions, markups, and markdowns must be fair and reasonable, and policies can't discriminate among customers. The items that firms should consider follow:

>> The market value of the securities at the time of the trade.

>> The total dollar amount of the transaction. Although you're going to charge more money for a larger transaction, the percentage charged is usually lower.

>> The difficulty of the trade. If you had to jump through hoops to make sure the trade was completed, you're entitled to charge more.

>> The fact that you and the firm that you work for are entitled to make a profit (which is, of course, the reason you got involved in the business to begin with).

You can't take race, ethnicity, religion, gender, sexual orientation, disability, age, funny accents, or how much you like (or dislike) the client into account.

Gathering Municipal Bond Info

As with other investments, you need to be able to locate information if you're going to sell municipal securities to investors. You may find that information about municipal bonds is not as readily available as it is for most other securities. Some municipal bonds are relatively *thin* issues (not many are sold or traded) or may be of interest only to investors in a particular geographic location. This section reviews some of the information that you have to know to ace the SIE exam.

The bond resolution (indenture)

A *bond resolution* (indenture) provides investors with contract terms including the coupon rate, years until maturity, collateral backing the bond (if any), and so on. Although not required by law, almost every municipal bond comes with a bond indenture, which is printed on the face of most municipal bond certificates. It makes the bonds more marketable because the indenture serves as a contract between the municipality and a trustee who's appointed to protect the investors' rights. Included in the indenture are the flow of funds (see "Dealing with Revenue Bonds: Raising Money for Utilities and Such," earlier in this chapter) and any assets that may be backing the issue.

Legal opinion

Printed on the face of municipal bond certificates, the legal opinion is prepared and signed by a *municipal bond counsel* (attorney). The purpose of the legal opinion is to verify that the issue is legally binding on the issuer and conforms to tax laws. Additionally, the legal opinion may state that interest received from the bonds is tax exempt.

REMEMBER

If a bond is stamped *ex-legal*, it does not contain a legal opinion.

Official statement

Municipal bonds don't have a prospectus; instead, municipalities usually provide an official statement. As with prospectuses, official statements come in *preliminary* and *final versions*. The preliminary version of the statement doesn't include an offering price or coupon rate. The *official statement* is the document that the issuer prepares; it states what the funds will be used for, provides information about the municipality, and details how the funds will be repaid. The official statement also includes

>> The offering terms

>> The underwriting spread (basically, who gets what)

>> A description of the bonds

>> A description of the issuer

>> The offering price

>> The coupon rate

>> The feasibility statement (for revenue bonds — how much sense the project makes)

>> The legal opinion

Any dealer selling municipal securities to a customer during the issue's underwriting period (see "The Primary Market: Bringing New Municipal Bonds to Market" earlier in this chapter) must deliver a final official statement, if there is one, to a customer by the settlement of the transaction. If a dealer is selling a new issue to another dealer, it must deliver the official statement to the purchasing dealer within one business day.

"G" That's a Whole Lot of Rules

Yes, there are a lot of "G" rules. There are even more that you'll have to study when you take some of the co-requisite exams such as the Series 7. Some of these rules would be taller than you if printed out, even if you're tall enough to give Shaquille O'Neal a run for his money.

TIP

The following list isn't as huge as it could be because many of the rules are already covered throughout this book. However, you're not expected to know the minute details of each rule, just the main idea. Fortunately, many of them just make sense. Also, don't worry about the rule numbers; pay more attention to the rule.

» **Rule G-2** (standards of professional qualifications): Prior to effecting any transaction in, or inducing or attempting to induce the purchase or sale of any municipal security, the dealer and every natural person associated with that dealer must be qualified in accordance with MSRB rules.

» **Rule G-3** (professional qualification requirements): Broker-dealers that conduct a business in general securities must have at least one associated person qualified as a municipal securities principal to oversee and supervise the broker-dealers' municipal securities business.

» **Rule G-7** (information concerning associated persons): Associated persons (municipal securities sales principal, municipal securities principal, general securities principal engaging in municipal securities business, municipal securities representative, limited representatives, and so on) must provide their employer with a form U-4 or MSD-4 for bank dealers. A U-4 form is an application form sent into the Central Registration Deposit (CRD) along with the applicant's fingerprints. Included in the form are the applicant's address, work history, arrest record (if any — hopefully not), education, previous addresses, and so on. A copy of the form must be kept by the employer. In addition, the employer is responsible for calling previous employers to find out if the information in the form is accurate. In the event that the applicant's information changes any time during employ, the employer is responsible for updating the information.

» **Rules G-8 and G-9** (books and records requirements): All brokers, dealers, and municipal securities dealers must keep records regarding municipal securities business. Among the many items they have to keep are the following:

- Records of original entry (blotters): Itemized daily records of all purchases and sales of municipal securities

- Account records: Account records for each customer account

- Securities records: Separate records showing all municipal securities positions

- Subsidiary records: Records of municipal securities in transfer, municipal securities borrowed or loaned, municipal securities transactions not completed by the settlement date, and so on

- Put options and repurchase agreements

- Records for agency transactions

- Records concerning primary offerings

- Copies of confirmations (for more on confirmations, see Chapter 16)
- Customer account information
- Customer complaints
- Records concerning political contributions

TIP

You aren't expected to remember the entire preceding list. Just get a general feeling for what's required. It looks like the MSRB wants the broker-dealer or municipal securities dealer to maintain records of just about everything.

>> **Rule G-9** (preservation of records): MSRB's record-keeping requirements are very similar to but not exactly the same as FINRA's requirements. Most records have to be kept either four or six years. To keep you from pulling your hair out (this coming from a bald man), look at the record-keeping requirements in Chapter 16, where I note how the MSRB rules and FINRA rules are different.

>> **Rule G-10** (delivery of investment brochure): Broker-dealers and municipal securities dealers must send yearly written statements (which may be electronic) to each customer stating that they are registered with the SEC and MSRB. The statement must also include the web address for the MSRB and a statement of how to receive an investment brochure on the website describing customer protections and how to file a complaint to the proper authority. The same information holds true of municipal advisors — they must also send yearly statements with the same information plus provide information on how to get the municipal advisory client brochure on the MSRB website.

>> **Rule G-13** (quotations): According to MSRB rules, all quotations for municipal securities published or distributed by any broker-dealer, municipal securities dealer, or person associated with a broker-dealer or municipal securities dealer must be bona fide (genuine).

>> **Rule G-17** (conduct of municipal securities and municipal advisory activities): Municipal securities broker-dealers, municipal securities dealers, municipal advisors, agents, and so on shall deal fairly with all persons and not engage in dishonest, deceptive, or unfair practices.

>> **Rule G-18** (best execution): When entering into a municipal securities transaction with a customer or customer of another broker, dealer, or municipal securities dealer, a broker must use reasonable diligence to attempt to get the best price for the security (lowest buying price or highest selling price for the customer). This rule is similar to Rule G-30, but G-30 includes markups, markdowns, and commission.

>> **Rule G-21** (advertising): Advertisements by municipal securities dealers, brokers, and dealers can't contain false or misleading statements. Advertisements include published material used in electronic or other public media, promotional literature (written or electronic) made available to customers or the public, circulars, market letters, seminar text, press releases, and so on. However, preliminary official statements, official statements, offering circulars, and so on are not considered advertisements.

>> **Rule G-25** (improper use of assets): Brokers, dealers, and municipal securities dealers shall not make improper use of municipal securities or funds held on behalf of another person. In addition, no broker, dealer, or municipal securities dealer can make a guarantee against loss. And, they may not share directly or indirectly in the profit or losses in a customer's account. However, an associated person may set up a partnership or joint account with a customer and share in the profits or losses based on the contribution made into the account. In that case, a proportionate sharing agreement should be in place.

>> **Rule G-30** (pricing and commissions): If buying or selling municipal securities for a customer on a principal basis (for or from the dealer's inventory), the aggregate price including the markdown or markup must be *fair and reasonable.* If buying or selling municipal securities

on an agency basis for a customer, the broker-dealer is responsible for making a reasonable effort to obtain the best price for the customer and the commission charged must be *fair and reasonable* in relation to prevailing market conditions.

» **Rule G-34** (CUSIP numbers, new issue and market information requirements): For new issues of municipal bonds (whether negotiated or competitive offerings), the managing underwriters must apply to the Committee on Uniform Security Identification Procedures (CUSIP) to receive identification numbers for the bonds for each maturity, if more than one. For negotiated offerings where the underwriter(s) is/are chosen directly, the managing underwriter must apply prior to the pricing of the new municipal issue. For competitive offerings, the managing underwriter must apply after winning the bid. In the event that the municipal issuer hired an advisor, the municipal advisor must apply no later than the business day after the Notice of Sale is published.

» **Rule G-37** (political contributions and prohibitions on municipal securities business): This rule prohibits brokers, dealers, municipal securities dealers, and municipal advisors from engaging in municipal advisory business with municipal entities if they've made political contributions to officials of such municipal entities. In the event that they did make political contributions, they must be disclosed to the public. In addition, if a political contribution was made as described in the first sentence, they are not allowed to engage in municipal securities business with that municipal entity for a period of two years after the contribution. However, municipal finance professionals (MFPs) are allowed to make political contributions of up to $250 per election to a candidate the MFP is entitled to vote for.

» **Rule G-47** (time of trade disclosure): Brokers, dealers, and municipal securities may not trade a municipal security (buy from or sell to) with a customer (whether solicited or unsolicited) without providing all material information about the trade. The information must be provided before or at the time of sale and can be disclosed orally or in writing. If you're dying to know, you can view a complete list of what the MSRB considers material information at `www.msrb. org/Rules-and-Interpretations/MSRB-Rules/General/Rule-G-47.aspx`. However, it shouldn't be necessary to commit them to memory.

3

Delving Deeper: Security Investments with a Twist

IN THIS PART . . .

Understand the role of investment companies in helping investors diversify their portfolios.

Become versed in limited partnerships — their formation, function, structure, tax advantages, and tax disadvantages.

Examine direct participation programs (DPPs) and real estate investment trusts (REITs).

Get to know options, an investment vehicle that allows investors to buy and sell securities at a fixed price.

Chapter **9**
Delivering Diversification with Packaged Securities

D iversification is key when you're helping customers set up a portfolio of securities, and it's fairly easy when your customer has a good deal of money to invest. But what if an investor has limited resources? Certainly, such investors can't afford to buy several different securities, and you don't want to limit your customer to only one (heaven forbid it should go belly up). Packaged securities to the rescue! These securities, such as open-end funds, closed-end funds, face-amount certificate companies, UITs, and annuities, offer variety within one security by investing a customer's money in a diversified pool of securities . . . for a cost, of course. A bit of profit-driven teamwork can ensure your customers' investments are much safer than, say, the blackjack tables in Vegas.

In this chapter, I cover topics relating to investment companies and annuities. Open-end (mutual) funds and closed investment funds are only the beginning. I also discuss face-amount certificate companies and trusts like unit investment trusts (UITs).

As with other non-exempt securities, investment companies must register with the Securities and Exchange Commission (SEC). When registering with the SEC, they must disclose:

» Whether the investment company will be open- or closed-end

» The names and addresses of affiliated persons

» If the company plans to raise money by borrowing

» If they plan on investing in commodities or real estate

» How they plan on investing (a single industry, many industries, debt securities, and so on)

» Conditions under which the investment plan can change (in other words, a vote or shareholder)

» The business experience of each director and officers

Diversifying through Management Investment Companies

In general, investment companies are ones whose business is investing in securities. As such, they take the money received from investors and invest in a large number of different securities. Each investor shares in the profits or losses based on his or her interest in the investment company. The Investment Company Act of 1940 divides investment companies into three main types: management investment companies, face-amount certificate companies, and unit investment trusts. This section focuses on management investment companies, which are the more heavily tested areas of this chapter. I cover the other types in the aptly named "Considering Other Investment Company Options" section later on.

Management companies are, by far, the most familiar type of investment company. The securities held by the management companies are actively managed by portfolio managers.

As a subclassification of management companies, they can be considered *diversified* or *non-diversified*. In order to be considered diversified, at least 75 percent of the company's assets must be spread out in the following way:

>> The management company cannot own more than 10 percent of the outstanding shares of a company.

>> No more than 5 percent of the management company's money can be invested in one company's securities.

REMEMBER

Since the diversified portion only relates to 75 percent of the management company's assets, the other 25 percent can be invested in any way. Whether the management company is diversified or non-diversified must be in the prospectus.

Comparing open- and closed-end funds

Management companies have to be either open-end or closed-end funds. Make sure you know the difference between the two.

Open-end (mutual) funds

An open-end fund is more commonly known as a mutual fund. As with closed-end funds, *mutual funds* invest in many different securities to provide diversification for investors. The key difference is that mutual funds are constantly issuing and redeeming shares, which provides liquidity for investors. Because open-end fund shares are continuous offerings of new shares, a mutual fund prospectus must always be available. You need to understand the makings of the net asset value and the public offering price when taking the SIE exam:

>> **Net asset value (NAV):** Fortunately, the net asset value or net asset value per share is determined the same way for both open- and closed-end funds — by dividing the value of the securities held by the fund by the number of shares outstanding; however, with open-end funds, the NAV is the bid price. When investors redeem shares of a mutual fund, they receive the NAV. Mutual funds can't ever trade below the NAV.

>> **Public offering price (POP):** For mutual funds, the public offering price (the ask price) is the NAV plus a sales charge.

If a mutual fund doesn't charge a sales charge, it's called a *no-load fund*.

REMEMBER

Because mutual funds are new issues, investors must receive a prospectus (for more on what a prospectus is, see Chapter 5) and/or a *summary prospectus*. Certainly prospectuses for mutual funds include their holdings, investment strategy, fees, expenses, graphs of the fund's performance, and so on. Every prospectus for every security must contain a disclosure stating that the SEC does not approve of the issue. I assume that this is the SEC's way of not being sued if investors lose money. The SEC just clears the issue.

If the fund provides a summary prospectus, it must include items like the fund's name and ticker symbol, the class of shares, the fund's investment strategies, investment objectives, costs of investing, investment advisors, financial compensation, risks, performance, and so on. The summary prospectus may include an application that investors can use to purchase shares. Potential investors can also request a full prospectus prior to investing. If an investor purchases via a summary prospectus, he must either receive or be provided online access to a full prospectus.

On an ongoing basis, funds must include in their prospectus annual report graphs comparing the performance of the fund to a proper index (S&P 500, NASDAQ composite, and so on), items and/or strategies that may have affected the performance in the past year, and the name of the fund's manager.

Note: Expenses of a mutual fund include salaries for the board of directors; management (investment advisor) fees for the person or persons making the investment decisions for the fund; custodial fees for the safeguarding of assets (cash, securities, and so on) held by the fund; transfer agent fees for keeping track of investors, sending distributions, and sending proxies; and 12b-1 fees, if any. *12b-1 fees* are fees paid by a mutual fund out of the fund assets to cover promotional expenses such as advertising, printing and mailing of prospectuses to new investors, and so on. If there are 12b-1 fees, they must be included in the prospectus.

Closed-end funds

Unlike open-end funds, closed-end funds have a fixed number of shares outstanding (hence the word *closed*). Closed-end funds act more like stock than open-end funds because they issue new shares to the public, and after that, the shares are bought and sold in the market. Because they trade in the market, they're often called *publicly traded funds*. Although the net asset value of closed-end and open-end funds is figured the same, the public offering price is determined a little differently:

>> **Net asset value (NAV):** The net asset value or net asset value per share is the parity price where the fund should be trading. You determine it by dividing the value of the securities held by the fund by the number of shares outstanding. Only closed-end funds may trade below the NAV (at a discount).

>> **Public offering price (POP):** For closed-end funds, the public offering price (the ask price) depends more on supply and demand than the NAV. Investors of closed-end funds pay the POP (current market price) plus a broker's commission.

Note: Although closed-end funds are not purchased from and redeemed with the issuer, they do offer a high degree of liquidity. After the initial offering, they can be purchased or sold either on an exchange or over-the-counter (OTC).

Open and closed: Focusing on their differences

You can expect at least a question or two on the SIE exam relating to investment companies to test you on the differences between open-end and closed-end funds. Table 9-1 should help you zone in on the major distinctions.

TABLE 9-1 Comparing Open-End and Closed-End Funds

Category	Closed-End	Open-End
Capitalization	One-time offering of securities (fixed number of shares outstanding).	Continuous offering of new shares (no fixed number of shares outstanding).
Pricing the fund	Investors purchase at the current market value (public offering price, or POP) plus a commission.	Investors purchase at the net asset value (NAV) plus a sales charge.
Issues	Common stock, preferred stock, and debt securities.	Common stock only.
Shares purchased	Shares can be purchased in full only.	Shares can be purchased in full or fractions (up to three decimal places).
Purchased and sold	Initial public offerings go through underwriters; after that, investors purchase and sell shares either over-the-counter or on an exchange (no redemption).	Shares are sold and redeemed by the fund only.

REMEMBER

The key difference between open-end and closed-end funds is the method of capitalization. An open-end (mutual) fund is a continuous offering of new securities, whereas a closed-end fund is a one-time offering of new securities.

Keeping your customer's investment objectives in mind

Unlike investors in face-amount certificate companies and unit investment trusts (see "Considering Other Investment Company Options," still to come), investors of open-end and closed-end funds have many choices available. Investors may be looking for safety, growth, a combination, and so on. This section gives you a glimpse into those investment choices.

REMEMBER

The single most important consideration for customers who invest in packaged securities is the fund's investment objectives. This feature surpasses even the sales charge or management fees. If you become a registered rep, one of your primary jobs will be to help investors decide which type of fund would be best for them. The test-designers want to know you can handle that job. Comparing like-type funds is secondary. So without further ado, here are the major types (although variables within each fund can make a fund riskier or safer, I've placed the list in the normal order from safest to riskiest):

>> **Money market fund:** This fund (as you've probably guessed) invests in money market instruments (short-term debt securities). You need to know the specifics of this fund more than other types of funds. Here are the key points:

- It usually provides a check-writing feature (you're given a checkbook) as a way of redeeming shares.

- It's always no-load (there's no sales charge).

- It computes dividends daily and credits them monthly.

- There's no penalty for early redemption.

>> **Income fund:** The primary objective of an income fund is to provide current revenue (not growth) for investors. This type of fund invests most of its assets in a diversified portfolio of debt securities that pay interest and in preferred and common stock of companies that are known to pay consistent dividends in cash.

Income funds are considered much safer (more conservative) investments than growth funds. You can assume for SIE exam (and real-life) purposes that income funds are better investment choices for retirees and investors who are looking for a steady cash flow without much risk.

» **Balanced fund:** A balanced fund is a combination of a growth fund and an income fund. Balanced funds invest in common stocks, preferred stocks, long-term bonds, and short-term bonds, aiming to provide both income and capital appreciation while minimizing risk. These funds don't get hammered too badly when the market is bearish but usually underperform when the market is bullish.

» **Growth fund:** This fund is exactly what you'd expect it to be; growth funds invest most of their assets in a diversified portfolio of the common stock of relatively new companies, looking for big increases in the stock prices. Growth funds offer a higher potential for growth but usually at a higher risk for the investor. This type of fund is ideal for an investor who's looking for long-term capital appreciation potential.

Because of the inherent risk of investing in growth funds, they're better for younger investors who can take the risk because they have more time to recover their losses.

» **Specialized (sector) fund:** A specialized or sector fund is a type of fund that invests primarily in the securities of a single industry or geographical area. A specialized fund may invest only in financial services, healthcare, automotive stocks, Japanese securities, and so on. Because specialized funds are limited in their investments, you can assume that they're a little riskier (more volatile) than the average fund.

» **International or global fund:** An international fund invests in companies based anywhere outside of the investor's home country. A global fund invests in securities located anywhere in the world, including the investor's home country. Although international and global funds may be good to round out a portfolio, they aren't without their risks. Along with the risk that investors face by just investing in securities in general, holders of international and global funds also face currency risk, which is the risk that the currency exchange rate between the U.S. and foreign issuers will hurt investors. There's also the additional risk that politics in a particular country will harm the value of the fund.

Hedge funds: What are they?

You've probably heard about hedge funds but aren't exactly sure what they are. For the SIE exam, you do need to know a little bit about them. Because they aren't open- or closed-end funds, unit investment trusts, or face amount certificate companies, they are an exception to the standard definition of investment company under the Investment Company Act of 1940. In addition, because they are considered *private* investment companies and are *only* open to sophisticated (accredited) investors, they are exempt from SEC registration. Hedge funds often require a very high initial investment — sometimes $500,000 or more.

Hedge funds hold a pool of investments and are professionally managed like mutual (open-end) funds but have a lot more flexibility. Hedge funds are typically much more aggressive in nature and may buy securities on margin, sell securities short, purchase or sell options, and so on in an attempt to maximize gains. I guess you can almost think of them as a "whatever it takes to make money" type of fund.

Private-equity funds

Private-equity funds are similar to hedge funds in that they're exempt from SEC registration and only available to sophisticated investors. However, hedge funds invest in securities and are able to buy and sell the securities held quickly, whereas private-equity funds invest directly in companies. They typically buy private companies but may buy enough stock of a publicly traded company to gain controlling interest. Private-equity funds are much more focused on the long-term potential of the companies they purchase, whereas hedge funds are typically looking to make a quick profit.

FUND OF A FUND

Many funds are actually funds of funds, such as life-cycle funds. Life-cycle funds are also called *targeted* or *age-based* funds. The idea behind life-cycle funds is to automatically adjust the composition of the fund so that investors take less risk as they get older. Typically, younger investors can afford to take more financial risk and therefore invest a larger percentage of their portfolio in equity securities and a lesser percentage in fixed-income securities. As investors get older, the percentages should change so that a larger percentage of the portfolio is in fixed-income securities and a lesser percentage is in equity securities. Life-cycle funds are set up with targeted retirement dates. Investors choose the life-cycle fund that matches their retirement date, and the fund adjusts its fund holdings occasionally so that equity funds gradually decrease and funds that invest in fixed-income securities gradually increase.

TIP

Don't let the variety of funds distract you too much. So many different funds are out there that the choices could drive you crazy. I list the main types, but funds can invest by objective (as previously listed) or composition, such as with foreign stock funds (which invest in foreign securities), tax-exempt funds (which invest in municipal bonds), U.S. government funds, and so on. The composition of the fund should help you match it with your customer's objectives. For instance, a customer looking for safety and income may invest in a U.S. government bond fund.

Dealing with discounts

Investors who have the extra funds available may be able to receive a reduced sales charge for large dollar purchases. Breakpoints and the letter of intent are available to investors of open-end funds and unit investment trusts. Because closed-end funds, after the initial offering, are traded in the market, investors do not receive breakpoints. Dollar cost averaging and fixed share averaging are most often used for open-end fund purchases but may apply to other investments as well.

Breakpoints

Funds have an investment advisor (portfolio manager) who gets paid a percentage of the value of the securities held in the fund. Therefore, one way to entice investors to spend more is to reduce the sales charge when they spend a certain minimum amount of money. That's where the breakpoint comes in.

Management investment companies divide purchase amounts into different tiers. Within a certain range, investors all pay the same sales charge percentage. But when investors spend enough to put them in the next tier (when they hit the *breakpoint*), they get a reduced sales charge. Breakpoints have no set schedule, so they vary from fund to fund.

Another discount, *rights of accumulation*, allows shareholders to receive a reduced sales charge when the amount of the funds held plus the amount purchased is enough to reach a breakpoint. There is no time limit for rights of accumulation.

Here are a few key points for you to remember for the SIE exam:

>> Breakpoints must be disclosed in the prospectus.

>> Breakpoints are not available to partnerships or *investment clubs* (several people pooling money together to receive reduced sales charges).

>> Breakpoints are generally available to individual investors, joint accounts with family members, and corporations.

Breakpoint sales

As an agent, you are responsible for letting investors know about the existence of breakpoints. A *breakpoint sale* is when you induce a sale just below the level where an investor would receive a breakpoint or an additional sales discount. As shown in Table 9-2, you would actually make more money if a client purchased $9,000 worth of a fund instead of $10,000 because of the discounted sales charge the customer would receive at $10,000. It is your responsibility to let the client know that by investing $1,000 more, she can reach a breakpoint. Not disclosing breakpoints and inducing sales just below breakpoints are both violations.

Letters of intent

A *letter of intent* (LOI) signed by an investor allows her to receive a breakpoint (quantity discount) right away with the initial purchase, even if the investor hasn't yet deposited enough money to achieve the breakpoint. This document states that as long as the investor deposits enough within a 13-month period, she will receive the discounted sales charge right away.

Here are a few specifics about the letter of intent that you need to know for the SIE:

» The investor has *13 months* after the first deposit to live up to the terms of the letter of intent in order to maintain the reduced sales charge.

» The LOI may be *backdated for up to 90 days,* meaning that it may apply to a previous purchase. However, remember that if the LOI applies to a previous purchase, the 13-month period starts from the date of that previous transaction.

» While the investor is under the letter of intent, shares are held in escrow to pay for the difference in the sales charge. If the investor doesn't live up to the terms of the obligation, the fund sells the shares held in escrow.

Here's how a letter of intent may work. Suppose, for instance, that Mr. Smith purchased $2,000 worth of ABC Growth Fund two months ago and has another $7,000 to invest in the fund right now. Mr. Smith believes that he'll keep investing in ABC Growth Fund and would like to get a reduced sales charge for investments of $10,000 and up (see Table 9-2 for the breakpoints).

TABLE 9-2   ## Breakpoints for ABC Growth Fund

Purchase Amount	Sales Charge
$1–$9,999	7%
$10,000–$19,999	6%
$20,000–$39,999	4%
$40,000 and up	2%

Mr. Smith signs a letter of intent and wants to apply it to his previous purchase. Because his previous purchase was two months ago, Mr. Smith has only another 11 months to invest the remaining $8,000 into ABC Growth Fund. Mr. Smith will receive the 6 percent sales charge on his $7,000 investment right now, which will be reduced by the overage he paid on the previous investment of $2,000. In other words, he'll pay only $400 sales charge on the current investment ($420 for this transaction minus the $20 overpaid from the previous investment) when he invests the $7,000. As long as Mr. Smith deposits the additional $1,000 by the end of the letter of intent's time frame, he'll pay the 6 percent sales charge. However, if Mr. Smith doesn't live up to the terms of the agreement, ABC Growth Fund will sell the shares held in escrow to pay for the difference in the sales charge.

REMEMBER

Investors may redeem their shares at any time, even if they're under a letter of intent.

Figuring the sales charge and public offering price of open-end funds

You need to know two basic formulas to determine the sales charge and public offering price of open-end funds. Yes, every chapter seems to have more formulas, but these formulas are pretty straightforward and shouldn't cause you too many sleepless nights.

Sales charge percent

The sales charge, which is set at a maximum of 8½ percent, is part of the public offering price (POP), or ask price, not something tacked on afterward like a sales tax. One of the tricks for calculating the sales charge for open-end funds is remembering that the POP equals 100 percent. Therefore, if the sales charge is 8 percent, the net asset value (NAV) is 92 percent of the POP. The formula for determining the sales charge percent is as follows:

$$\text{sales charge \%} = \frac{\text{ask} - \text{bid}}{\text{ask}} = \frac{\text{POP} - \text{NAV}}{\text{POP}}$$

The following question tests your expertise in calculating the sales charge of a mutual fund.

EXAMPLE

ABC Aggressive Growth Fund has a net asset value of $9.20 and a public offering price of $10.00. What is the sales charge percent?

(A) 6.8 percent

(B) 7.5 percent

(C) 8 percent

(D) 8.7 percent

The right answer is Choice (C). The first thing that you have to do is set up the equation. Start with the POP of $10.00 and subtract the NAV of $9.20 to get $0.80. Next, divide the $0.80 by the POP of $10.00 to get the sales charge of 8 percent:

$$\text{sales charge \%} = \frac{\text{POP} - \text{NAV}}{\text{POP}} = \frac{\$10.00 - \$9.20}{\$10.00} = \frac{\$0.80}{\$10.00} = 8\%$$

TIP

To help you remember that the ask (offer) price of a fund is the same as the POP, remember to ask your POP about it.

Public offering price (POP)

When taking the SIE exam, you may be asked to figure out the public offering price of a mutual fund when you're given only the sales charge percent and the NAV.

Remember, the sales charge is already a part of the POP, so the sales charge is *not* equal to the sales charge percent times the NAV. Use the following formula to figure out how much an investor has to pay to buy shares of the fund when you know only the NAV and the sales charge percent:

$$\text{public offering price} = \frac{\text{net asset value}}{100\% - \text{sales charge \%}}$$

The following question tests your ability to answer a POP question.

EXAMPLE

DEF Aggressive Growth Fund has a NAV of $9.12 and a POP of $9.91. If there is a 5 percent sales charge for investments of $30,000 and up, how many shares can an investor who is depositing $50,000 purchase?

(A) 5,045.409 shares

(B) 5,208.333 shares

(C) 5,219.207 shares

(D) 5,482.456 shares

The answer you want is Choice (B). Don't let the decimals throw you off; mutual funds can sell fractional shares. This investor isn't going to be paying the POP of $9.91 per share because she's receiving a breakpoint for a large dollar purchase (see "Breakpoints," earlier in this chapter). To figure out the POP for this investor, set up the formula:

$$POP = \frac{NAV}{100\% - \text{sales charge }\%} = \frac{\$9.12}{100\% - 5\%} = \frac{\$9.12}{95\%} = \$9.60 \text{ per share}$$

After working out the formula, you see that the investor is paying $9.60 per share instead of $9.91. Next, determine the number of shares the investor can purchase by dividing the amount of the investment by the cost per share:

$$\frac{\$50,000 \text{ invested}}{\$9.60 \text{ per share}} = 5,208.333 \text{ shares}$$

This investor is able to purchase 5,208.333 shares because of the breakpoint. Without the breakpoint, the investor would have been able to purchase only 5,045.409 shares.

Loads

As I explain earlier in this chapter, most mutual funds charge a sales charge (also known as a *load*) that's built into the public offering price (POP). However, most charge up front, some charge constantly, some charge when redeeming, and some don't charge a load at all. Depending on how investors are charged, mutual funds are broken down into classes:

>> **Class A (front-end load):** The investor pays the load when purchasing shares of the fund.

>> **Class B (back-end load):** The investor pays the load when redeeming shares of the fund.

>> **Class C (level load):** The investors pay a periodic fee (usually annually) over the time period that they hold the fund.

>> **Class D (no load):** Investors don't pay a sales charge but may be charged some sort of transaction fee.

Considering Other Investment Company Options

A couple of other types of investment companies — face-amount certificate companies and unit investment trusts (UITs) — aren't as popular as they used to be. Unfortunately, even though you may never sell any, you do need to know them for the SIE exam. You probably won't see more than a question or two on these topics. However, exchange-traded funds (ETFs) are becoming increasingly popular, and your chance of having a question on ETFs and/or inverse ETFs is around 100 percent.

Face-amount certificate companies

A *face-amount certificate* is a type of packaged security that's similar to a zero-coupon bond (see Chapter 7); investors make either a lump-sum payment or periodic payments in return for a larger future payment. The issuer of a face-amount certificate guarantees payment of the face amount (a fixed sum) to the investor at a preset date. Very few face-amount certificate companies are around today.

Unit investment trusts (UITs)

A *unit investment trust* (UIT) is a registered investment company that purchases a fixed (unmanaged) portfolio of income-producing securities (typically bonds) and holds them in trust, which means that a UIT acts as a holding company for its investors. Then the company issues redeemable shares (units) that represent investors' interest in the trust. Unlike mutual funds, UITs are set up for a specific period of time and have a set termination date. Any capital gains, interest, and/or dividends are passed on to shareholders at regular intervals.

UITs have a finite number of shares outstanding and are distributed in the primary market at the initial public offering (IPO) price. Because a limited number of shares are outstanding and they must be redeemed with the issuer or sponsor, liquidity is very limited.

Like mutual (open-end) funds, UITs can be purchased by type, such as growth, income, balanced, international, and so forth.

Here are the two main categories of these trusts:

>> **Fixed investment trusts:** These companies invest in a portfolio of debt securities, and the trust terminates when all the bonds in the portfolio mature.

>> **Participating trusts:** These companies invest in shares of mutual funds. The mutual funds that the trust holds don't change, but the securities held by the underlying mutual funds do.

REMEMBER

Because the portfolio of securities is fixed, UITs don't employ investment advisors and therefore have no investment advisor fees during the life of the trust. Nice break!

Exchange-traded products (ETPs)

Exchange-traded products (ETPs) include exchange-traded funds (ETFs) and exchange-traded notes (ETNs). ETPs are considered an alternative to investing in mutual funds because they not only provide diversification like mutual funds but can also be sold short and be purchased on margin. However, investors should be aware that they will typically be charged a commission for buying and selling ETPs, which can really cut into any potential profits.

Most ETFs are *passive*, meaning that they are designed to be a single security that tracks certain indices such as the S&P 500, the S&P 100, the DJIA, NASDAQ securities, and so on. However, some ETFs are *active*, meaning that the securities they hold may change. Quite often ETFs are designed to mirror securities held by certain mutual funds.

Exchange-traded funds (ETFs)

Exchange-traded funds, or ETFs, are closed-end index funds that are traded on an exchange. ETFs provide investors with diversification along with the ability to sell short and purchase shares on margin. Since these are exchange-traded funds, they can be traded during the day, unlike mutual funds, which have forward pricing (if you buy or redeem, you get the closing price at the end of the day). Even though they trade more like closed-end funds, ETFs are registered as open-end funds or unit investment trusts.

Inverse ETFs (also known as *Short ETFs* or *Bear ETFs*) are exchange-traded funds that are designed using many derivative products, such as options to attempt to profit from a decline in the value of the underlying securities (for example, the S&P 500). Inverse ETFs can be used to profit from a decline in a broad market index or in a specific sector, such as the energy or financial sector.

REMEMBER

Because ETFs are traded on an exchange, their market price is not only based on the value of the underlying securities but also on market forces (supply and demand). In addition, because they are traded on an exchange instead of being purchased from the issuer like open-end mutual funds, investors are charged commissions for trades of ETFs.

Exchange-traded notes (ETNs)

Exchange-traded notes have characteristics of ETFs and fixed-income securities. ETNs are unsecured debt securities issued by a bank or financial institution. Their return is linked to a particular market index. Exchange-traded notes don't receive dividends or coupon payments, so investors receive income at a specified maturity date. Since they are traded on an exchange, they may be purchased on margin or sold short. If an investor holds the ETN until the maturity date, the investor will receive a principal amount based on the performance of the index the note is tracking.

Investment company rules 17a-6 and 17a-7

According to *Rule 17a-6*, affiliated persons of investment companies (persons affiliated with the manager of the fund, the custodian bank, and owners of 5 percent or more of the outstanding shares of the fund) are not allowed to trade securities within the fund's portfolio of securities. However, affiliated persons are certainly allowed to buy and redeem shares of the fund like regular public investors.

Rule 17a-7 says that advisors, officers, or directors may trade securities held by funds within the same family of funds (for example, trading securities held from the portfolio of securities of one of Fidelity's Large Value Funds to one of Fidelity's Large Blend Funds or vice versa).

Adding Annuities to a Portfolio

Annuities are similar to mutual funds, except annuities are designed to provide supplemental retirement income for investors. Life insurance companies issue annuities, and these investments provide guaranteed payments for the life of the holder. The SIE exam tests you on the two basic types of annuities: fixed and variable. Because variable annuities are considered securities and fixed annuities are not (because of the guaranteed payout by the insurance company), most of the annuity questions on the SIE exam are about variable annuities.

REMEMBER

Gather very specific information about your client before making recommendations. In addition, before recommending annuities, make sure you really understand the ins and outs and know what you're talking about. Annuities have been under the watchful eye of State Insurance Commissions and the SEC due to inappropriate recommendations from some brokers. Annuities typically aren't recommended for younger clients (most annuity purchasers are over the age of 50), for clients older than 75, or for a client's entire investment portfolio. For information on portfolio and securities analysis, see Chapter 13.

Looking at fixed annuities

The main thing for you to remember about *fixed annuities* is that they have fixed rates of return that the issuer guarantees. Investors pay money into fixed annuities, and the money is deposited into the insurance company's general account. After the investor starts receiving payments from the fixed annuity (usually monthly), the payments remain the same for the remainder of the investor's life. Because of the guaranteed payout, fixed annuities are *not* considered securities and therefore are exempt from SEC registration requirements.

REMEMBER

Because the payouts associated with a fixed annuity remain the same, they're subject to *purchasing power risk* (the risk that the investment won't keep up with inflation). An investor who received payments of $1,000 per month in the 1970s may have been able to survive; however, that amount today is not even likely to pay your monthly grocery bill.

Checking out variable annuities

Insurance companies introduced variable annuities as a way to keep pace with (or hopefully exceed) inflation. In a fixed annuity, the insurance company bears the inflation risk; however, in a variable annuity, the investment risk is borne by the investor. Because the investors assume the investment risk, variable annuities are considered securities and must be registered with the SEC. All variable annuities have to be sold with a prospectus, and only individuals who hold appropriate securities and insurance licenses can sell them.

The money that investors deposit is held in a *separate account* (separate from the insurance company's other business) because the money is invested differently. The separate account is invested in securities such as common stock, bonds, mutual funds, and so on, with the hope that the investments will keep pace with or exceed the inflation rate.

The *assumed interest rate* (AIR) is a projection of the performance of the securities in the separate account over the life of the variable annuity contract. If the assumed interest rate is 4 percent and the performance of the securities in the separate account is equal to 4 percent, the investor receives the payouts that she expects. However, if the securities outperform the AIR, the investor receives higher payouts than expected. And unfortunately, if the securities held in the separate account underperform the AIR, the investor gets lower payouts than expected.

Putting money into (and receiving money from) annuities

Investors have choices when purchasing annuities and getting distributions. Investors may choose a lump-sum payment or multiple payments, depending on their needs. Investors also have a choice regarding how they want to get their distributions at retirement.

Looking at the pay-in phase

Payments into both fixed and variable annuities are made from after-tax dollars, meaning that the investor can't write the payments off on her taxes. However, payments into both fixed and variable annuities grow on a tax-deferred basis (they aren't taxed until the money is withdrawn). If an investor has contributed $80,000 into a variable annuity that's now worth $120,000, the investor is taxed only on the $40,000 difference because she has already paid taxes on the contribution. If an annuitant dies during the pay-in phase, most annuity contracts require a *death benefit* to be paid to the annuitant's beneficiary. The death benefit is typically the greater of all the money in the account or some guaranteed minimum.

Note: During the pay-in phase, an investor of a variable annuity purchases *accumulation units*. These units are similar to shares of a mutual fund.

Investors have a few payment options to select when purchasing fixed or variable annuities. Here's the rundown of options:

>> **Single payment deferred annuity:** An investor purchases the annuity with a lump-sum payment, and the payouts are delayed until some predetermined date.

>> **Periodic payment deferred annuity:** An investor makes periodic payments (usually monthly) into the annuity, and the payouts are delayed until some predetermined date; this is the most common type of annuity.

>> **Immediate annuity:** An investor purchases the annuity with a large sum, and the payouts begin within a couple months.

REMEMBER

Most annuities in which investors are making scheduled deposits provide a *waiver of premium* during the pay-in phase if the annuitant becomes disabled or is confined to long-term care.

Getting the payout

Investors of both fixed and variable annuities have several payout options. These options may cover just the *annuitant* (investor) or the annuitant and a survivor. No matter what type of payout option the investor chooses, she will be taxed on the amount above the contribution. The earnings grow on a tax-deferred basis, and the investor is not taxed on the earnings until withdrawal at retirement.

Note: During the payout phase of a variable annuity, accumulation units are converted into a fixed number of *annuity units*. Investors receive a fixed number of annuity units periodically (usually monthly) with a variable value, depending on the performance of the securities in the separate account.

When an investor purchases an annuity, she has to decide which of the following payout options works best for her:

>> **Life annuity:** This type of payment option provides income for the life of the *annuitant* (the individual covered by the annuity); however, after the annuitant dies, the insurance company stops making payments. This type of annuity is riskiest for the investor because if the annuitant dies earlier than expected, the insurance company gets to keep the leftover annuity money. Because it's the riskiest type of annuity for the annuitant, it has the highest payouts of all the options.

>> **Life annuity with period certain:** This payout option guarantees payment to the annuitant for a minimum number of years (10, 20, and so on). For example, if the annuitant were to purchase an annuity with a 20-year guarantee and die after 7 years, a named beneficiary would receive the payments for the remaining 13 years.

>> **Joint life with last survivor annuity:** This option guarantees payments over the lives of two individuals. As you can imagine, this type of annuity is typically set up for a husband and wife. If the wife dies first, the husband receives payments until his death. If the husband dies first, his wife receives payments until her death. Because this type of annuity covers the lifespans of two individuals, it has the lowest payouts.

REMEMBER

All annuities have a *mortality guarantee.* This guarantee means that the investor receives payments as long as she lives, even if it's beyond her life expectancy.

Early withdrawal penalty

As with most other retirement plans, annuity investors are hit with a 10 percent early withdrawal penalty if they withdraw the money prior to age 59½. Yes, that's correct — the 10 percent penalty is added to the investor's tax bracket. Typically, retirement plans include a waiver of the 10 percent penalty in cases such as the purchase of a first home, age 55 and separated from work, death, or disability.

Exploring Variable Life and Variable Universal Life Insurance

You may wonder what life insurance is doing in the SIE, which is mainly about investments. Well, the answer is that certain life insurance products (specifically, *variable life* [VLI] and *variable universal life* [VUL]) have an investment component. Like variable annuities, variable life and variable universal life insurance policies have a separate account for investing. That separate account is kept separate from the insurance company's general fund. You won't need to know too much about the aforementioned insurance products, so I'll keep it brief.

REMEMBER

Persons selling variable annuities, variable life insurance, and variable universal life insurance must have not only an appropriate securities license but also an insurance license. Prior to recommending any of the previously mentioned products, you should do an analysis of the client's needs and make appropriate recommendations.

Variable life

Variable life policies have a fixed premium. As with variable annuities, the investor chooses the investments held in a separate account. The death benefit (face amount) on the policy is fixed to a minimum but not to a maximum. The death benefit may increase depending on the performance of the securities held in the separate account. If the separate account performs poorly, there may be limited or no cash value built up. Policyholders may borrow up to 75 percent of the cash value.

Variable universal life

Unlike variable life policies, variable universal life policies do not have fixed premiums. As such, they are sometimes called flexible premium variable life policies. As with variable life policies, the investors can pick the securities held in the separate account. In this case, since the premium is not fixed and the securities held in the separate account may perform poorly, the minimum death benefit and cash value are not guaranteed.

IN THIS CHAPTER

» Understanding the specifics of DPPs

» Distinguishing a limited partner from a general partner

» Getting a handle on the paperwork and taxes involved

» Looking at the different types of DPPs

» Mitigating real-estate risk with REITs

Chapter **10**

Working with Direct Participation Programs and REITs

D irect participation programs (DPPs) can raise money to invest in real estate, oil and gas, equipment leasing, and so on. More commonly known as limited partnerships, these businesses are somewhat similar to corporations (stockholder-owned companies). However, limited partnerships have some specific tax advantages (and disadvantages) that a lot of other investments don't have. According to tax laws, limited partnerships are not taxed directly; the income or losses are passed directly through to the investors.

DPPs were once known as tax shelters because of the tax benefits to investors; however, tax law changes have taken away a lot of these advantages. As a result, DPPs have somewhat fallen out of favor for investors (though not entirely for the SIE designers).

In this chapter, I explain the differences between limited and general partners as well as the types of partnerships, their particular risks, and potential rewards. The info here can help you examine those risks and rewards and determine the suitability of DPPs for investors. I also explain two inevitable facts of life as they apply to partnerships: the filing of paperwork and the payment of taxes. Finally, I explain the ins and outs and some of the specifics you need to know about real-estate investment trusts (REITs). Unlike mutual funds that invest in a pool of securities, REITs invest in real estate. If you can't wait, they're toward the end of the chapter.

Searching for Identity: What DPPs Are (and Aren't)

Just as stockholders are owners of a corporation, limited (and general) partners are owners of a *direct participation program* (DPP). The key difference for people investing in DPPs is that they're required to tie up their investment dollars for a long period of time, though they receive tax advantages for doing so. Most DPPs are set up for real-estate projects, oil and gas projects, or equipment leasing.

REMEMBER

The IRS determines whether an enterprise is a corporation or a limited partnership. For a limited partnership to actually be considered (and taxed) as a limited partnership, it has to *avoid* at least two of the following corporate characteristics (usually the last two):

>> **Having a centralized management:** Corporations have management in one place. The challenges of managing a limited partnership from several locations make this corporate trait quite difficult for a partnership to avoid.

>> **Providing limited liability:** Corporate shareholders have limited liability; well, so do limited partners. The liability of corporate shareholders is limited to the amount invested, and the liability of limited partners is limited to the amount invested plus a portion of any recourse loans taken out by the partnership (if any). Providing limited liability is pretty much unavoidable.

>> **Having perpetual (never-ending) life:** Unlike corporations, which hope to last forever, limited partnerships are set up for a definite period of time. Limited partnerships are dissolved at a predetermined time — for example, when their goals are met or after a set number of years.

>> **Having free transferability of partnership interest:** DPPs are difficult to get in and out of. Unlike shares of stock, which can be freely bought and sold by anyone, limited partners not only have to pass the scrutiny of a registered rep, but they also require approval of the general partner. DPP investors (limited partners) must show that they have enough money to invest initially, plus have liquidity in other investments in the event that the partnership needs a loan.

REMEMBER

For SIE exam purposes, you need to remember that the easiest corporate characteristics for a partnership to avoid are perpetual life (continuity of life) and having free transferability of shares; the most difficult to avoid are providing limited liability and having a centralized management.

The DPP Characters: General and Limited Partners

By law, limited partnerships require at least one limited partner and one general partner. Limited partners are the investors, and general partners are the managers. When you're looking at general and limited partners, you want to focus on *who can and can't do what*.

General partners are responsible for the day-to-day decision making (overseeing operations, deciding when to buy or sell, choosing what to invest in, and so on) for the partnership. Limited partners (the investors) provide the bulk of the money for the partnership but, unlike general partners, can't make any of the partnership's investment decisions. Table 10-1 lays out the key things to remember about general and limited partners for the SIE.

TABLE 10-1 **Comparing General and Limited Partners**

Category	General Partners	Limited Partners
Decision making	Are legally bound to make decisions in the best interest of the partnership; make all the partnership's day-to-day decisions	Have voting rights but can't make decisions for the partnership
Tasks	Buy and sell property for the partnership; manage the partnership's assets	Provide capital; vote; can keep general partners in check by reviewing books
Liability and litigation	Have unlimited liability (can be sued and held personally liable for all partnership debts and losses)	Have limited liability (limited to the amount invested and a proportionate share of any recourse loans taken by the partnership); can inspect *all* the partnership books; can sue the general partner or can sue to dissolve the partnership
Financial involvement	Maintain a financial interest in the partnership	Provide money contributed to the partnership, recourse debt of the partnership, and nonrecourse debt for real-estate DPPs
Financial rewards	Receive compensation for managing the partnership	Receive their proportion of profits and losses
Conflicts of interest	Can't borrow money from the partnership; can't compete against the partnership (for example, they can't manage two buildings for two different partnerships in close proximity to each other)	None; can invest in competing partnerships

Partnerships are usually set up as *tenants in common* (TIC). What this means is that each limited partner owns an undivided interest in the property held by the partnership. In addition, in the event that one of the limited partners dies, his partnership interest will be passed to a beneficiary or to his estate.

Pushing through Partnership Paperwork

For the SIE, you need to know about certain paperwork that's specific to limited partnerships. In the following sections, I discuss the three required documents necessary for a limited partnership to exist.

Partnership agreement

The *partnership agreement* is a document that includes the rights and responsibilities of the limited and general partners. Included in the agreement are basics that you would probably guess such as the name of the partnership, the location of the partnership, the name of the general partner, and so on. In addition, the partnership agreement addresses the general partner's rights to

>> Charge a management fee for making decisions for the partnership

>> Enter the partnership into contracts

>> Decide whether cash distributions will be made to the limited partners

>> Accept or decline limited partners

Certificate of limited partnership

The *certificate of limited partnership* is the legal agreement between the general and limited partners, which is filed with the Secretary of State in the home state of the partnership. The certificate of limited partnership includes basic information such as the name of the partnership and its primary place of business, the names and addresses of the limited and general partner(s), and the following items:

>> The objectives (goals) of the partnership and how long the partnership is expected to last

>> The amount contributed by each partner, plus future expected investments

>> How the profits are to be distributed

>> The roles of the participants

>> How the partnership can be dissolved

>> Whether a limited partner can sell or assign his interest in the partnership

If any significant changes are made to the partnership, such as adding new limited partners, the certificate of limited partnership must be amended accordingly.

Subscription agreement

The *subscription agreement* is an application form that potential limited partners have to complete. The general partner uses this agreement to determine whether an investor is suitable to become a limited partner. The general partner has to sign the subscription agreement to officially accept an investor into the DPP.

One of your jobs as a registered rep is to prescreen the potential limited partner to make sure that the partnership is a good fit for the individual. Consider the following questions:

>> Does he have enough money to invest?

>> Does he have enough cash or liquidity in other investments in case the partnership needs more money?

>> Is he okay with tying up his money for a long period of time?

>> Can he handle the risks?

Also, you need to review the agreement to ensure (to the best of your ability) that the information the investor provides is complete and accurate. Besides the investor's payment, the subscription agreement has to include items such as the investor's net worth and annual income, a statement explaining the risks of investing in the partnership, and a power of attorney that allows the general partner to make partnership investment decisions for the limited partner.

Passive Income and Losses: Looking at Taxes on Partnerships

DPPs used to be called *tax shelters* because DPPs flow through (or pass through) not only income but also losses to investors (corporations only flow through income). Prior to 1986, investors could write off these losses against income from other investments. Then the IRS stepped in because it felt that this write-off was too much of an advantage for investors (or the IRS wasn't making enough money) and decided to give DPPs their own tax category. Now, because investors are not actively involved in earning the income, taxes on DPPs are classified as *passive income* and *passive losses*. (See Chapter 15 for more info on taxes and types of income.)

REMEMBER

The key thing to remember for SIE purposes is that investors can write off passive losses only against passive income from other DPP investments.

Evaluating Direct Participation Programs

Direct participation programs can be offered *publicly* or *privately*. Public offerings of DPPs must be registered with the Securities and Exchange Commission (SEC) whereas private offerings (offerings to mostly wealthy investors) are not. Typically, publicly offered DPPs have a lower unit (buy-in) cost than that of privately offered DPPs.

Certainly direct participation programs do provide some advantages, but they also have additional risks that investors don't face with other types of investments, such as having to loan additional money to the partnership if needed. Therefore, when evaluating whether an investment in a DPP may be right for one of your clients, not only do you need to determine whether investing in a partnership is wise for that client, but you also need to consider the following items:

>> The economic soundness of the program

>> The expertise of the general partner

>> The basic objectives of the program

>> The start-up costs involved

Checking Out Types of Partnerships

Certainly partnerships can be formed to run any sort of business that you can imagine, but the SIE exam focuses on the big three: real estate, equipment leasing, and oil and gas. You need to be able to identify the risks and potential rewards for each of the following types of partnerships.

REMEMBER

Because of the risks associated with some of the different types of DPPs, investors should have the ability to tie up their money for a long period of time and be able to recover from a loss of all the money invested in case the partnership never becomes profitable.

Building on real-estate partnership info

Real-estate partnerships include programs that invest in raw land, new construction, existing properties, or government-assisted housing. You need to know the differences among the types of programs, along with their risks and potential rewards. Here are the types of real-estate DPPs, from safest to riskiest:

>> **Public housing (government-assisted housing programs):** This type of real-estate DPP develops low-income and retirement housing. The focus of this type of DPP is to earn consistent income and receive tax credits. The U.S. government (through U.S. government subsidies),

via the department of Housing and Urban Development (HUD), makes up any deficient rent payments. Appreciation potential is low and maintenance costs can be high, but the DPP does benefit from a little government security. Public housing DPPs are backed by the U.S. government and, therefore, are considered the safest real-estate DPP.

>> **Existing properties:** This type of DPP purchases existing properties, and the intent is to generate a regular stream of rental income. Because the properties already exist, this DPP generates immediate cash flow. The risk with this type of DPP is that the maintenance or repair expenses will eat into the profit or that tenants won't renew their leases. The properties already exist and are producing income, so the risk for this type of DPP is relatively low.

>> **New construction:** This type of DPP purchases property for the purpose of building. After completing the construction, the partnership's goal is to sell the property and structure at a profit after all expenses. Building costs may be more than expected, and the partnership doesn't receive income until the property is sold, but the DPP can benefit from appreciation on both the land and the structure. Although this investment is speculative, it's not as risky as a raw land DPP.

>> **Raw land:** This type of DPP invests in undeveloped land in anticipation of long-term capital appreciation; raw land DPPs don't build on or rent out the property. The partnership hopes the property purchased will appreciate in value so that the DPP can sell the property for more than the purchase price plus all expenses.

Raw land DPPs are considered the riskiest real-estate DPP because the partnership doesn't have any cash flow (no rental or sales income), and the value of the land may not increase — it may actually decrease.

The main thing to remember with real-estate DPPs is that depending on which type you invest in, they can provide capital growth potential through the appreciation of property held by the DPP; cash flow for DPPs that hold rentals; tax deductions for mortgage interest, depreciation, and capital improvements; and tax credits for DPPs that hold government-assisted housing.

Gearing up with equipment leasing

Although you may be tested on equipment leasing programs on the SIE exam, it's typically the least-tested type of DPP on securities exams. Equipment leasing programs purchase equipment (trucks, heavy machinery, computers . . . you name it) and lease it out to other businesses. The objective is to obtain a steady cash flow and depreciation write-offs. The two types of leasing arrangements you need to be aware of are the operating lease and the full payout lease:

>> **Operating lease:** This type of equipment leasing program purchases equipment and leases it out for a short period of time. The DPP doesn't receive the full value of the equipment during the first lease. This type of arrangement allows the DPP to lease out the equipment several times during the life of the machinery.

>> **Full payout lease:** This type of equipment leasing program purchases the equipment and leases it out for a long period of time. The DPP receives enough income from the first lease to cover the cost of the equipment and any financing costs. Usually, the initial lease lasts for the useful life of the equipment.

The main thing to remember about equipment leasing is that the operating lease is riskier because the equipment becomes less valuable or outdated over time and, therefore, less rentable.

Strengthening your grasp on oil and gas

Oil and gas partnerships include programs that produce income, are speculative in nature, or are a combination of the two. You need to know how the types of programs differ, along with their risks and potential rewards. Oil and gas partnerships also have certain tax advantages that are unique:

>> **Intangible drilling costs (IDCs):** IDCs are write-offs for drilling expenses. The word *intangible* is your clue that you're not talking about actual equipment. These costs include wages for employees, fuel, repairs, hauling of equipment, insurance, and so on. IDCs are usually completely deductible in the tax year in which the intangible costs occur. IDC deductions are only for the drilling and preparing of a well for the production of oil and gas. Therefore, when a well is producing, IDC write-offs are not allowed.

>> **Tangible drilling costs (TDCs):** TDCs are write-offs on items purchased that have salvage value (items that can be resold). All oil and gas DPPs have TDCs, which include costs for purchasing items such as storage tanks, well equipment, and so on. These costs are not immediately written off but are *depreciated* (deducted) over seven years. Depreciation may be claimed on either a straight-line basis (writing off an equal amount each year) or an accelerated basis (writing off more in the early years and less in the later years).

IDCs are fully deductible in the current year; TDCs are depreciated (deductible) over several years.

>> **Depletion:** Depletion is a tax deduction that allows partnerships that deal with natural resources (such as oil and gas) to take a deduction for the decreasing supply of the resource. Partnerships can claim depletion deductions only on the amount of natural resources sold (not extracted and put in storage for future sale).

Depletion deductions are only for DPPs that deal with natural resources. On the SIE exam, the only DPP with depletion deductions that you need to be concerned with is oil and gas.

When investing in oil, partnerships can pioneer new territory, drill near existing wells, buy producing wells, or try a combination of those methods. For SIE exam purposes, exploratory programs are the riskiest oil and gas DPPs because oil may never be found, and income programs are the safest oil and gas DPPs. To make your life easier (hopefully), I've composed a DPP comparison chart (see Table 10-2) to help you focus on the main points of each type of oil and gas DPP.

TABLE 10-2 Advantages and Risks of Various Oil and Gas DPPs

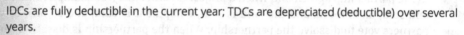

Type	Objective	Advantages	Risks
Exploratory (wildcatting)	To locate and drill for oil in unproven, undiscovered areas	Long-term capital appreciation potential; high returns for discovery of new oil or gas reserves	Riskiest oil and gas DPP because new oil reserves may never be found; high IDCs because the DPP isn't working with producing wells
Developmental	To drill near producing wells with the hope of finding new reserves	Long-term capital appreciation potential with less risk than exploratory programs; oil will likely be found	The property's expensive; the drilling costs may be higher than expected; the risk of dry holes (non-producing wells) is still somewhat high; medium level of IDCs
Income	To provide immediate income by purchasing producing wells	The partnership generates immediate cash flow; the least risky of the oil and gas DPPs; no IDCs	High initial costs; the well could dry up; gas prices could go down
Combination	To provide income to help pay for the cost of finding new oil reserves	The ability to offset the costs of drilling new wells by using income generated by existing wells	Carries the risks of all the programs combined

The following question concerns different DPP investments.

EXAMPLE

Mr. Smith has money invested in a limited partnership that's expecting to have a significant amount of income over the next one to two years. Which of the following programs would BEST help Mr. Smith shelter the MOST of that income?

(A) Oil and gas exploratory

(B) Raw land purchasing

(C) Equipment leasing

(D) Existing real-estate property

The answer you want is Choice (A). Oil and gas exploratory programs spend a lot of money attempting to find and drill for oil. These programs have high IDCs (intangible drilling costs), which are fully tax-deductible when the drilling occurs. Therefore, the oil and gas exploratory programs have the largest write-offs in the early years, which could help Mr. Smith offset some or all of his passive income from the other limited partnership.

REMEMBER

Unlike corporations, DPPs have an ending date. That date could be either predetermined as placed in the partnership agreement, when a project is completed (for example, when buildings are built and sold, oil is found and the land is sold, equipment is sold, and so on), or when the limited partners vote to dissolve the partnership. When the partnership is dissolved, the first to be paid out of the partnership assets are secured creditors, then general creditors are paid, after that limited partners are paid, and the last to be paid are the general partners.

Reducing Real-Estate Risk with REITs

A *real-estate investment trust* (REIT) is a trust that invests in real-estate-related projects such as properties, mortgage loans, and construction loans. REITs pool the capital of many investors to manage property and/or purchase mortgage loans. As with other trusts, they issue shares to investors representing their interest in the trust. REITs may be listed on an exchange or can trade over-the-counter (OTC) (see Chapter 14 for more info on markets). They also provide real-estate diversification and liquidity for investors.

REITs are distributed in the primary market at the IPO price. Unlike mutual funds, which are redeemed with the issuer, REITs are traded (bought and sold) in the secondary market to other investors. In addition, REITs have a finite number of shares outstanding, like closed-end funds. Because REITs are traded in the secondary market, their price may be at a discount or premium to the NAV (Net Asset Value; see Chapter 9), depending on investor sentiment.

Equity REITs take equity positions in real-estate properties; the income is derived from rent collected or profits made when the properties are sold. *Mortgage REITs* purchase construction loans and mortgages. The trust receives the interest paid on the loans and in turn passes it on to the owners of the trust (the investors). *Hybrid REITs* are a combination of equity and mortgage REITs. Hybrid REITs generate income derived from rent and capital gains (like an equity REIT) and interest (like a mortgage REIT).

REITs can *avoid* being taxed like a corporation if

>> At least 75 percent of the income comes from real-estate-related activities

>> At least 75 percent of the REIT's assets are in real estate, government securities, and/or cash

>> At least 90 percent of the net income received is distributed to shareholders (who pay taxes on the income)

WARNING

Don't get REITs confused with real-estate limited partnerships. Limited partnerships pass on (the industry term is *pass through*) income and write-offs to investors to claim on their own personal tax return; REITs pass only income through to investors.

Don't kill yourself worrying too much about REITs (not that you would); you won't get more than one or two questions on the SIE relating to REITs.

Private (private placement) REITs

REITs may be sold privately. Private REITs are exempt from SEC registration, and their shares don't trade on a national securities exchange such as the NYSE. As such, they are not subject to the same disclosure requirements as exchange-listed or public non-listed REITs. Private REITs are exempt from SEC registration under Regulation D of the Securities Act of 1933 (see Chapter 5). In general, private REITs can only be sold to accredited investors and institutional investors. Since they aren't sold on an exchange and cannot be sold to just any investor, private REITs are not liquid investments.

Registered non-listed REITs

Registered non-listed REITs are also known as public non-listed REITs (PNLRs). PNLRs are registered with the SEC but do not trade on a major exchange. PNLRs are similar to listed REITs in every way, including disclosure requirements, except that they're not as liquid. PNLRs may be purchased and sold over-the-counter (OTC), and some issuers have periodic (daily or less frequent) repurchase options that allow investors to sell shares back to the issuer at the net asset value (NAV).

Listed REITs

As you can imagine, listed REITs are ones that have to register with the SEC and are also listed on one or more national exchanges. So, listed REITs provide the highest degree of liquidity to investors.

Chapter **11**

Options: The Right to Buy or Sell at a Fixed Price

Welcome to the wonderful world of options. I'm sure you've heard stories about the difficulty of options. Put your mind at ease — I'm here to make your life easier. Maybe I'm a little warped, but options are my favorite part of the SIE exam!

You don't have to do a lot of calculations relating to options on the SIE, but the ones that you do have to do are relatively simple. More of the option questions on this exam are about understanding the terminology and rules. But, in this chapter I make facing any math questions you may encounter as simple as possible for you.

TIP

There are certainly many more complex options strategies such as straddles, spreads, combinations, and so on. However, you won't need to calculate any of them on the SIE exam. However, if you're planning on taking the Series 7 exam after this one . . . be prepared.

Brushing Up on Option Basics

Options are just another investment vehicle that (hopefully) more-savvy investors can use. An owner of an *option* has the right, but not the obligation, to buy or sell an underlying security (stock, bond, and so on) at a fixed price; as derivatives, options draw their value from that underlying security. Investors may either *exercise* the option (buy or sell the security at the fixed price) or trade the option in the market.

All option strategies (whether simple or sophisticated), when broken down, are made up of simple call and/or put options. After going over how to read an option, I explain a basic call option and help you figure out how to work with that before moving on to a put option. Next, I discuss options that are in-, at-, or out-of-the-money, and the cost of options. After you've sufficiently mastered the basics, the rest (the more difficult strategies later in this chapter) becomes easier.

Reading an option

To answer SIE questions relating to options, you have to be able to read an option. The following example shows you how an option may appear on the SIE exam:

Buy 1 XYZ Apr 60 call at 5

Here are the seven elements of the option order ticket and how they apply to the example:

1. Whether the investor is buying or selling the option: Buy

When an investor buys (or *longs, holds,* or *owns*) an option, she is in a position of power; that investor controls the option and decides whether and when to exercise the option. If an investor is selling (*shorting* or *writing*) an option, she is obligated to live up to the terms of the contract and must either purchase or sell the underlying stock if the holder exercises the option.

2. The contract size: 1

You can assume that one option contract is for *100 shares* of the underlying stock. Although this idea isn't as heavily tested on the SIE exam, an investor may buy or sell multiple options (for example, five) if she's interested in having a position in more shares of stock. If an investor owns five option contracts, she's interested in 500 shares of stock, which you will need to know in more detail when taking other exams such as the Series 7.

3. The name of the stock: XYZ

In this case, XYZ is the underlying stock that the investor has a right to purchase at a fixed price.

4. The expiration month for the options: Apr

All options are owned for a fixed period of time. The initial expiration for most options is *9 months* from the issue date. In the preceding example, the option will expire in April. Options expire at 4 p.m. EST (3 p.m. CST) on the third Friday of the expiration month. Remembering the EST (Eastern Standard Time) is generally easier than recalling the CST (Central Standard Time) and is more often tested.

5. The strike (exercise) price of the option: 60

When the holder (purchaser or owner) *exercises* the option, she uses the option contract to make the seller of the option buy or sell the underlying stock at the strike price (see the next step for info on determining whether the seller is obligated to buy or sell). In this case, if the holder were to exercise the option, the holder of the option would be able to purchase 100 shares of XYZ at $60 per share.

6. The type of option: call

An investor can buy or sell a call option or buy or sell a put option. Calls give holders the right to buy the underlying security at a set price; puts give holders the right to sell. So in the example scenario, the holder has the right to buy the underlying security at the price stated in the preceding step.

7. The premium: 5

Of course, an option investor doesn't get to have the option for nothing. An investor buys the option at the premium. In this case, the premium is 5, so a purchaser would have to pay $500 (5 × 100 shares per option).

Looking at call options: The right to buy

REMEMBER

A *call option* gives the holder (owner) the right to buy 100 shares of a security at a fixed price and the seller the obligation to sell the stock at the fixed price. Owners of call options are bullish (picture a bull charging forward) because the investors want the price of the stock to increase. If the price of the stock increases above the strike price, holders can either exercise the option (buy the stock at a good price) or sell the option for a profit. By contrast, sellers of call options are bearish (imagine a bear hibernating for the winter) because they want the price of the stock to decrease.

For example, assume that Ms. Smith buys 1 DEF October 40 call option. Ms. Smith bought the right to purchase 100 shares of DEF at 40. If the price of DEF increases to over $40 per share, this option becomes very valuable to Ms. Smith, because she can purchase the stock at $40 per share and sell it at the market price or sell the option at a higher price.

If DEF never eclipses the 40 strike (exercise) price, then the option doesn't work out for poor Ms. Smith and she doesn't exercise the option. However, it does work out for the seller of the option, because the seller receives a premium for selling the option, and the seller gets to pocket that premium.

Checking out put options: The right to sell

REMEMBER

You can think of a put option as being the opposite of a call option (see the preceding section). The holder of a *put option* has the right to sell 100 shares of a security at a fixed price, and the writer (seller) of a put option has the obligation to buy the stock if exercised. Owners of put options are bearish because the investors want the price of the stock to decrease (so they can buy the stock at market price and immediately sell it at the higher strike price or sell their option at a higher premium). However, sellers of put options are bullish (they want the price of the stock to increase), because that would keep the option from going in-the-money (see the next section) and allow them to keep the premiums they received.

For example, assume that Mr. Jones buys 1 ABC October 60 put option. Mr. Jones is buying the right to sell 100 shares of ABC at 60. If the price of ABC decreases to less than $60 per share, this option becomes very valuable to Mr. Jones. If you were in Mr. Jones's shoes and ABC were to drop to $50 per share, you could purchase the stock in the market and exercise (use) the option to sell the stock at $60 per share, which would make you (the new Mr. Jones) very happy.

If ABC never drops below the 60 strike (exercise) price, then the option doesn't work out for Mr. Jones and he doesn't exercise the option. However, it does work out for the seller of the option, because the seller receives a premium for selling the option that she gets to keep.

Getting your money back: Options in-, at-, or out-of-the-money

To determine whether an option is in- or out-of-the-money, you have to figure out whether the investor would be able to get at least some of his premium money back if the option were exercised.

REMEMBER

You can figure out how much an option is in-the-money or out-of-the-money by finding the difference between the market value and the strike price. Here's how you know wherein-the-money an option is:

>> When an option is *in-the-money,* exercising the option lets investors sell a security for more than its current market value or purchase it for less — a pretty good deal.

   The *intrinsic value* of an option is the amount that the option is in-the-money; if an option is out-of-the-money or at-the-money, the intrinsic value is zero.

>> When an option is *out-of-the-money,* exercising the option means investors can't get the best prices; they'd have to buy the security for more than its market value or sell it for less. Obviously, holders of options that are out-of-the-money don't exercise them.

>> When the strike price is the same as the market price, the option is *at-the-money;* this is true whether the option is a call or a put.

Call options — the right to buy — go in-the-money when the price of the stock is above the strike price. Suppose, for instance, that an investor buys a DEF 60 call option and that DEF is trading at 62. In this case, the option would be in-the-money by two points (the option's intrinsic value). If that same investor were to buy that DEF 60 call option when DEF was trading at 55, the option would be out-of-the-money by five points (with an intrinsic value of zero).

A put option — the right to sell — goes in-the-money when the price of the stock drops below the strike price. For example, a TUV 80 call option is in-the-money when the price of TUV drops below 80. The reverse holds as well: If a put option is in-the-money when the price of the stock is below the strike price, it must be out-of-the-money when the price of the stock is above the strike price.

WARNING

Don't take the cost of the option (the premium) into consideration when determining whether an option is in-the-money or out-of-the-money. Having an option that's in-the-money is not the same as making a profit. (See the next section for info on premiums.)

TIP

Use the phrases *call up* and *put down* to recall when an option goes in-the-money. *Call up* can help you remember that a *call* option is in-the-money when the market price is *up,* or above the strike price. *Put down* can help you remember that a *put* option is in-the-money when the market price is *down,* or below the strike price.

The following question tests your knowledge of options being in- or out-of-the-money.

EXAMPLE

Which TWO of the following options are in-the-money if ABC is trading at 62 and DEF is trading at 44?

   I. An ABC Oct 60 call option

   II. An ABC Oct 70 call option

   III. A DEF May 40 put option

   IV. A DEF May 50 put option

   (A) I and III

   (B) I and IV

   (C) II and III

   (D) II and IV

The correct answer is Choice (B). Start with the strike (exercise) prices. You're *calling up* or *putting down* from the strike prices, not from the market prices. Because call options go in-the-money when the market price is above the strike price, Statement I is the only one that works for ABC.

An ABC 60 call option would be in-the-money when the price of ABC is above 60. ABC is currently trading at 62, so that 60 call option is in-the-money. For the ABC 70 call option to be in-the-money, ABC would have to be trading higher than 70. Next, use *put down* for the DEF put options, because put options go in-the-money when the price of the stock goes below the strike price. Therefore, Statement IV makes sense because DEF is trading at 44, and that's below the DEF 50 put strike price but not the 40 put strike price.

REMEMBER

When people purchase an option, it is said that they are *long* the option. An investor who is long an option is paid the premium for the option so he needs the option to go in-the-money (the price of the underlying security to go in the correct direction) enough for him to not only recoup his premium but also make a few bucks.

When someone is *short* an option, it means that he sold the option. This person is on the opposite side of the transaction than the person who is long the option. In this case, the seller received a premium for selling the option. So, someone who is short an option is doing so for income and is hoping that the option expires out-of-the-money so that he gets to keep the premium.

Paying the premium: The cost of an option

The *premium* of an option is the amount that the purchaser pays for the option. The premium may increase or decrease depending on whether an option goes in- or out-of-the-money, gets closer to expiration, and so on. The premium is made up of many different factors, including

>> Whether the option is in-the-money (see the preceding section)

>> The amount of time the investor has to use the option

>> The volatility of the underlying security

>> Investor sentiment (for example, whether buying calls on ABC stock is the cool thing to do right now)

One of the simple options math questions you may run across on the SIE exam requires you to figure out the time value of an option premium. *Time value* has to do with how long you have until an option expires. There's no set standard for time value, such as every month until an option expires costs buyers an extra $100. However, you can assume that if two options have everything in common except for the expiration month, the one with the longer expiration will have a higher premium. Hopefully, the following equation can help keep you from getting a "pit" in your stomach:

$$P = I + T$$

In this formula, P is the premium or cost of the option, I is the intrinsic value of the option (the amount the option is in-the-money), and T is the time value of the option.

For example, here's how you find the time value for a BIF Oct 50 call option if the premium is 6 and BIF is trading at 52: Call options (the right to buy) go in-the-money when the price of the stock goes above the strike price (*call up* — see the preceding section). Because BIF is trading at 52 and the option is a 50 call option, it's two points in-the-money; therefore, the intrinsic value is two. Because the premium is six and the intrinsic value is two, the premium must include four as a time value:

$$P = I + T$$

$$6 = 2 + T$$

$$T = 4$$

The following question tests your knowledge of using the formula $P = I + T$.

Use the following chart to answer the next question.

Stock	Strike Price	Calls		Puts	
		July	Oct	July	Oct
LMN					
40.50	30	13	14.5	0.25	0.50
40.50	40	2.5	4.5	1.5	2.75
40.50	50	0.25	0.75	10.5	12

What is the time value of an LMN Oct 30 call?

(A) 2.5

(B) 4

(C) 6.25

(D) 9.5

The answer you're looking for is Choice (B). I threw you a curveball by giving you a chart similar to what you may see on the SIE exam. I hope you're able to find the premium that you need to answer the question. Most of the exhibits you get on the SIE are simple, and solving the problem is just a matter of locating the information you need.

Using the chart, the first column shows the price of the stock trading in the market, the second column shows the strike prices for the options, and the rest of the chart shows the premiums for the calls and puts and the expiration months. Scan the chart under the October calls, which is in the fourth column; then look for the 30 strike price, which is in the first row of data. The column and row intersect at a premium of 14.5.

Now you need to find the intrinsic value (how much the option is in-the-money). Remember that call options go in-the-money when the price of the stock is above the strike price (call up). This is a 30 call option and the price of the stock is 40.50, which is 10.5 above the strike price. Plug in the numbers, and you find that the premium includes a time value of 4:

P (premium) = I (intrinsic value) + T (time value)

$14.5 = 10.5 + T$

$T = 4$

Incorporating Standard Option Math

I'm here to make your life easier. Prep courses use several different types of charts and formulas to figure out things such as gains or losses, break-even points, maximum gain or loss, and so on. I believe that the easiest way is to use the options chart that follows. It's a simple *Money Out, Money In* chart you can use to plug in numbers. What's great about this chart is that you don't even necessarily have to understand what the heck is going on to determine the answers to most options questions. As this chapter progresses, I show you how incredibly useful the options chart can be.

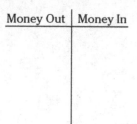

Money Out	Money In

If it looks basic, it is — and that's the idea. Any time an investor spends money, you place that value in the Money Out side of the options chart, and any time an investor receives money, you place the number in the Money In side of the chart.

Calls same: Buying or selling call options

The most basic options calculations involve buying or selling call or put options. Although using the options chart may not be totally necessary for the more basic calculations (such as the one that follows in the next section), working with the chart now can help you get used to the tool so you'll be ready when the SIE exam tests your sanity with more-complex calculations.

As you work with options charts, you may notice a pattern when determining maximum losses and gains. Table 11-1 gives you a quick reference concerning the maximum gain or maximum loss an investor faces when buying or selling call options. Notice that the buyer's loss is equal to the seller's gain (and vice versa).

TABLE 11-1 **Maximum Gains and Losses for Call Options**

Buying or Selling	Maximum Loss	Maximum Gain
Buying a call	Premium	Unlimited
Selling a call	Unlimited	Premium

TIP

The key phrase to remember when working with call options is *calls same*, which means that the premium and the strike price go on the same side of the options chart.

Buying call options

The following steps show you how to calculate the maximum loss and gain for holders of call options (which give the holder the right to buy). I also show you how to find the break-even point. Here's the order ticket for the example calculations:

Buy 1 XYZ Oct 40 call at 5

1. Find the maximum loss.

The holder of an option doesn't have to exercise it, so the most she can lose is the premium. The premium is five, so this investor purchased the option for $500 (5 × 100 shares per option); therefore, you enter that value in the Money Out side of the options chart (think "money out of the investor's pocket"). According to the chart, the maximum loss (the most this investor can lose) is $500.

Money Out	Money In
$500	

2. Determine the maximum gain.

To calculate the maximum gain, you have to exercise the option at the strike price. The strike price is 40, so you enter $4,000 (40 strike price × 100 shares per option) under its premium (which you added to the chart when calculating maximum loss); exercising the call means buying the stock, so that's Money Out. When exercising call options, always put the multiplied strike price under its premium. (Remember *calls same*: The premium and the strike price go on the same side of the options chart.)

Money Out	Money In
$500	
$4,000	

Because you've already determined the maximum loss, look at the Money In portion of the options chart. The Money In is empty, so the maximum gain (the most money the investor can make) is unlimited.

When you see a question about the break-even point, the SIE examiners are asking, "At what point does this investor not have a gain or loss?" The simplest way to figure out this point for a call option is to use *call up* (remember that call options go in-the-money when the price of the stock goes above the strike price — see the section "Getting your money back: Options in-, at-, or out-of-the-money"). When using *call up*, you add the strike price to the premium:

$$\text{strike price} + \text{premium} = 40 + 5 = 45$$

For this investor, the break-even point is 45. This number makes sense because the investor paid $5 for the option, so the option has to go $5 in-the-money for the investor to recoup the amount she paid. *Note:* The break-even point is always the same for the buyer and the seller.

Selling call options

Here, I show you how to find the maximum gain and loss, as well as the break-even point, for sellers of call options. Here's the order ticket for the example calculations:

Sell 1 ZYX Oct 60 call at 2

1. Determine the maximum gain.

The seller makes money only if the holder fails to exercise the option or exercises it when the option is in-the-money by less than the premium received. This investor sold the option for $200 (2 × 100 shares per option); therefore, you enter that amount in the Money In side of the options chart. According to the chart, the maximum gain (the most that this investor can make) is the $200 premium received. **Note:** The exercised strike price of $6,000 ($60 \times 100$ shares) doesn't come into play when determining the maximum gain in this example because the holder of the option would exercise the option only if it were in-the-money.

Money Out	Money In
	$200

2. **Find the maximum loss.**

To calculate the maximum loss, you need to exercise the option at the strike price. The strike price is 60, so you enter $6,000 (60 strike price $\times$ 100 shares per option) under its premium. The $6,000 goes in the Money In side of the options chart because this investor had to sell the stock to the holder at the strike price (60×100 shares). When exercising call options, always enter the multiplied strike price under its premium. (Remember *calls same:* The premium and the strike price go on the same side of the options chart.)

Money Out	Money In
	$200
	$6,000

You've already determined the maximum gain; now look at the Money Out portion of the options chart. The Money Out is empty, so the maximum loss (the most money the investor can lose) is unlimited.

When you see a question about the break-even point, the examiners are asking you, "At what point does this investor not have a gain or loss?" The simplest way to figure this out for a call option is to use *call up*. When using *call up,* you add the strike price to the premium:

$$\text{strike price} + \text{premium} = 60 + 2 = 62$$

For this investor, the break-even point is 62. This makes sense because the investor received $2 for the option, so the option has to go $2 in-the-money for this investor to lose the amount that she received for selling the option. Call options go in-the-money when the price of the stock goes above the strike price.

Puts switch: Buying or selling put options

Fortunately, when you're calculating the buying or selling of put options (which give the holder the right to sell), you use the options chart in the same way but with a slight change (see the preceding section for info on call options). Instead of using *calls same* as you do with call options, you use *puts switch* — in other words, you place the premium and the strike price on opposite sides of the options chart.

Table 11-2 serves as a quick reference regarding the maximum gain or maximum loss an investor faces when buying or selling put options.

TABLE 11-2   Maximum Gains and Losses for Put Options

Buying or Selling	Maximum Loss	Maximum Gain
Buying a put	Premium	(strike – premium) × 100 shares
Selling a put	(strike – premium) × 100 shares	Premium

Buying put options

This section explains how to find the maximum loss, maximum gain, and the break-even point for buyers (holders) of put options. Here's the ticket order for the calculations:

Buy 1 TUV Oct 55 put at 6

1. Find the maximum loss.

Exercising an option is, well, optional for the holder, so buyers of put options can't lose more than the premium. Because this investor purchased the option for $600 (6 × 100 shares per option), you enter that value in the Money Out side of the options chart. The maximum loss (the most that this investor can lose) is the $600 premium paid.

Money Out	Money In
$600	

2. Determine the maximum gain.

To find the maximum gain, you have to exercise the option at the strike price. The strike price is 55, so you enter $5,500 (55 strike price × 100 shares per option) on the opposite side of the options chart. (Remember *puts switch:* The premium and the strike price go on opposite sides of the options chart.) Exercising the option means selling the underlying stock, so that $5,500 is Money In.

Money Out	Money In
$600	$5,500

You've already determined the maximum loss; now look at the Money In portion of the options chart. Because you find $4,900 more Money In than Money Out ($5,500 – $600), the maximum gain is $4,900.

The break-even point is the security price where the investor doesn't have a gain or loss. The simplest way to figure this point out for a put option is to use *put down* (put options go in-the-money when the price of the stock goes below the strike price). When using *put down*, you subtract the premium from the strike price:

strike price − premium = 55 − 6 = 49

For this investor, the break-even point is 49. The investor paid $6 for the option, so the option has to go $6 in-the-money in order for this investor to recoup the amount that she paid. As with call options, the break-even point is always the same for the buyer and the seller.

Selling put options

The following steps show you how to calculate the maximum gain and loss for the seller of a put option. I also demonstrate calculations for the break-even point. Here's the ticket order for the example:

Sell 1 TUV Sep 30 put at 8

1. Determine the maximum gain.

The seller makes money only if the holder of the option fails to exercise it. This investor sold the option for $800 (8 × 100 shares per option); you put that number in the Money In side of the options chart. The maximum gain (the most this investor can make) is $800.

Money Out	Money In
	$800

2. Find the maximum loss.

To calculate the maximum loss, you have to exercise the option at the strike price. The strike price is 30, so you place $3,000 (30 strike price × 100 shares per option) on the opposite side of the options chart. (Remember *puts switch:* The premium and strike price go on opposite sides of the options chart.)

Money Out	Money In
$3,000	$800

You've already determined the maximum gain; now look at the Money Out portion of the options chart and compare it to the Money In. The maximum potential loss for this investor is the $2,200 difference between the Money Out and the Money In.

You calculate the break-even point for buying or selling puts the same way: You use *put down* (the strike price minus the premium) to figure out the break-even point:

$$\text{strike price} - \text{premium} = 30 - 8 = 22$$

For this investor, the break-even point is 22. Because this investor received $8 for the option, the option has to go $8 in-the-money for this investor to lose the amount she received for selling the option. Put options go in-the-money when the price of the stock goes below the strike price (put down).

Trading options: Opening and closing transactions

Although some investors hold onto their options long enough to actually exercise them, a lot of investors trade options the way that they trade other investments. On the SIE exam, not only do you need to know the difference between opening and closing transactions, but you also have to be able to calculate the profit or loss for an investor trading options. This process is actually pretty easy when you break it down.

Putting things back where you found them: Doing opposite transactions

When distinguishing between opening and closing transactions, your key is to know whether this transaction is the first time or the second time the investor is buying or selling an option: The first time is an *opening*, and the second time is a *closing*.

Here are your opening transactions:

>> **Opening purchase:** An opening purchase occurs when an investor first buys a call or a put.

>> **Opening sale:** An opening sale is when an investor first sells a call or a put.

If an investor already has an option position, the investor has to close that position by doing the opposite — through a closing transaction. If the investor originally purchased the option, she has to sell to close it. By contrast, if she originally sold the option, she has to purchase to close. Here are the two types of closing transactions:

>> **Closing purchase:** A closing purchase occurs when an investor buys herself out of a previous option position that she sold. For example, if an investor sold an XYZ Oct 40 call (opening sale), she would have to buy an XYZ Oct 40 call to close out the position. The second transaction is a closing purchase.

>> **Closing sale:** A closing sale occurs when an investor sells herself out of a previous option position that she purchased. For example, if an investor bought an ABC Sep 60 put (opening purchase), she would have to sell an ABC Sep 60 put to close out the position. The second transaction is a closing sale.

REMEMBER

When determining opening or closing transactions, whether the transactions are both calls or both puts doesn't matter.

The following question tests your knowledge of opening and closing transactions.

EXAMPLE

Mr. Dimpledell previously bought 1 XYZ Oct 65 call at 8 when the market price of XYZ was 64. XYZ is currently trading at 69, and Mr. Dimpledell decides that now would be a good time to sell the option that he previously purchased. The second option order ticket would be marked

(A) opening sale

(B) opening purchase

(C) closing sale

(D) closing purchase

The right answer is Choice (C). This is the second time that Mr. Dimpledell does something with the option that he owns; therefore, the move has to be a closing transaction, and you can immediately eliminate Choices (A) and (B). Mr. Dimpledell has to sell himself out of the position because he owns the option. The second order ticket would have to be marked *closing sale*.

Tricks of the options trade: Calculating gains and losses

In addition to knowing how to mark the order ticket, you have to be able to figure out an investor's gain or loss when trading options. This task isn't difficult after you master the options chart. The key thing to remember is that when an investor closes, she does the opposite of what she did before.

The following question tests your mastery of options trades.

EXAMPLE

Mrs. Cleveland purchased 100 shares of DPY stock at $50 per share. Two weeks later, Mrs. Cleveland sold 1 DPY Oct 55 call at 6. Mrs. Cleveland held that position for three months before selling the DPY stock at $52 per share and closing the DPY Oct 55 call at 4. What is Mrs. Cleveland's gain or loss on the transactions?

(A) $400 gain

(B) $400 loss

(C) $600 gain

(D) no gain or loss

The correct answer is Choice (A). This question introduces stock trades as well as options transactions, but that's no problem. The options chart works for questions involving actual stocks and options or just options.

When you approach the transactions one at a time, the problem-solving process is actually pretty straightforward. Mrs. Cleveland purchased 100 shares of DPY stock at $50 per share for a total of $5,000; therefore, you enter $5,000 in the Money Out side of the options chart. Next, she sold the DPY 55 call for a premium of 6, so you need to enter $600 (6 × 100 shares per option) on the Money In side of the chart because she received money for selling that option.

Three months later, Mrs. Cleveland sold the stock for $5,200 ($52 per share × 100 shares) and received money for selling the stock. Place the $5,200 in the Money In side of the options chart. When closing the option, the customer has to do the opposite of what she did before. Originally, Mrs. Cleveland sold the option, so to close, she has to buy the option (make a closing purchase). She purchased the option for $400 (4 × 100 shares per option), so enter $400 in the Money Out side of the options chart. All that's left for you to do is total up the two sides. Mrs. Cleveland has $5,800 in and $5,400 out for a gain of $400.

Money Out	Money In
$5,000	$600
$400	$5,200
$5,400	$5,800

Gaining Additional Option Info

To help you get a deeper understanding of options, you need to know a few additional things that you will most certainly see on the real-deal SIE exam. Some of these items include who issues the options, what an ROP is, what a risk disclosure document is, and so on.

Clearing through the OCC

The Options Clearing Corporation (OCC) is the issuer and guarantor of all listed options. The OCC decides which options will trade and their strike prices. In addition, when an investor decides to exercise her option, it's the OCC that randomly decides which firm on the other end will be responsible for fulfilling the terms of the option.

REMEMBER

The OCC does not determine the premium for options; the premium is determined by investors based on supply and demand, the options intrinsic value (how much it's in the money — or away from the money), and the amount of time until the option expires.

That's ODD: Options risk disclosure document

Because options have a risk that is greater than almost any other investment, all investors must receive an options risk disclosure document (ODD) prior to their first options transaction. This ODD explains to investors the risk involved in investing in options, such as the chance of losing all money invested or, if selling call options, facing an unlimited maximum loss potential.

Getting the go-ahead: Registered options principal

Because of the extra risk of investing in options, all new accounts and option order tickets must be approved and signed by a registered options principal (ROP), which is a manager with a Series 4 license. The registered options principal determines the amount of risk that each investor can take. Certainly, sophisticated investors with a lot of money are able to handle more risk than new option investors with a limited supply of funds.

Options account agreement

Within 15 days after approval of the account by an ROP, the customer must sign and return an options account agreement (OAA). Basically, the OAA just states that the customer has read the ODD, understands the risk associated with trading options, and will abide by the rules and regulations regarding options trading. Should anything change (such as the customers, investment objectives, financial situation, and so on), the customer agrees to notify the firm. In the event that the OAA is not received within 15 days after approval of the account, the customer cannot open any new options positions.

Order ticket

You can find out more about what is required on an order ticket in Chapter 16. However, a few things are required on an order ticket that are unique to options. Besides the option that is being bought or sold, you have to write down whether the customer is establishing a long position (if he's buying) or a short position (if he's selling). In addition, for option sellers, you need to put down whether the seller is covered or uncovered (naked). The seller of a call option is considered covered if he owns the underlying security or owns an option on the same security with the same or longer expiration that will be in-the-money first. And, of course an uncovered (naked) position is when the seller owns neither the underlying stock nor an option on the same security that will be in-the-money first with an equal or longer expiration date.

Last trade, last exercise, and expiration of an option

Unlike stock certificates, options do expire after a certain period of time. In addition, investors are limited as to when they can trade and exercise an option. Here's the timeline to keep in mind:

» **Last trade:** The last time an investor can trade an option is 4:00 p.m. EST on the business day of expiration.

» **Last exercise:** The last time an investor can exercise an option is 5:30 p.m. EST on the business day of expiration. If an option is in-the-money by at least 1 point at expiration, it will be automatically exercised. A vast majority of options can be exercised any time up till expiration — this is known as *American style*. However there are also *European-style* options that can only be exercised on the expiration date. European-style options include capped index options and some foreign currency options.

» **Option expiration:** Options expire at 11:59 p.m. EST on the third Friday of the expiration month.

Exercise and assignment

When taking the SIE exam, you will be expected to have a basic understanding of how options are exercised and assigned. Options are cleared through the OCC. Here's how an option is *exercised:*

When a client wants to exercise an option she owns, she contacts her broker-dealer. The broker-dealer contacts the OCC. The trade settles in two business days after the OCC is notified because when the investor is exercising an option, she is actually trading stock (the right to buy or sell stock). Stock trades settle in two business days, so exercises of options settle in two business days (trades of options settle in one business day).

The steps involved look like this:

1. Client #1 tells her broker-dealer (Broker A) to exercise the option.

2. Broker A notifies the Options Clearing Corporation.

3. The Options Clearing Corporation chooses the contra broker (the broker-dealer on the other side of the transaction — Broker B) randomly.

4. Broker B assigns (chooses the client — Client #2) either randomly, first-in-first-out (FIFO), orby any other method which is fair and reasonable. However, Broker B cannot choose the assignment based on size (the one with the most options, the one with the least options, and so on).

5. Client #2 sends the proceeds (stock or cash) to Broker B.

6. Broker B sends the proceeds directly to Broker A (the OCC doesn't handle stock or cash).

So, if you were to look at a flow chart, it would look something like this:

Flow Chart

Client #1 ⟷ Broker A
(owns the option)

OCC

Client #2 ⟷ Broker B
(seller of the option)

TIP

Although most exercises of options are settled by the delivery of the underlying security, there are some that are settled by the delivery of *cash*. Specifically, *index* (options on an index of securities) and *foreign currency options* are always settled in cash. This just makes sense because investors can't be expected to deliver an entire index for index options nor be expected to deliver the underlying foreign currency for foreign currency options.

Additional definitions

For some reason, the SIE exam writers decided you need to know some additional option-specific definitions. I cover several of them earlier in this chapter, but there are several more that you need to be aware of. I will try to make this as painless as possible.

>> **Aggregate exercise price:** The exercise (strike) price of an option multiplied by the number of units (usually shares) of the underlying security covered by the option contract (usually 100 shares).

>> **Class of options:** All option contracts of the same type (puts or calls) covering the same underlying security or index.

>> **Clearing member:** A FINRA member that has been admitted to membership in the OCC (Options Clearing Corporation).

>> **Closing sale transaction:** An option transaction in which the seller wants to reduce or eliminate a long position. So, for argument's sake, say an investor is long (owns) 1 ABC Oct 40 call. To close that position, the investor would short (write or sell) the 1 ABC Oct 40 call.

>> **Conventional index option:** An option that overlies a basket (nine or more equity securities) or index of securities providing that no one security comprises more than 30 percent of the basket or index.

>> **Conventional option:** (A) Any option contract not issued or subject to issuance by the OCC, or (B) an OCC-cleared OTC option.

>> **Delta neutral:** An equity options position that has been fully hedged. For example, owning 100 shares of ABC stock and owning an at-the-money put on ABC stock. Basically, offsetting long and short positions.

>> **Net delta:** The number of shares that must be maintained (either long or short) to offset the risk the investor is facing having an equity option position.

- **>> Opening writing (opening sale) transaction:** The initial sale of an option in which the seller receives the premium paid.

- **>> Outstanding:** An option contract that has been neither closed (closing sale) nor exercised, and has not reached the expiration date.

- **>> Series of options:** All option contracts that are of the same class, same expiration date, and same exercise price, and cover the same number of units of the underlying security or index.

- **>> Type of option:** Either a call or a put.

Some additional option rules

Yes, I know . . . even more? Don't blame me; I didn't design the test. Anyway, as with the preceding section, I think a quick perusal of the following items will give you enough of a general understanding of some of the additional rules that you should be able to pick them out of any multiple-choice questions posed on the exam.

- **>> Position limits:** A number placed on the amount of option contracts that a person can hold or write on the same side of the market (bullish or bearish) on the same security. This will be covered more in depth if you are taking the Series 7.

- **>> Exercise limits:** A number placed on the amount of option contracts that a person can exercise on the same side of the market (bullish or bearish) within five consecutive business days. This will be covered in more detail if you are taking the Series 7 exam.

- **>> Limit on uncovered short positions:** FINRA may decide to limit the amount of uncovered short positions on option contracts of a given class if deemed necessary for the protection of investors.

- **>> Restrictions on option transactions and exercises:** As with the limit on uncovered short positions, FINRA may also place restrictions on option transactions or the exercise of option contracts in one or more series of options of any class when deemed necessary to help maintain a fair and orderly market.

- **>> Open order on the "ex-date" (ex-dividend date):** Since the underlying stock price will be lowered due to a dividend, the OCC will adjust option contracts accordingly unless otherwise instructed by the customer.

- **>> Confirmations:** Members are responsible for providing a written confirmation of each option transaction for each customer's account. The confirmation must include the type of option (call or put); the underlying security or index; the expiration month; the exercise (strike) price; the number of option contracts; the premium, trade, and settlement dates; whether it was a purchase or sale (long or short); opening or closing transaction; whether it was done on a principal or agency basis; the amount of commission; and so on. There's more on confirmations in Chapter 16 — yippee!

- **>> Statements of account (account statements):** All clients must receive account statements at least monthly if there has been any trading in the account for the previous month and at least quarterly (once every three months) when there has been no trading in the previous month. The account statements must show the security and money positions, entries, interest charges, and any other charges assessed against the account. Account statements are covered in more detail in Chapter 16.

- **Opening of accounts:** In order to open an options account for a client, the client must receive an ODD, and you must exercise due diligence by getting the customer's investment objectives, employment status, estimated annual income, estimated net worth, estimated liquid net worth, marital status, number of dependents, age, investment experience and knowledge, and so on. In addition, the account and all transactions must be approved by a registered options principal (ROP), branch office manager, or limited principal-general securities sales supervisor. All options accounts must be approved or disapproved within ten business days. Please note that all option accounts may not be approved for all transactions — depending on the client, he may be approved for buying covered writing, uncovered writing, spreading, discretionary transactions, and so on.

- **Options account agreement (OAA):** Within 15 days after approval of the account, a member must obtain from the customer a written account agreement, which states that the customer understands that he is aware of and agrees to be bound by FINRA rules regarding option trading.

- **Uncovered short option contracts:** Since uncovered short option contracts are the riskiest of all option contracts, member firms must create standard rules for evaluating the suitability of customers who plan on writing uncovered options.

- **Maintenance of records:** Each member must keep a current log, index, or other file for options-related complaints. Each complaint should be easily identified and easy to retrieve if necessary. Each complaint file (hopefully there aren't many) must contain the identification of the complaint, the date the complaint was received, the name of the registered rep handling the account, a description of the complaint, any action taken (if any), and so on.

- **Discretionary account:** As with any discretionary account in which the client gives you the right to trade his account without pre-approval, it must be approved by a principal (manager). Options discretionary accounts must be approved in writing by a registered options principal (ROP) or limited principal-general securities sales supervisor, and written approval must be received from the client. In addition, discretionary accounts must be reviewed frequently by an ROP.

- **Suitability:** You may not recommend any option transaction(s) to a customer unless you believe that the transaction is suitable for the customer. Remember that you should already know the customer's investment objectives, financial information, and so on. In other words, you should not be recommending a risky option transaction for someone you deem incapable of handling the risk.

- **Supervision of accounts:** Members conducting an options business must have a written supervisory system in place to adequately address the public customer's option business. In addition, each branch office must have either a registered options principal or a limited principal-general securities sales supervisor in order to conduct options business.

4

Playing Nicely: Serving Your Customers and Following the Rules

Chapter **12**

Serving Your Customers: Customer Accounts

I f you're going to have a successful business, you have to be able to open accounts. Beyond "smiling and dialing," you need to know what to do once you hook your first big one. Next, you need to get the account form filled out. The account form and conversations with your customers and potential customers help you make appropriate recommendations. Hopefully, the securities you recommend will do well, and your customer will rent a van with a huge speaker on top so he can drive through town telling everyone how great you are.

In this chapter, I cover topics related to opening accounts. First, I help you understand the information required on a new account form. Then I go over investment objectives, I cover margin accounts, and finally, I discuss when you can call potential customers. I also include a couple of questions to give you an idea of potential questions you may see on the exam.

Following Protocol When Opening Accounts

The SIE examiners seem to be focusing more and more on the handling of customer accounts. You need to know what to do to open accounts, how to take customer orders, the rules for sending out confirmations, and so on.

Filing the facts on the new account form

When you're opening any new account for a customer, the new account form needs some basic information. Broker-dealers may, in accordance with the Patriot Act (covered later in this chapter), require a customer to provide proof of identification. Getting this information is your responsibility (or the responsibility of the broker-dealer). Here's a list of the items that need to be on the new account form:

>> The name(s) and address(es) of the individual(s) who'll have access to the account

>> The customer's date of birth (the customer must be of legal age to open an account)

>> Contact number(s)

>> Marital status and number of dependents (if any)

>> Whether the person opening the account or any immediate family member is employed or associated with the securities industry, and if so, how

>> The type of account the customer is opening (cash, margin, retirement, day trading, prime brokerage, DVP/RVP, advisory or fee-based, discretionary, options, and so on)

>> The customer's Social Security number (if the customer is an individual) or tax ID number (if the customer is a business)

>> The customer's occupation, employer, address of employer, and type of business (certain limitations are placed on customers who work for banks, broker-dealers, insurance companies, SROs, and so on)

>> Domestic or foreign residency and/or citizenship (including ID info per the customer's driver's license, passport, state ID, government ID, and so on)

>> Bank references and the customer's net worth, liquid net worth, tax rate, and annual income

>> Whether the customer is an insider of a company

>> Investment objectives and risk tolerance

>> Financial investment experience

>> The signatures of the registered representative and a principal

REMEMBER

You need this information to open an account. If anything changes (for example, a customer's address), the account records need to be updated. Additionally, only individuals who are legally competent may open accounts. You also have to pay close attention to the investor's age and/or mental or physical ability. FINRA has additional rules specifically put in place for older people and/or those with some sort of disability; these rules, regarding "financial exploitation of specified adults" are covered in Chapter 16.

TIP

When you're filling out a new account form, you can determine whether your client is accredited (see Chapter 14 for more on the topic of accredited investors).

EXAMPLE

The following question tests your ability to answer a question about opening a new account.

Which of the following people must sign a new account form?

   I. The customer

  II. The customer's spouse

 III. The registered representative

 IV. A principal

(A) I and II only

(B) III and IV only

(C) I and IV only

(D) I, III, and IV only

The correct answer is Choice (B). When you're opening a new account for a customer, the new account form requires only your signature and a principal's (manager's) signature. Make sure you don't assume extenuating circumstances. You need the customer's signature on a new account form only if the customer is opening a margin account. Additionally, you need the spouse's signature only if you're opening a joint account. Because the question doesn't say that the account is a margin or joint account, you can't assume that it is.

REMEMBER

You should be able to gather the information you need for making recommendations based on the customer's account form and your conversations with the person. It is your duty to know your customer (also conveniently called the "Know Your Customer Rule") in order to make recommendations that are suitable and effectively handle the account. Your recommendations should be fair and reasonable based on the customer's profile and within the customer's financial ability. Basically, don't recommend buying $100,000 of a penny stock to a customer who's risk averse and has limited funds. Some of the things you should know to accurately make recommendations are

>> The customer's age

>> Other investments he has

>> His financial situation and needs (for example, is he buying a house soon or sending a kid to college?)

>> His tax rate (investors with a high tax rate are more suitable for municipal bonds)

>> His investment objectives, such as retirement funding, generating current income, preservation of capital, capital growth, total return (growth and income), tax-advantaged investments, liquidity, speculation, trading profits, long-term versus short-term risk, and so on

>> His investment experience (how much do you need to explain to him?)

>> His time horizon (expected time to reach a financial goal, if any)

>> His risk tolerance (should you recommend speculative securities or only safer ones?)

>> His liquidity needs (should you only recommend securities that he can get in and out of easily?)

Word on the street: Numbered accounts

A *street name* or *numbered account* is an account registered in the name of the broker-dealer with an ID number. Street name accounts give the investor a certain degree of privacy and help facilitate the trading of securities (because the brokerage firm, not the customer, signs the certificates). You need to know a few rules about street name accounts for the SIE:

>> You need a written statement from the customer attesting to the ownership of the account.

>> With the exception of margin accounts, a street name account may be changed by the customer into a regular account at any time.

>> All margin accounts must be in street name.

The Patriot Act

The Patriot Act was enacted in 2001 to help identify and catch terrorists. As part of the Patriot Act, broker-dealers are required to

>> Keep records of the information used to identify the customer (via customer identification programs, or CIPs). The CIP is a program used by financial institutions to verify the identity of customers who want to conduct financial transactions.

>> Verify that a customer doesn't appear on any list of known terrorists or terrorist organizations. (The U.S. Treasury keeps this list.)

Selecting the appropriate type of account

Investors can open many different types of accounts through a broker-dealer. Besides knowing a customer's investment profile, you need a basic understanding of the types of accounts for the SIE exam. Fortunately, most of them are pretty straightforward.

Single and joint accounts

Some investors prefer to share; others like to go it alone. Whatever their preference, adults can open up accounts that fit their needs:

>> **Single (individual) accounts:** Naturally, this account is in the name of one person. The key thing for you to remember is that individuals may not open accounts in other people's names without written permission (power of attorney).

>> **Joint accounts:** This account is in the name of more than one person. All individuals named on the account have equal trading authority for the account. For SIE exam purposes, you need to be familiar with two types of joint accounts:

  • **Joint tenants with rights of survivorship (JTWROS):** With this type of joint account, when a joint tenant named on the account dies, his portion of the account passes on to the surviving joint tenant. These accounts are usually set up almost exclusively for husbands and wives. In states where *community property laws* exist (currently Arizona, California, Idaho, Louisiana, Nevada, New Mexico, Texas, Washington, and Wisconsin), investments acquired during the marriage are automatically presumed to be jointly owned by the husband and wife.

  • **Joint with tenants in common (JTIC):** With this type of account, when one tenant of the account dies, his portion of the account becomes part of his estate. JTICs are usually set up for individuals who aren't related.

The following question tests your knowledge of account types.

EXAMPLE

All the following people may open a joint account EXCEPT

(A) Two friends

(B) A husband and wife

(C) A parent and minor son

(D) Three strangers

The right choice here is (C). A joint account is an account in the name of more than one adult. Choices (A), (B), and (D) are all possible for joint accounts; however, an account opened for a minor must be a custodial account, which I discuss in the next section.

Trust accounts

Trust accounts are managed by one party for the benefit of another party. A specific type of trust account that you're most likely to see on the SIE exam is a custodial account. A *custodial account* is set up for a child who's too young to have his own account. A custodian (adult) makes the investment decisions for the account. Any adult can open a custodial account for a minor, so the people named on the account don't have to be related.

REMEMBER

Custodial accounts are trust accounts and may be referred to on the SIE exam as UGMA or UTMA accounts because they fall under the Uniform Gifts to Minors Act or Uniform Transfer to Minors Act. A *UTMA account* is an extension of the UGMA account that allows gifts in addition to cash and securities to be transferred to the minor. The additional gifts allowed are art, real estate, patents, and royalties.

Additionally, because the minor is too young to make investment decisions for himself, some rules are specific to custodian accounts:

>> There can only be one custodian and one minor per account.

>> The minor is responsible for the taxes (the minor's Social Security number is registered for the account).

>> The account is registered in the name of the custodian for the benefit of the minor (the custodian is responsible for endorsing all certificates).

>> The account can't be held in street name (in the name of the broker-dealer with an ID number — see the earlier section "Word on the street: Numbered accounts").

>> Securities can't be traded on margin or sold short.

>> Anyone may give a gift of cash or securities to the minor. The gift is irrevocable (can't be refused by the custodian).

>> If an account receives rights, the custodian can't let the rights expire. (See Chapter 6 for info on rights.) Because rights have value, a custodian can exercise or sell the rights.

REMEMBER

Custodial accounts are for minors, so as soon as a minor reaches the age of majority, which is determined by the minor's state of residence, the custodial account is terminated and the account is transferred to a single account in the name of the (former) minor.

Discretionary accounts

Decision making can be stressful, and some investors don't want to deal with it. With a *discretionary account*, an investor can give you (the registered rep) the right to make trading decisions for the account. All discretionary accounts need a *written power of attorney* signed by the investor, which gives trading authorization to the registered rep.

REMEMBER

If a customer places an order but doesn't specify the security, the number of shares or units, and/or whether the customer wants to buy or sell, you need a written power of attorney. If you don't have a written power of attorney, you can't do anything but decide when to place the order (timing). For example, suppose one of your customers calls you and says that he wants to sell 100 shares of ABC common stock and you believe you can get a better price later in the day. The customer can give you verbal permission to place the order at your discretion. This type of order is called a *market not held order* and is usually good only for the rest of the day.

Here are some specific rules for discretionary orders that you're likely to see on the SIE exam:

>> Each discretionary order must be marked as *discretionary* on the order ticket.

>> As with other orders, principals must sign each order ticket.

>> A principal needs to review discretionary accounts regularly to make sure reps don't trade excessively to generate commissions, which is called *churning*.

REMEMBER

A *fiduciary* is anyone who can legally make decisions for another investor. Examples of fiduciaries are custodians (UGMA accounts), a registered rep having power of attorney, an executor of an estate, a trustee, and so on. Fiduciaries are subject to the *Prudent Man* or *Prudent Investor Rule,* which means that they must invest the fund's money in securities designated by their state's *legal list.* If their state does not have a legal list, fiduciaries should invest in securities that only a prudent person who's seeking reasonable income and preservation of capital would invest in.

Corporate accounts

Only incorporated businesses can open corporate accounts. If you're opening a corporate account, you need to obtain the tax ID number of the corporation, which is similar to an individual's Social Security number. Additionally, you need to obtain a copy of the *corporate resolution,* which lets you know whom you should be taking trading instructions from (so you don't get a call like, "Hi, I'm Joe Blow, the janitor for XYZ Corporation, and I'd like to purchase 1,000 shares of ABC for our company").

If a corporation wants to open a margin account (accounts where it's borrowing some money from the broker-dealer to purchase securities — see "Cash or margin?" later in the chapter), you also need a copy of the corporate charter (bylaws). The corporate charter has to allow the corporation to purchase securities on margin.

Unincorporated associations

An unincorporated association is sometimes called a voluntary organization. An unincorporated association is a group of two or more individuals who form an organization for a specific purpose (in this case, investing). If an unincorporated association has too many characteristics of a corporation, such as having a board of directors, limited liability, and so on, it may be treated and taxed at a higher rate, as if it were a corporation.

Institutional accounts

Accounts set by institutions such as banks, mutual funds, insurance companies, pension funds, hedge funds, and investment advisors are considered institutional accounts. Their role is to act as specialized investors on behalf of others.

Partnership accounts

Two or more individual owners of a business that's not set up as a corporation may set up a partnership account. All partnerships must complete a partnership agreement, which the broker-dealer has to keep on file. The *partnership agreement,* like a corporate resolution, states who has trading authorization for the account so you know whom you're supposed to be taking orders from.

REMEMBER

Accounts can be opened for many reasons other than to just buy and sell stocks. They may be opened to trade options, which is covered in Chapter 11. They may be opened to provide a family member with a means to pay for his or her education, which is covered in Chapter 8. Or, maybe they're set up to provide income for retirement, which is covered in Chapter 15. In addition, if you're registered as an investment adviser, you may be setting up a fee-based account rather than one in which you make a commission on trades (see the following section). No matter which type of account you open, portfolio diversification is key.

Investment advisers

If you're working for a broker-dealer as an agent, you'll receive commission when one of your clients makes a trade using your expert services. However, there is a different way to make money other than commission (or markups or markdowns, if your employer trades securities from inventory). More and more broker–dealers are requiring their agents to get a Series 66 (for those with a Series 7 license) or 65 license, which allows them to receive a fee for giving investment advice. To do so, you have to pass an exam and be registered as an investment adviser under the Investment Advisers Act of 1940. Advisers must have a written contract that explains to clients how and when fees will be charged. Fees may be charged as a percentage of managed assets for every time the adviser offers services or as wrap fees, whereby a client is charged fees for unlimited trading, advice, and/or custody of funds and securities. People who provide investment advice that is incidental to their business (teachers, accountants, lawyers, and so on) do not have to register as investment advisers.

Cash or margin?

When one of your clients is opening a *cash account*, it means that she must pay for each trade in full. It doesn't mean that she has to drop off a suitcase full of cash; the trades are typically paid for via check or wire transfer. When a customer opens a cash account, she cannot purchase securities on margin.

You don't necessarily need cold cash to buy securities. Thanks to the wonder of *margin accounts*, you can borrow money from a broker–dealer to purchase securities or borrow the securities themselves. Margin accounts allow customers to buy more securities from you (as a registered rep) than they otherwise would, thus leading to more money in your pocket (a greater commission). However, margin accounts are not without an additional degree of risk (which a lot of people found out back in 1929). Margin accounts are great if the securities held in the account are going in the right direction but horrible if they aren't.

Getting Margin Paperwork Out of the Way

Because purchasing or selling short on margin involves extra risk, all customers must receive a risk disclosure document, which outlines those risks and some of the broker–dealer's rules. Besides receiving the margin risk disclosure document, the customer must sign a *margin agreement* before any securities can be purchased or sold short on margin. The margin agreement is broken down into three main sections:

>> **The credit agreement:** Because the investors are borrowing money from the broker-dealer to purchase the securities, they're going to be charged interest on that money. The credit agreement discloses the terms for that borrowing, including the interest rate charged, the broker-dealer's method of computation, and situations under which the interest rate may change.

>> **The hypothecation agreement:** This agreement states that all the margined securities must be held in street name (in the name of the broker-dealer for the benefit of the customer). In addition, it allows the broker-dealer to use a portion of the customer's margined securities as collateral for a bank loan *(rehypothecation)*. The hypothecation agreement also allows the broker-dealer to sell securities from the account in the event that equity falls below a certain level.

>> **The loan consent form:** The loan consent form gives permission to the broker-dealer to loan a customer's margined securities to other investors or broker-dealers, typically for the short sale of securities.

REMEMBER

Besides receiving the paperwork listed above, investors opening margin accounts also receive a *margin risk disclosure document*. Some of the things included in that document let the client know that she can lose more money than deposited into the margin account, the firm can force the sale of securities or other assets in the account without contacting the client, the client cannot choose which securities in the account are liquidated, the firm can increase the house maintenance requirement in the account at any time, a client is not entitled to additional time to meet a margin call, and so on.

Introducing Long and Short Margin Accounts

In margin accounts, investors either borrow some money to buy securities or borrow the securities themselves. As a result, margin accounts come in two varieties: long and short.

As you may remember, *long* means *to buy*. With a *long margin account*, the customer buys securities by coming up with a certain percentage of the purchase price of the securities and borrowing the balance from the broker-dealer. These optimistic investors are hoping for a bull market, because they want to sell the securities sometime later for a profit.

With a *short margin account*, an investor is borrowing securities to immediately sell in the market. The process sounds a bit backwards, but the investor is selling things he doesn't actually own yet. Hopefully, for this bearish customer, the price of the security will decrease so the investor can purchase the shares in the market at a lower price and then return them to the lender.

REMEMBER

When a customer buys securities, he can purchase the securities in a cash or margin account, but when a customer sells short securities, the transaction must be executed in a margin account.

Playing by the Federal Reserve Board's Rules

The Securities Exchange Act of 1934 gives the Federal Reserve Board (FRB) the authority to regulate the extension of credit to customers in the securities industry. In addition to Regulation T (see the following section), the FRB decides which securities can be purchased on margin. (Chapter 13 can tell you more about the FRB and its role in influencing money supply.)

Regulation T

Regulation T is the Federal Reserve Board rule that covers the credit broker-dealers may extend to customers who are purchasing securities. Currently for margin accounts both long and short, Regulation T (Reg T) requires customers to deposit at least 50 percent of the current market value of the securities purchased on margin, and the balance is borrowed from the broker-dealer.

REMEMBER

Regulation T is currently set at 50 percent; however, firms not willing to take as much risk may increase the house margin requirement to 55 percent, 60 percent, 65 percent, and so on. When you're taking the SIE exam, you should assume 50 percent unless the question states a different percentage.

Regulation T applies not only to margin accounts but also to cash accounts (see Chapter 16). When customers are purchasing securities in cash accounts, they have a certain number of business days to pay for the trade. This delay is an extension of credit; therefore, it falls under Regulation T.

Reg T also identifies which securities can be purchased on margin and which ones can't.

Margin call

A *margin call* (also known as a *Fed call*, *federal call*, or *Reg T call*) is the broker–dealer's demand for a customer to deposit money in a margin account when purchasing or shorting (selling short) securities. If a customer is buying securities on margin, the customer may deposit fully paid securities in lieu of cash to meet the margin call.

For both long and short margin accounts, the margin call is the dollar amount of securities purchased (or shorted) multiplied by Regulation T (50 percent). So, for example, if an investor purchases $50,000 worth of securities on margin, the margin call would be $25,000. Here's how you figure that:

$$\text{margin call} = \text{the current market value of the securities} \times \text{Reg T}$$

$$\text{margin call} = \$50,000 \times 50\% = \$25,000$$

Opening a Margin Account: The Initial Requirements

The initial margin requirements for short and long accounts apply to the *first* transaction in a margin account only. After the account is established, the investor can purchase or short securities just by depositing Regulation T of the current market value of the securities purchased or shorted.

For an initial purchase in a margin account, customers must deposit a minimum of equity in their margin accounts. Currently, Regulation T calls for a minimum deposit of 50 percent of the current market value of the securities purchased or sold short. However, the Financial Industry Regulatory Authority (FINRA) and the New York Stock Exchange (NYSE) call for a minimum deposit of $2,000 or ask customers to pay for the securities in full (see the section "Starting long accounts" for more on how this works).

TIP

When you're taking the SIE, pay attention to the wording of the question. Phrases like "opens a margin account," "in an initial transaction in a margin account," and so on indicate that the question is asking for the initial margin requirement rather than a margin call (see the preceding section for info on margin calls).

REMEMBER

The following sections are based on the initial margin requirements for regular long and short margin accounts. If an investor wants to open a *day trading account*, the initial margin requirement is $25,000, and the investor must keep at least $25,000 in equity to continue trading. A day trading (pattern day trader) account is one in which the investor buys and sells the same security on the same day or sells short and buys the same security on the same day at least four times in five consecutive days.

Starting long accounts

To open a long margin account, the customer is required to deposit Regulation T or $2,000, whichever is greater. The exception to this rule occurs when a customer is purchasing less than $2,000 worth of securities on margin. In this case, the customer pays for the transaction in full. It certainly wouldn't make sense for a customer to purchase $1,000 of securities on margin and pay $2,000 when he could pay $1,000 if it were purchased in a cash account. Even if the customer pays in full, the account is still considered a margin account because the customer can make future purchases on margin as soon as he has over $2,000 in equity.

Table 12-1 shows you how Regulation T and the FINRA/NYSE requirements affect how much customers have to deposit when opening long margin accounts.

TABLE 12-1 **Deposit Requirements for Long Margin Accounts**

Dollar Amount of Purchase	Regulation T Requirement	FINRA/NYSE Requirement	Amount Customer Must Deposit
$6,000	$3,000	$2,000	$3,000
$3,000	$1,500	$2,000	$2,000
$1,000	$500	$1,000	$1,000

REMEMBER

In short, here's how much an investor has to deposit:

Purchase Price	Amount Owed
Initial purchase < $2,000	Full purchase price
$2,000 ≤ initial purchase ≤ $4,000	$2,000
Initial purchase > $4,000	Reg T (50% of market value)

Opening short accounts

The minimum deposit for short accounts is fairly easy to remember. The $2,000 minimum required by the FINRA and NYSE applies to short margin accounts. Because of the additional risk investors take when selling short securities, the $2,000 minimum always applies, even if the customer is selling short only $300 worth of securities. In this case, the customer must deposit 50 percent of the current market value of the securities or $2,000, whichever is greater. Here's the breakdown:

Purchase Price	Amount Owed
Initial purchase ≤ $4,000	$2,000
Initial purchase > $4,000	Reg T (50% of market value)

Obeying the Telephone Act of 1991

Since this chapter is about opening customer accounts, it makes sense to cover the Telephone Act of 1991. So, if you're opening the account, you likely called them first unless you happen to be one of those blokes or blokettes lucky enough to have a customer call you to open an account. To make sure that certain standards are used when calling potential customers (such as not calling them at midnight), the Telephone Act of 1991 was created. When you're dealing with *potential customers* on the phone, you need to know these rules:

>> You can't make calls before 8 a.m. or after 9 p.m. local time of the potential customer.

>> You have to give your name, company name, company address, and phone number.

>> If you get a potential customer who's tired of being called, you should place that person on a *do not call list.* Each firm must maintain its own do not call list and have the U.S. government's National Do Not Call List available.

>> You may not send unsolicited ads by fax machine.

REMEMBER

The Telephone Act of 1991 *does not* apply to existing customers (customers who have executed a trade or had a security in the firm's account in the previous 18 months) or calls from nonprofit organizations. Existing customers who want to be placed on the "do not call" list after opening an account cannot be solicited but can be updated on the status of their account.

IN THIS CHAPTER

» Doing some fundamental analysis

» Showing what a technical analyst does

» Looking at the money supply

» Understanding economic indicators

» Reviewing some economic terms and principles you need to know

Chapter **13**

Doing a Little Market Research: Securities Analysis

I n terms of choosing securities, throwing darts at a list of stocks seems to have fallen out of favor. So has drawing company names out of a hat. But hey, no problem. Your psychic powers may not be the most reliable, but you still have tons of tools that can help you get a good idea of where the market's heading and how certain securities may perform.

One of your main jobs as a registered representative is to figure out the best investments for your customers. To help lead people down the path of riches, you have to analyze your customer's portfolio and the market and try to find a good fit. In many cases firms hire analysts to provide registered reps with investment information, which helps you determine the best recommendations for each customer.

In this chapter, I cover topics relating to securities analysis and money supply. The majority of this chapter is about analyzing companies and the market, and seeing what happens with the money supply. Don't worry, though — I don't leave out technical and fundamental analysis; I just focus on the information that can help you get the best score on the SIE.

Knowing Your Securities and Markets: Securities Analysis

Although many brokerage firms have their own analysts, you do need to know some of the basics of securities analysis to pass the SIE and co-requisite exams. In this section, I cover investment risks that your customers face and show you the differences between technical and fundamental analysis.

Regarding risk

Investors face many risks (and hopefully many rewards) when investing in the market. You need to understand the risks because not only can this knowledge make you sound like a genius, but it can also help you score higher on the SIE exam:

>> **Market (systematic) risk:** The risk of a security declining due to negative market conditions. All securities have market risk.

>> **Business (nonsystematic) risk:** The risk of a corporation failing to perform up to expectations.

>> **Credit risk:** The risk that the principal and interest aren't paid on time. Moody's, Standard & Poor's, and Fitch are the main bond-rating companies.

>> **Liquidity (marketability) risk:** The risk that the security is not easily traded. Long-term bonds and limited partnerships have more liquidity risk.

>> **Interest (money rate) risk:** The risk of bond prices declining with increasing interest rates. (Use the idea behind the seesaw from Chapter 7: When interest rates increase, outstanding bond prices decrease.) All bonds (even zero-coupon bonds) are subject to interest risk.

>> **Reinvestment risk:** The risk that interest and dividends received will have to be reinvested at a lower rate of return. Zero coupon bonds, T-bills, T-STRIPS, and so on have no reinvestment risk because they don't receive interest payments.

>> **Purchasing power (inflation) risk:** The risk that the return on the investment is less than the inflation rate. Long-term bonds and fixed annuities have high inflation risk. To avoid inflation risk, investors should buy stocks and variable annuities.

>> **Capital risk:** The risk of losing all money invested (for options [Chapter 11] and warrants [Chapter 6]). Because options and warrants have expiration dates, purchasers may lose all money invested at expiration. To reduce capital risk, investors should buy investment-grade bonds.

>> **Regulatory (legislative) risk:** The risk that law changes will affect the market.

>> **Currency risk:** The risk that an investment's value will be affected by a change in currency exchange rates. Investors who have international investments are the ones most affected by currency risk.

>> **Nonsystematic risk:** A risk that is unique to a certain company or a certain industry. To avoid nonsystematic risk, investors should have a diversified portfolio.

>> **Political (legislative) risk:** The risk that the value of a security could suffer due to instability or political changes in a country (for example, the nationalization of corporations).

>> **Prepayment risk:** The type of risk mostly associated with real-estate investments such as mortgage-backed securities (Chapter 7). Mortgage-backed securities have an average expected life, but if mortgage interest rates decrease, more investors will refinance and the bonds will be called earlier than expected.

>> **Timing risk:** The risk of an investor buying or selling a security at the wrong time, thus failing to maximize profits.

TIP

On the SIE exam, to determine the best investment for a customer, pay close attention to the investor's risk tolerance, financial considerations, non–financial considerations, risk(s) mentioned, and so on.

Mitigation of risk

Certainly, all investments have a certain degree of risk. Younger investors, sophisticated investors, and wealthy investors can all afford to take more risk than the average investor. However, when you are talking to your clients, you should help them make decisions that will help them mitigate their risk. Following are a few topics that you may potentially be asked about on the SIE exam.

Diversification

You've probably heard the expression, "Don't put all your eggs in one basket." Well, the same holds true for investing. Suppose for instance that one of your customers has everything invested in DIMP Corporation common stock. All of a sudden, DIMP Corporation loses a big contract or is being investigated. Your customer could be wiped out. However, if your customer had a diversified portfolio, DIMP Corporation would likely only be a small part of her investments and she wouldn't be ruined. This is the reason that having a diversified portfolio is so important. There are many ways to diversify, including:

- » **Geographical:** Investing in securities in different parts of the country or world.

- » **Buying bonds with different maturity dates:** Buying a mixture of short-term, intermediate-term, and long-term debt securities.

- » **Buying bonds with different credit ratings:** You may purchase high-yield bonds (ones with a low credit rating) with highly rated bonds with lower returns so that you get a mixture of high returns with the safety of the highly rated bonds.

- » **Investing in stocks from different sectors:** Often, certain sectors of the market perform better than others. By spreading your investments out among these different sectors, you can minimize your risk and hopefully make a profit if one or more sector happens to be performing well. The sectors include financials, utilities, energy, healthcare, industrials, technology, and so on.

- » **Type of investment:** Investing in a mixture of different types of stocks, bonds, DPPs, real estate, options, and so on.

TIP

There are certainly many more ways to diversify a portfolio than the ones listed previously — use your imagination. In addition, they aren't mutually exclusive. Remember that mutual funds (packaged securities) provide a certain amount of diversification within an individual stock. This is why smaller investors who may not be able to afford to diversify their portfolio are ideal candidates for mutual funds.

Portfolio rebalancing

Say that you and one of your clients determine that it is best for her to have a portfolio of 50 percent equity securities and 50 percent debt securities. After setting up and purchasing the portfolio, one year later, due to appreciation, your client now has 60 percent in equity securities and 40 percent in debt securities. At that point, your client may decide to rebalance her portfolio by selling some equity securities and purchasing more debt securities to help maintain her original desired level of asset allocation (50-50). As a matter of fact, there are mutual funds called *asset allocation funds* that will rebalance the portfolio of securities held by the fund without needing to contact the shareholders.

REMEMBER

Typically, as investors age, they can't afford to take as much risk and should change their asset allocation to include fewer equity securities and more debt securities.

Hedging

I'm sure you've heard of the saying, "Hedge your bets." In the gamblers' world, this may mean taking insurance to protect oneself against the possibility of the dealer getting a 21 when playing blackjack. What it means is that you are trying to reduce your risk. The problem is that by doing so, you may be limiting your upside potential. In the investors' world, there are several ways to hedge depending on what you're investing in.

To hedge against market volatility (the risk that the market will fluctuate in price), you can hedge (protect) by having a diversified portfolio. In this case, although some of your investments may be subject to big swings in price, others will remain stable or increase when the market decreases. A well-diversified portfolio may include short- and long-term bonds of varying credit risk, cash equivalents (in other words, money-market funds), all sorts of equity securities (value, growth, large-cap, small-cap, and so on), real-estate investments, commodities, and so on.

To hedge against credit risk (the risk that bond issuers default), you can purchase some more secure debt securities issued by the U.S. government (T-bills, T-notes, T-bonds, and so forth), debt securities issued by local governments (municipal bonds and municipal notes), debt securities by higher-rated corporations, and so on.

Inflation risk is the risk that a security doesn't keep pace with inflation. To hedge against inflation risk, you can purchase stocks, variable annuities, real estate, commodities (raw materials or agricultural products), or even TIPS (Treasury Inflation Protected Securities).

REMEMBER

There are many different types of risk, as you can see from the previous section. There are different ways to hedge against risk depending on which risk you're concerned about. The preceding are just a few examples. Options can also be used to hedge against the risk of a security you own going in the wrong direction. The best way to limit risk for most investors is to have a diversified portfolio. You must also understand that in most cases, older investors can't afford to take as much risk. For SIE exam purposes, the main thing you need to remember is that *hedge* means to protect and work it from there.

Deciding what to buy: Fundamental analysis

Although most analysts use some combination of fundamental analysis and technical analysis to make their securities recommendations, for SIE exam purposes, you need to be able to differentiate between the two types. This section discusses fundamental analysis; I cover technical analysis later in the section "Deciding when to buy: Technical analysis."

Fundamental analysts perform an in-depth analysis of companies. They look at the management of a company and its financial condition (balance sheets, income statements, the industry, management, earnings, and so on) and compare it to other companies in the same industry. They can also compare many years of financial statements to help determine whether a company is heading in the right direction. In addition, fundamental analysts even look at the overall economy and industry conditions to determine whether an investment is good to buy.

REMEMBER

In simplest terms, fundamental analysts decide *what to buy*.

A fundamental analyst's goal is to determine the value of a particular security and decide whether it's underpriced or overpriced. If the security is underpriced, a fundamental analyst recommends buying the security; if the security is overpriced, he recommends selling or selling the security short.

The following sections explain some of the fundamental analyst's tools of the trade and how to use them.

Balance sheet components

The *balance sheet* provides an image of a company's financial position at a given point in time. The SIE exam tests your ability to understand the components (see Figure 13-1) and how financial moves that the company makes (buying equipment, issuing stock, issuing bonds, paying off bonds, and so on) affect the balance sheet. In general, understanding how a balance sheet works is more important than being able to name all the components.

Assets	*Liabilities*
Current assets	Current liabilities
Fixed assets	Long-term liabilities
Intangible assets	
	Stockholder's equity (net worth)
	Par value (common)
	Par value (preferred)
	Paid-in capital
	Treasury stock
	Retained earnings

FIGURE 13-1: Components of a balance sheet.

REMEMBER

People call this statement a balance sheet because the assets must always balance out the liabilities plus the stockholders' equity.

Assets are items that a company owns. They include

>> **Current assets:** Owned items that are easily converted into cash within the next 12 months; included in current assets are cash, securities, accounts receivable, inventory, and any prepaid expenses (like rent or advertising).

   Note: Fundamental analysts also look at methods of inventory valuation, such as *LIFO* (last in first out) or *FIFO* (first in first out). In addition, they look at the methods of depreciation, which are either *straight line* (depreciating an equal amount each year) or *accelerated* (depreciating more in earlier years and less in later years).

>> **Fixed assets:** Owned items that aren't easily converted into cash; included are property, plant(s), and equipment. Because fixed assets wear down over time, they can be depreciated.

>> **Intangible assets:** Owned items that don't have any physical properties; included are items such as trademarks, patents, formulas, goodwill (a value based on the reputation of a company — for example, the name McDonald's is probably worth more than Fred's Sloppy Burgers), and so on.

Liabilities are what a company owes. They may be current or long-term:

>> **Current liabilities:** Debt obligations that are due to be paid within the next 12 months; included in current liabilities are *accounts payable* (what a company owes in bills), wages, debt securities due to mature, *notes payable* (the balance due on money borrowed), declared cash dividends, and taxes.

>> **Long-term liabilities:** Debt obligation due to be paid after 12 months; included in long-term liabilities are mortgages and outstanding corporate bonds.

Stockholders' equity (net worth) is the difference between the assets and the liabilities (basically, what the company is worth). This value includes

>> **Par value of the common stock:** The arbitrary amount that the company uses for bookkeeping purposes. If a company issues 1 million shares of common stock with a par value of $1, the par value on the stockholders' equity portion of the balance sheet is $1 million.

>> **Par value of the preferred stock:** The value that the company uses for bookkeeping purposes (usually $100 per share). If the company issues 10,000 shares of preferred stock, the par value on the stockholders' equity portion of the balance sheet is $1 million.

>> **Paid in capital:** The amount over par value that the company receives for issuing stock. For example, if the par value of the common stock is $1 but the company receives $7 per share, the paid in capital is $6 per share. The same theory holds true for the preferred stock.

>> **Treasury stock:** Stock that was outstanding in the market but was repurchased by the company.

>> **Retained earnings:** The percentage of net earnings the company holds after paying out dividends (if any) to its shareholders.

Income statement components

An income statement tells you how profitable a company is right now. *Income statements* list a corporation's expenses and revenues for a specific period of time (quarterly, year-to-date, or yearly). When comparing revenues to expenses, you should be able to see the efficiency of the company and how profitable it is. I don't think you need to actually see a detailed balance sheet from a company, but knowing the components of an income statement is important. Take a look at Figure 13-2 to see how an income statement is laid out. Most of the items are self-explanatory.

> *Net sales*
> - Cost of goods sold (earnings before interest, taxes, depreciation, and amortization) (EBITDA)
> - Operating expenses (including depreciation)
>   Operating profit (earnings before interest and taxes) (EBIT)
> - Interest expenses
>   Taxable income (earnings before taxes) (EBT)
> - Taxes
>   Net income (earnings after taxes) (EAT)
> - Preferred dividends
>   Earnings available to common stockholders
> - Common dividends
>   Retained earnings

FIGURE 13-2: Components of an income statement.

Deciding when to buy: Technical analysis

Technical analysts look at the market to determine whether the market is bullish or bearish. They look at trendlines, trading volume, market sentiment, market indices (S&P 500, DJIA, and so on), options volatility, market momentum, available funds, index futures, new highs and lows, the advance-decline ratio, odd lot volume, short interest, put-to-call ratio (options trading), and so on. These analysts believe that history tends to repeat itself and that past performance of securities and the market indicate its future performance.

Fundamental analysts decide *what to buy*, and technical analysts decide *when to buy* (timing).

Not only do technical analysts chart the market, but they also chart individual securities. Technical analysts try to identify market patterns and patterns of particular stocks in an attempt to determine the best time to purchase or sell. Even though a stock's price may vary a lot from one day to another, when plotting out stock prices over a long period of time, the prices tend to head in a particular direction (up, down, or sideways) and create a *trendline*.

Benchmark and indices

If you watch news stations, read the newspaper, listen to the radio, and so on, you can't help but see or hear about the DJIA (Dow Jones Industrial Average) or the NASDAQ being up or down. Well, those are indices (indexes) or benchmarks. Benchmarks are typically used to evaluate the performance of individual investments or a group of investments. Most investors compare their investments to certain broad-based indices or narrow-based indices.

>> **Narrow-based:** Narrow-based indices indicate the performance of a particular industry such as the Dow Jones Transportation Index.

>> **Broad-based:** Broad-based indices are more indicative of the overall market. Broad-based indices measure securities from many different industries.

There are certainly more indices than the ones listed, but for SIE exam purposes, you shouldn't need to memorize them but mainly understand what indices are and that they are often used as benchmarks.

Here are examples of some of the broad-based stock indices:

>> **Standard & Poor's 500 Index** (S&P 500): Includes 500 large-cap listed common stocks.

>> **Wilshire 5000 Total Market Index:** The largest of all stock indexes; includes 5,000 listed common stocks.

>> **Russell 2000 Index:** An index of 2,000 small-cap (smaller-sized) companies.

>> **Lipper Indexes:** Track the financial performance of different mutual funds based on their investment strategy. Each Lipper Index tracks the performance of only the largest fund in each category (large-cap growth, mid-cap value, international fund, and so on).

>> **Dow Jones Composite Average:** An index that tracks 65 stocks from some of the most prominent companies. The Dow Jones Composite is broken down into:

- **Dow Jones Industrial Average (DJIA):** Tracks 30 stocks from the industrial sector. The DJIA is the most commonly used index to indicate the performance of the market in general.

- **Dow Jones Transportation Average:** Tracks 20 stocks from the transportation sector.

- **Dow Jones Utility Average:** Tracks 15 stocks from the utility sector.

Proponents of the *Dow Theory* believe that major market trends are confirmed if the Dow Jones Industrial Average and the Down Jones Transportation Average are trending in the same direction (that is, both advancing or both declining). Logic dictates that if industrial companies are producing more goods, then those same goods need to be transported.

Most of the indices listed previously are weighted toward the larger companies. This means that price movement of the larger companies will have a greater impact on the particular index than a smaller company would.

Stages of the business cycle

The business cycle is the natural rise and fall of goods and services (Gross Domestic Product, or GDP) that occur over time. The business cycle has four phases that will occur over and over again. Please see Figure 13-3.

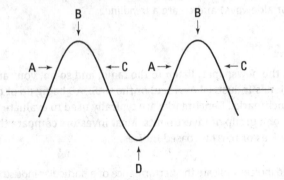

FIGURE 13-3:
The four phases of the business cycle.

>> **Expansion** (*A* in Figure 13-3): *Expansion* is characterized by increasing demand for goods and services. During expansion, the stock market is generally increasing (bullish), property values are increasing, and industrial production is increasing. Expansion also can be characterized as recovery.

>> **Peak** (*B* in Figure 13-3): The *peak* occurs at the top of the expansion phase and happens right before the economy starts to contract.

>> **Contraction** (*C* in Figure 13-3): *Contraction* is characterized by higher levels of consumer debt, a stock market that is generally decreasing (bearish), a decreasing demand for goods and services, and an increasing number of bond defaults and bankruptcies.

>> **Trough** (*D* in Figure 13-3): *Trough* is the lowest part of the contraction phase and happens right before the economy starts to expand (recover) again.

TIP

If asked to place them in order on the SIE exam, you can put them in order just as they're given in the preceding list.

Bullish versus bearish

When thinking of whether the market is bullish or bearish, think of the terms. You can think of bullish as charging ahead. So if the market is bullish, it is generally increasing in value. If the market is bearish, it is generally hibernating or sleeping. When the market is bearish, it is generally decreasing in value.

Individuals can be bullish or bearish on the market in general or bullish or bearish on certain securities.

>> **Bullish** strategies include buying individual stocks, buying mutual funds, buying call options, selling uncovered [naked] put options, and so on.

>> **Bearish** strategies include selling short individual stocks, buying bearish funds (funds that generally increase in value in a declining market), buying inverse exchange-traded funds, selling uncovered [naked] call options, buying put options, and so on.

Following the Green: Money Supply

The money supply heavily affects the market. If the money supply is higher than average, interest rates go down, people borrow more money, and people spend more money. That all sounds great, but the situation can lead to some negatives, such as higher inflation and the weakening of U.S. currency in relation to foreign currency. The Federal Reserve Board (the Fed or FRB) has to do a balancing act to help the economy grow at a slow and steady rate. This section deals with how the money supply affects the market and the tools that the Fed uses to control the money supply.

REMEMBER

The Fed controls the monetary policy but the *fiscal policy* is controlled by government politicians (the House, the Senate, and ultimately signed by the President). The monetary policy is typically included in budget decisions and includes how much the U.S. government will borrow (and how), how much it will spend (and on what), how much money will be raised through taxes, and so on.

TIP

To put it in a nutshell so to speak, you can think of it like this:

>> Monetary policy = money supply, interest rates

>> Fiscal policy = borrowing, spending, taxes

Influencing the money supply

Changes in money supply can affect rates of economic growth, inflation, and foreign exchange, so knowing a bit about monetary policy can help you predict how certain securities will fare and how interest rates will change. Take a look at Table 13-1 to see what easing and tightening the money supply can do.

TABLE 13-1 **Effects of Easing and Tightening the Money Supply**

Category	Easing the Money Supply	Tightening the Money Supply
Economy	Easy money helps the U.S. avoid or get out of a recession. Consumers can borrow money at lower interest rates.	The economy slows down because people aren't spending as much money; the rate of small business failure increases.
Market	As a result of lower interest rates, investors have more money to invest and can purchase more goods. Additionally, businesses don't have to pay as much interest to borrow money, which increases their profits. Both elements can lead to a bullish market.	High interest rates hurt the market because investors don't have extra money to spend. Additionally, corporations have to pay higher interest on loans and, therefore, report lower earnings. The market becomes bearish.
Inflation	Lower interest rates lead to higher inflation. If companies see that customers are spending money freely, they raise their prices.	A tighter money supply helps curb high inflation.
Strength of the U.S. dollar	The U.S. dollar weakens. U.S. exports increase because foreign currency strengthens (people can trade fewer units of foreign currency for more dollars); therefore, buying U.S. products is cheaper for foreign consumers. However, the U.S. dollar loses value when purchasing foreign goods, so foreign imports decrease.	The value of the U.S. dollar rises in relation to foreign currency. The U.S. dollar is subject to supply and demand, so if our money supply is tight, the value of our currency increases. Because the U.S. dollar is strong, importing foreign goods is cheaper for U.S. companies. However, U.S. exports decline because buying U.S. goods becomes more expensive for foreign companies.

When the money supply is eased (resulting in *easy money*), interest rates in general decrease. The Fed can ease the money supply by

>> Buying U.S. government securities in the open market

>> Lowering the discount rate, reserve requirements, and/or Regulation T (although changing Reg T isn't likely)

>> Printing U.S. currency

Occasionally, the Fed has to tighten the money supply. (Remember, the Fed wants the U.S. economy to grow at a slow, steady pace.) When the money supply is tightened (resulting in *tight money*), interest rates across the board increase. The Fed can tighten the money supply by

>> Selling U.S. government securities (pulling money out of the banking system)

>> Increasing the discount rate, reserve requirements, and/or Regulation T

The following section tells you more about these tools.

Opening the Federal Reserve Board's toolbox

The Federal Reserve Board, or the Fed, has the authority on behalf of the U.S. government to lend money to banks; it determines the interest rate charged to banks for these loans. You probably remember the chairman of the Fed (currently Jerome Powell) coming on TV to announce an increase or decrease in the *discount rate* (the rate the Fed charges banks for loans) and what a big deal it was. The rate the Fed charges impacts the rates banks charge each other and their public customers. Because banks charge customers higher rates than the Fed charges banks, the Fed policy affects consumers as well (through credit card fees, mortgage loans, auto loans, and so on):

Fed $ → banks $ → customers $

The Fed has a few tools in its arsenal to help control the money supply (the preceding section explains the effects of tightening and easing the supply). Here's what you need to understand about these tools for the SIE:

>> **Open market operations:** Besides the printing of money, this is the tool the Fed uses most often. *Open market operations* are the buying or selling of U.S. government bonds or U.S. government agency securities to control the money supply. Open market operations are performed by the Federal Open Market Committee (FOMC). If the Fed sells securities, it pulls money out of the banking system; if the Fed purchases securities in the open market, it puts money into the banking system.

>> **The discount rate:** This value is the rate that the 12 Federal Reserve Banks charge member banks for loans. If the discount rate increases, the money supply tightens; by contrast, if the discount rate decreases, the money supply eases.

>> **Reserve requirement:** The *reserve requirement* is the percentage of customers' money that banks are required to keep on deposit in the form of cash. In line with the theory of supply and demand, if the Fed increases the reserve requirement, banks have less money to lend to customers, so interest rates increase.

>> **Regulation T:** *Reg T* is the percentage that investors must pay when purchasing securities on margin (see Chapter 12 for details). Regulation T is currently set at 50 percent, and it doesn't change very often. If the Fed raises the rate, investors have less cash, which tightens up the money supply.

HOW THE FED IS SET UP

Here's a quick lesson in government: Congress established the Federal Reserve System in 1913 to stabilize the country's chaotic financial system. The Fed controls our money supply and, therefore, our economy.

The nation is divided into 12 Federal Reserve Districts, each with its own bank. Each bank prints currency to meet the business needs of its district, and each district is distinguished by a letter printed on the face of the bill.

The Federal Reserve Board in Washington is the parent organization that oversees and controls each of the 12 Federal Reserve District Banks. The members of the board, including the chairman, are nominated by the President of the United States, subject to confirmation by the Senate.

Exchange rates

Exchange rates are the rates at which one currency can be converted into another. As you can imagine, exchange rates are constantly changing as the value or currency in different countries appreciates, stays the same, or depreciates. Some investors even speculate in foreign currencies hoping to be able to purchase a foreign currency when its value is low with the hope that it appreciates so that they can sell it at a higher value. Certainly, many things can affect the value of a currency, such as a change in a country's social policies, taxing policies, economy, government, and so on.

You can assume for SIE exam purposes that the value of the U.S. dollar and foreign currency go in opposite directions. The exchange rate is considered a *floating rate* because it changes constantly.

U.S. balance of payments

The *U.S. balance of payments* (BoP) is an accounting of the United States' economic transactions between us and the world over a given period of time (typically quarterly or annually). The balance of payments may show a deficit (more money flowing out of the U.S. than in) or a credit (more money flowing into the U.S. than out). As such, the value of our currency (strong or weak dollar) greatly affects our balance of trade and thus the U.S. balance of payments.

If the U.S. dollar is strong in comparison to other currencies, it will be cheaper for us to buy foreign goods and services. Thus, more money will likely be going out of the U.S.

If the U.S. dollar is weak in comparison to other currencies, it will be cheaper for foreign corporations, governments, individuals, and so on to purchase U.S. goods and services. As such, more money will be flowing into the U.S.

Reading Economic Indicators

Economic indicators are statistics that help show the performance or direction of the economy and help predict the direction of the economy in the near future. The economic indicators are broken down into leading indicators, coincident indicators, and lagging indicators.

For the following section, you should pay attention to the indicators in bold because those are the ones most likely to be tested.

Leading indicators

Leading indicators are statistics that indicate how the economy is going to (or likely to) do. Leading indicators include:

» **M2 Money supply** (cash, checking deposits, savings deposits, money market instruments, and so on)

» **Stock prices**

» **Fed Funds rate** (rates depository institutions [banks and credit unions] charge each other for overnight loans)

» **Discount rate** (the rate the Fed charges banks for loans)

» Reserve requirements (the percentage of customer deposits that the banks must hold)

» Housing; new construction (building permits)

» Unemployment claims

» Average hours per workweek

» Orders for durable goods (durable goods are ones not for immediate consumption)

» Consumer sentiment

» Yield curves (lines that plot interest rates for bonds of different maturities)

Coincident (coincidental) indicators

Coincident (coincidental) indicators are statistics that indicate how the economy is performing right now. Coincident indicators include:

» **Industrial production**

» Personal income

» Gross Domestic Product (GDP)

» Number of employees on non-agricultural payrolls and employment levels

» Retail sales

Lagging indicators

Lagging indicators are statistics that mirror leading indicators but reach their peaks and troughs somewhat later. Lagging indicators include:

» **The prime rate** (the rate that banks charge their best customers for loans)

» Outstanding industrial and commercial loans

» Corporate profits

» Ratio of consumer credit to personal income

» Duration of employment

» Unemployment rate

» Ratio of inventories to sales

GDP versus GNP

As you can imagine, GNP (Gross National Product) and GDP (Gross Domestic Product) are closely related terms. When you are taking the SIE exam, you should understand the difference between the two. Because the SIE is mainly taken by U.S. residents, I focus on the GDP and GNP in U.S. terms.

>> **Gross Domestic Product (GDP):** To cut the information down to what you need to know for the SIE exam, think of the GDP as the total of all goods produced and all services provided by the U.S. in a one-year period.

>> **Gross National Product (GNP):** Gross National Product includes the GDP plus the investments made by U.S. businesses and residents inside and outside of the U.S. However, the GNP doesn't count income earned by foreign businesses or residents in the U.S. It also excludes products from overseas firms manufactured in the U.S.

Since inflation occurs over time, the GDP and GNP are measured in *constant dollars,* which includes the cost of inflation. This is necessary to help determine whether the economy is expanding or contracting from year to year.

How Economic Factors Affect Securities

Economic factors affect securities differently. When taking the SIE exam, you will be expected to understand how the economy affects *cyclical, defensive,* and *growth* companies.

Cyclical

A cyclical corporation is one in which the performance depends on the economy. If the economy is expanding, cyclical companies will do well. If the economy is contracting, cyclical companies will be heavily affected. Some examples of cyclical corporations are household appliances, automobile companies, tourism, construction, and manufacturing. Obviously, when the economy is not doing well, people will wait to buy that new refrigerator or that new car, wait to go on vacation, and so on. As such, cyclical companies' stock will likely decrease, and these companies may have problems paying interest on their debt securities.

There are counter-cyclical stocks such as alcohol, fast food, auto parts, discount retailers, and so on that may actually do better as the economy gets worse.

Defensive

Defensive corporations are ones whose sales remain relatively stable no matter how the economy performs. The corporations offer products or services that people will purchase even in a contracting economy. Examples of defensive companies include utilities, food, clothing, alcohol, tobacco, and cosmetics.

Growth

Growth companies such as technology companies are ones that are growing at a more rapid pace than other comparable companies or the market as a whole. Growth companies are typically the newer companies and are more likely to do extremely well during periods where the economy is expanding but will underperform other stocks such as value stocks when the economy is contracting and the market is bearish. Because growth companies invest a lot of money back into their business, they typically don't pay much (or anything) in dividends.

Principal Economic Theories

The principal economic theories are Keynesian (demand side), supply side (Reaganomics), and monetarist. Economists typically believe in one of them, and there has been much debate over which one is best for the economy. Fortunately for you, you don't have to figure that out; you only need to understand the basics of each theory.

Keynesian (demand side)

The basis of the Keynesian theory is that government intervention through fiscal policy is good to help stimulate consumer demand for goods and services. Keynesian policy typically involves raising taxes, deficit spending, borrowing money, and the printing of currency.

Supply side (Reaganomics)

Supply-side economics is the theory that the government should remain relatively inactive and the economy will grow by itself. According to this theory, the lower the taxes are, the more businesses will reinvest and the more people they will hire.

Monetarist

Monetarists believe that the economy's performance is largely determined by the money supply (controlled by the Fed). The money supply can be used to fight inflation or to stimulate the economy.

IN THIS CHAPTER

» **Understanding the differences between the primary and secondary markets**

» **Comparing stock exchanges to the over-the-counter market**

» **Seeing the role of the broker-dealer**

» **Looking at order qualifiers**

» **Getting to know market participants**

Chapter **14**

Going to Market: Orders and Trades

P art of your function as a registered rep will be to understand and explain to customers (and potential customers) how the stock market works. I designed this chapter with that in mind (along with the fact that you need to know this stuff for the SIE, of course).

In this chapter, I cover the basics of exchanges and the over-the-counter market, along with some of the active participants who help the market run smoothly (at least most of the time). Pay particular attention to the sections "Talking about order types" and "Factoring in order features," because you'll definitely use that information every day after you pass the SIE and co-requisite tests.

Shopping at Primary and Secondary Markets

Depending on whether the securities are new or outstanding, they trade in either the primary or secondary market. This section deals with the differences between the two.

Buying new in the primary market

The primary market (new issue market) is broken down into two categories, depending on whether the company has ever issued securities before. A security that has never been offered or sold to the public is considered a *new issue.* When securities are sold in the primary market, a bulk of the sales proceeds go to the issuer, and the balance goes to the underwriter (who buys the securities from the issuer and sells them to the public). Here are the two types of offerings on the primary market:

>> **Initial public offering (IPO):** An IPO is the first time a company ever sells stock to the public to raise money. When a company is in the process of issuing securities for the first time, it's said to be *going public*.

>> **Primary offering:** When a company initially offers securities, it usually holds some back for future use; it later pulls those securities out of storage and sells them in a primary offering. For example, a company may be authorized to sell 2 million shares of common stock, but in its initial public offering, it may sell only 800,000. At this point, 1,200,000 new shares remain that have never been offered to the public. One year later, when the company needs to raise additional capital to build a new warehouse, it can sell some of the remaining 1,200,000 shares in a primary offering.

Buying used in the secondary market

When the securities are already trading in the market, the sales proceeds go to another investor instead of to the issuer. The secondary market, also called the *aftermarket*, consists of four categories (see the following section for info on trading on exchanges versus over-the-counter markets):

>> **First market (auction market):** The first market is the trading of listed securities on the exchange floor, such as the New York Stock Exchange (NYSE).

>> **Second market (over-the-counter market):** This market is the trading of unlisted securities over-the-counter (by phone or computer).

>> **Third market:** The third market is comprised of exchange-listed securities trading over-the-counter (OTC) — traders are calling in their orders or ordering online. All NYSE Amex Equities and NYSE securities and most of the securities listed on other exchanges can be traded OTC.

>> **Fourth market:** The fourth market is the trading of securities between institutions without the use of a brokerage firm. Fourth-market trades are typically executed through ECNs (electronic communication networks).

TIP

You're more likely to get a question on the third or fourth market than the first or second.

Making the Trade

After securities are issued publicly, they may trade on an exchange or on the over-the-counter (OTC) market.

Auctioning securities at securities exchanges

Exchanges are auction markets, where bidders and sellers get together to execute trades. I'm sure you've seen movies or TV shows featuring the New York Stock Exchange. It definitely looks very chaotic (and like it's a good place to have a heart attack or develop an ulcer). However, some sort of order is definitely there: All exchanges have a trading floor where all trades are executed. Each security listed on an exchange has its own *trading post* (location) on the floor where the auction takes place. Brokers looking to purchase shout out and/or make hand signals to indicate the price they're willing to spend to buy a particular security. Sellers, in turn, shout out the price they're willing to sell a security for. If buyers and sellers can come to an agreement, a trade is made.

The main exchange that the SIE tests you on is the New York Stock Exchange (NYSE), but there are others, such as NYSE Amex Equities (formerly the American Stock Exchange [AMEX]), NASDAQ, CBOE (Chicago Board Options Exchange), Boston Stock Exchange, and so on. *Listed securities* are ones that satisfy minimum requirements and are traded on a regional or national exchange like the NYSE. Listed securities may trade on the exchange or in the OTC market.

Although thousands of people may seem to be on the floor of the exchange, you don't need to be aware of too many titles. Most of the people on the floor of the exchange fall into one of three categories:

>> **Floor brokers:** These individuals act as agents in executing buy or sell orders on behalf of their firm's customers. A floor broker may also facilitate buying and selling for her firm. Floor brokers receive buy or sell orders from their firms and either transfer the orders to a specialist or trade with another floor broker.

>> **Two-dollar brokers (independent brokers):** These people assist floor brokers in getting their orders executed on busy days. (By the way, they're called two-dollar brokers because many, many years ago, they used to receive $2 per trade. Commissions may have gone up a bit since then.)

>> **Designated market makers (DMMs; formerly specialists):** These market professionals manage the auction market trading for a particular security (or for a few securities, if not actively traded).

Negotiating trades over-the-counter

Unlike exchanges, the OTC market is a negotiated market. Instead of yelling out bid and ask prices, traders buy and sell securities by way of telephone or computer transactions. There's no central location for trading OTC securities. Thousands of securities — both listed and unlisted — are traded this way. In fact, *unlisted securities*, which aren't listed on an exchange, can only trade OTC. Unlisted securities are ones that either don't meet the listing requirements of the exchanges or that the corporation decided it didn't want to list for whatever reason.

The OTCBB (Over the Counter Bulletin Board) is a quotation service operated by FINRA for unlisted (non-NASDAQ) securities. Corporations too small to be placed on the OTCBB may still sell their securities in the Pink Market. Corporations on the Pink Market are not required to meet the listing requirements or file with the SEC.

REMEMBER

U.S. government and municipal bonds trade only over-the-counter.

Understanding the Role of a Broker-Dealer

REMEMBER

I would guestimate that a large percentage of people like you taking the SIE exam will be working for a broker-dealer. In order for a firm to be considered a broker-dealer, it must buy and sell securities from its own account and act as a middleman for securities not in inventory. Here are the differences between brokers and dealers:

>> **Broker:** A firm is acting as a broker when it doesn't use its own inventory to execute a trade. A broker charges a *commission* (sales charge) for acting as a middleman between a buyer and a seller.

For SIE exam purposes, the term *broker* and *agent* may be used interchangeably. A registered representative is sometimes called an agent or stockbroker because he acts as an intermediary between buyers and sellers.

>> **Dealer:** A firm is acting as a dealer when it uses its own inventory to execute a trade. When a dealer sells securities to a customer using its own inventory, it charges a *markup* (sales charge). When a dealer buys securities from a customer for its own inventory, it charges a *markdown* (reducing the price a customer receives by charging a sales charge). A firm becomes a dealer in the hopes that the securities it has in its own inventory will increase in price so that the dealer can benefit from the appreciation.

The terms *dealer, principal,* and *market maker* may be used interchangeably on the SIE and co-requisite exams.

Capacity refers to whether a firm is acting as a broker or dealer, and it must always be disclosed on the *confirmation* (receipt of trade). If a firm is acting as a broker, the commission always needs to be disclosed on the confirmation. However, if a firm is acting as a dealer, the markup or markdown doesn't always have to be disclosed.

REMEMBER

A firm can't act as a broker and a dealer for the same trade. In other words, charging a markup (or markdown) and a commission on the same trade is a violation. (For info on rules and regulations, see Chapter 16.)

TIP

To help you remember the differences between a broker and a dealer, think of a real-estate broker. A real-estate broker (or agent) acts as an intermediary between sellers and buyers and charges a commission, just like a stockbroker does. Conversely, a dealer like a used-car dealer, sells from his own inventory, charges a markup, and buys in the hopes of making a profit on that inventory.

Introducing broker (IB)

Although introducing brokers (IBs) are more commonly referred to in commodities and futures trading, an IB is a person or business that does not actually handle the transactions but just provides investment advice or counsel to investors. In general, an introducing broker will recommend trades to clients while handing over the job of executing the trade to a clearing firm. In general, the IB and the clearing firm that executes the trade split the trading fees and/or commission.

Clearing (carrying) broker

Clearing brokers (clearing firms) handle orders to buy and sell securities. In addition, clearing brokers maintain custody of clients' assets (securities and cash). Clearing firms are responsible for segregating (separating) clients' cash and securities held in their custody.

Prime broker

Prime brokers are used mainly by institutional accounts or large retail clients. Prime brokerage accounts are ones set up for individuals or entities with more complex financial needs. Besides helping the client combine information from all firms they are using into one statement, they also provide services such as lending, leveraged trade execution, and cash management. Often hedge funds use a prime brokerage account.

Receiving Orders from Customers

Here's where the rubber meets the road. You can receive several types of orders from customers along with numerous order qualifiers. This section explains the types of orders and how to execute them.

Talking about order types

You can definitely expect a question or two on the SIE exam relating to orders. The following sections explore the order types.

Market order

A market order is for immediate execution at the best price available. A majority of the orders that you'll receive will be market orders. Here are the varieties they come in:

- » **Buy order:** When an investor places a market order to buy, she's not price-specific; the investor purchases the security at the lowest ask price (the lowest price at which someone's willing to sell the security). An investor who's purchasing a security wants the price to increase (after the sale, of course) and is establishing a bullish position.

- » **Sell order:** When an investor places a market order to sell, she's not price-specific; she sells the security at the highest bid price (the highest price someone's willing to pay for the security).

- » **Selling short:** Selling short occurs when an investor sells securities she doesn't own. The investor is actually borrowing securities from a lender to sell. Here's how it works: Say an investor borrows 100 shares of ABC stock and sells them short at $40 per share, thus receiving $4,000. The borrower doesn't owe the lender $4,000; she owes the lender 100 shares of ABC stock. After a month or two, when ABC is trading at $20 per share, the borrower can purchase the 100 shares for $2,000 and return them to the lender, making a nice $2,000 profit (excluding commission costs). A short seller is bearish (wants the price of the security to decrease). If the price increases instead, the short seller has to buy the stock in the market at a higher price, thus losing money. All short sales must be executed in margin accounts. Short sales are subject to short-sale regulations under Regulation SHO (see the nearby sidebar).

  Note: Investors may sell short for *speculation* (believing the price of the security will decrease), *hedging* (protecting a security or several securities in the event of a market decline), or *arbitrage* (taking advantage of a price disparity on the security in different markets).

REMEMBER

When you purchase a security, the most you can lose is the amount you invest. When you're short a security, your maximum loss potential is unlimited because the price of the stock could keep climbing, in which case you'd have to spend more money to cover your short position. Additionally, because of the additional risk, all short sales must be executed in a margin account. Chapter 12 tells you a little more about margin accounts.

REGULATION SHO AND SHORT SALES

According to *Regulation SHO*, all order tickets must be marked as *short sale* rather than long sale, which is when a customer is selling securities she owns. Additionally, all brokerage firms must establish rules to locate, borrow, and deliver securities that are to be sold short. Brokerage firms must be sure that the security can be located and delivered on the date the delivery is due before executing the short sale.

Stop order

A stop order is used for protection; it tries to limit how much an investor can lose. Depending on whether an investor has a long or short stock position, he may enter a buy stop order or a sell stop order:

>> **Buy stop orders:** These orders protect a short position (when an investor sells borrowed securities). A buy stop tells you to buy a security if the market price touches a particular price or higher. Investors who are short the stock make money when the price of the stock decreases; however, if the price increases, they lose money. For example, an investor who's short ABC stock currently trading at $25 could enter a buy stop order on ABC at $30. If ABC reaches $30 or more, the order is triggered and the order becomes a market order for immediate execution at the next price.

>> **Sell stop orders:** These orders protect a long position (when an investor purchases stock); they tell you to sell a security if the market price touches a particular price or lower. Investors who are long stock make money when the price of the stock increases; if the price decreases, they lose money. For example, say an investor who is long DEF stock currently trading at $50 enters a sell stop order on ABC at $45. If DEF reaches $45 or below, the order is triggered and the order becomes a market order for immediate execution at the next price, whether higher or lower than $45.

Limit order

A customer who's specific about the price she wants to spend or receive for a security places a limit order; this order says the customer doesn't want to pay more than a certain amount or sell for less. Depending on whether an investor is interested in buying or selling, she can enter a buy limit or a sell limit order:

>> **Buy limit orders:** Investors who want to purchase a security place these orders. A buy limit order is a directive to buy a particular security at the limit price or lower. For example, suppose DEF stock is trading at $35 per share but one of your customers doesn't want to pay more than $30 per share. You could place a buy limit order at $30. If the price of DEF ever reaches $30 or less, chances are good that your customer will end up with the stock.

>> **Sell limit orders:** Investors who want to sell a security place sell limit orders. A sell limit order is a directive to sell a particular security at the limit price or higher. For example, suppose one of your customers owns LMN stock, which is currently trading at $62 per share, but he wants to receive at least $70 per share if he's going to sell it. This customer could place a sell limit on LMN at $70 per share. If LMN touches or goes above $70 per share, chances are good that the stock will be sold.

Stop limit order

A *stop limit order* is a combination of a stop and limit order (see the preceding sections); it's a buy stop or sell stop order that becomes a limit order after the stop price is reached. For example, an order that reads "sell 1,000 HIJ at 41 stop, 40.75 limit" means that the sell stop order will be triggered as soon as HIJ reaches $41 or below (the stop price). If this were just a stop order, the stock would be sold on the next trade (no matter what the price). But because this is a stop limit order, after the order is triggered, it becomes a limit order to buy at $40.75 or above (the limit price). In other words, this customer is interested in selling her stock if it drops to $41 but wants to receive at least $40.75 per share.

SELLING SHORT AGAINST THE BOX

Selling short or *shorting against the box* is when an investor sells short a security that she already owns. This type of sale typically happens when an investor wants to sell a security at the current price but can't get possession of her securities right away because she's traveling or whatever. By selling short against the box, the investor is locking in the price of the security because no matter which way it goes, she will be offsetting a gain or loss on the securities owned with a loss or gain on the securities sold short.

REMEMBER

Because stop and limit orders are price-specific, they may or may not be executed. Additionally, even if limit orders do reach or surpass the limit price, the order may not be executed if more orders were placed ahead of the investor's.

Factoring in order features

Besides knowing the basic types of orders (market, stop, and limit — see "Talking about order types"), you should have a handle on some additional features that may be added to the order to make your customers happy. A lot of them exist, but for the most part, the name of the order feature pretty much explains what it is:

» **Day:** If a day order hasn't been filled by the end of the trading day, it's canceled. All price-specific orders (stop and limit) are assumed to be day orders unless marked to the contrary. Most of the orders you'll receive will be market orders for immediate execution at the best price available (highest bid and lowest ask prices).

» **Good-till-canceled (GTC):** Good-till-canceled orders are also called *open orders* because the order is kept open until executed or canceled. For example, say that an investor wants to purchase ABC stock at $30. While the price of ABC is at $35, she enters an open buy limit order for ABC at $30. If the price of ABC ever hits $30 or below, the order will likely be executed; however, if the price of ABC never hits $30 or below, the order stays open until canceled.

   Note: An investor may specify that she wants the order canceled next week, next month, in two months, and so on. Many exchanges no longer take GTC orders but customers can place them with their broker-dealers and they will handle it internally. In actual practice, because customers may forget about their GTC orders, many broker-dealers will set them to expire in 30 days, 60 days, 90 days, and so on.

» **Not held (NH):** This order gives the broker discretion about when to execute the trade. Typically, investors use not held orders when the broker believes she can get the customer a better price later in the day.

   Not held orders deal only with timing. For registered reps to choose the security, number of shares, and/or whether to buy or sell, the customer needs to open a discretionary account, which requires a written power of attorney. See "Discretionary versus non-discretionary accounts," later in this chapter, for details.

» **Fill or kill (FOK):** This order instructs a floor broker either to immediately execute an entire order at the limit price or better, or to cancel it.

» **Immediate or cancel (IOC):** These limit orders are similar to FOK orders except that the order may be partially filled. Any portion of the order that's not completed is canceled.

» **All or none (AON):** These limit orders have to be executed either in their entirety or not at all. AON orders don't have to be filled immediately (several attempts to fill the order completely are allowed) and may be day orders or good-till-canceled orders.

- **At the open:** These orders are to be executed at the security's opening price. At the open orders can be market or limit orders, but if they aren't executed at the opening price, they're canceled. These orders allow for partial execution.

- **At the close (market on close):** This order is to be executed at the closing price (or as near as possible). If this order isn't completed, it's canceled.

- **Do not reduce (DNR):** This order says not to reduce the price of a stop or limit order in response to a dividend. For example, say that QRS stock is currently trading at $50 on the day prior to the ex-dividend date. If QRS previously announced a $0.50 dividend, the next day's opening price would be $49.50. If a customer had placed a DNR limit order to buy 1,000 shares of QRS at $45, the order wouldn't be reduced by the $0.50 dividend.

- **Alternative:** The alternative order is also known as a *one cancels the other order* or an *either/or order*. This type of order instructs the broker to execute one of two orders and then cancel the other. For example, say Mr. Smith owns stock at $60 per share. He enters a sell stop order at $55 for protection and a sell limit order at $70 in the event that the stock price increases. If one of the orders is executed, the other order is canceled immediately.

- **Bid wanted:** This order is an indication or notice that an investor or broker-dealer wants to sell a security at a specific price. Bid wanted is used most often when no current buyers of a security are available.

- **Offer wanted:** This order is an indication or notice that an investor or a broker-dealer wants to buy a particular security at a specific price. Offer wanted is used particularly when no current sellers of a security are available.

Discretionary versus non-discretionary orders

To be sure, most of the orders you will receive from your clients will be non-discretionary orders. For example, if one of your clients tells you to purchase 100 shares of ABC common stock, he is giving you a non-discretionary order. It is non-discretionary because he is giving you all the components of an order: purchase or sell, how many shares or dollar amount, and what security. If the client does not provide that information, it is considered discretionary, meaning that you must use your discretion. Here are some examples of discretionary orders:

"Buy or sell 100 shares of ABC common stock"

"Buy as many shares of ABC common stock as you think I should"

"Buy 100 shares of pharmaceutical stock"

REMEMBER

Discretionary orders may be executed by a registered rep or brokerage firm without prior verbal permission from the client. Because they don't require verbal approval, the registered rep is required to have a written power of attorney signed by the customer prior to executing any discretionary orders. The power of attorney remains in effect until the account is closed or it is removed by the client. As you can imagine, discretionary orders must be marked as such on the order ticket. In addition, these accounts must be closely watched by a principal of the firm to make sure that there's no excessive trading (churning) for the purpose of generating commission.

TIP

A client may give you approval to place the order at a later time in the day without discretionary authority. Say a client tells you to purchase 100 shares of DIM stock at the market price. You may tell your client that you believe that the price will drop later in the day and you might be able to get him a better price. This is allowed as long as the customer gives verbal approval, and it's not considered a discretionary order.

Solicited versus unsolicited orders

As with non-discretionary orders, most of the orders you receive from clients will be solicited by you, meaning that you may call up one of your clients and say, "DEF Corporation seems to be on the move, so I think it would be wise for you to buy 100 shares of DEF common stock." Because you called and suggested what the client should buy (or sell), you actually solicited that order.

Unsolicited orders are ones in which your client tells you what he wants to buy or sell. You may not think that this is the best idea for him and may tell him that, but you are not going to turn down the order and lose commission. In this case, because it was not your suggestion, you need to mark the order ticket in the box that says "unsolicited." This basically takes you off the hook in the event that the client loses money.

REMEMBER

No matter what the type of order, your job and your firm's job is to get your customers the best price available for their orders. As such, your customers orders cannot be split into multiple smaller orders for execution with the primary purpose of maximizing the amount of money (credits, commissions, gratuities, fees, and so on) that you or your firm make. In addition, "reasonable diligence" must be used to get the customer the best price. Here are some of the factors involved to determine if reasonable diligence was used: the price of the security, the volatility of the security, the liquidity of the security, the size and type of transaction, the number of markets checked, and accessibility of the quotation.

Looking at Market Participants

As a financial professional, you'll be working with all different types of investors: some smaller investors, some larger investors, corporations, and so on. Part of the SIE exam is knowing that you understand who's who when it comes to these different types of investors.

Retail investors

You are more likely to deal with retail investors than accredited or institutional investors. These guys (or gals) are nonprofessionals who trade (buy or sell) for their own accounts. Retail investors typically purchase or sell a much smaller amount of securities than accredited or institutional investors.

Accredited investors

Some investors just have access to more money than others do. The bigger guys or gals are called accredited investors. As such, they are typically able to handle more risk than retail investors. Accredited investors include

>> Financial institutions (banks, insurance companies, pension funds, and so on)

>> Insiders (officers, directors, or owners of 10 percent or more of the outstanding shares of the corporation and their immediate family members)

>> Investors who have an annual income of at least $200,000 (joint $300,000) for the previous two years and are expected to meet that requirement this year

>> Investors who have a net worth of at least $1 million excluding primary residence

>> Corporations, partnerships, or organizations with a net worth of at least $5 million

Institutional investors

Institutional investors are the big guys. They are the ones that invest a lot of money on behalf of their entity. They are generally considered to be knowledgeable about the market. Institutional investors include

>> Commercial banks

>> Mutual funds

>> Pension funds

>> Insurance companies

>> Real-estate investment trusts

>> Hedge funds

>> Endowment funds

DEPOSITORY TRUST AND CLEARING CORPORATION (DTCC)

The DTCC provides safeguards to the world's financial markets. Its role is to provide clearing, settlement, institutional matching, asset servicing, collateral management, global data management, information services, and so for equity securities, corporate bonds, municipal bonds, government securities, mortgage-backed securities, mutual funds, money market instruments, derivatives, and so on. The DTCC is absolutely massive and processes more than 100 million financial transactions each trading day. Its key roles are to provide reliability to the global financial system, to provide after-trade services, to limit risk, to lower cost, to provide transparency, and to promote greater market efficiency. The services offered by the DTCC are

• Clearing services

• Matching, settlement, and asset services

• Collateral management

• Wealth management services

• Derivative services

• Data services

IN THIS CHAPTER

» Outlining the breakdown of taxes
and income

» Seeing how the IRS taxes securities

» Comparing the different types of
retirement plans

Chapter **15**

Making Sure the IRS Gets Its Share

Yes, it's true what they say: The only sure things in life are death and taxes. Although taxes are an annoying necessity, investors do get tax breaks if they invest in securities for a long period of time, and you need a good understanding of the tax discounts investors receive. Additionally, the SIE exam tests your ability to recognize the different types of retirement plans, the specifics about each one, and the tax advantages.

In this chapter, I cover tax categories and rules, from distinguishing between types of taxes to calculating capital gains for securities received as gifts. And although enjoying retirement isn't quite as certain as pushing up daisies, I explain Uncle Sam's claim on the cash investors put into IRAs, Keoghs, and other retirement plans. As always, you can also count on some example questions and suggestions for further review.

Everything in Its Place: Checking Out Tax and Income Categories

The many lines you see on tax forms clue you in to the fact that the IRS likes to break things down into categories. The following sections explain progressive and regressive taxes, as well as types of personal income.

Touring the tax categories

The supreme tax collector (the IRS) has broken down taxes into a couple categories according to the percentage individuals pay. Your mission is to understand the different tax categories and how they affect investors:

» **Progressive taxes:** These taxes affect high-income individuals more than they affect low-income individuals; the more taxable money individuals have, the higher their income tax bracket.

Progressive taxes include taxes on personal income (see the next section), gift taxes, and estate taxes. The SIE contains more questions on progressive taxes than on regressive taxes.

>> **Regressive taxes:** These taxes affect individuals earning a lower income more than they affect people earning a higher income; everyone pays the same rate, so individuals who earn a lower income are affected more because that rate represents a higher percentage of their income. Examples of regressive taxes are payroll, sales, property, excise, gasoline, and so on.

Looking at types of income

The three main categories of income are earned, passive, and portfolio. (If you're especially interested in the details of how investments are taxed, you can find more information at www.irs.gov/.) You need to distinguish among the different categories because the IRS treats them differently:

>> **Earned (active) income:** People generate this type of income from activities that they're actively involved in. Earned income includes money received from salary, bonuses, tips, commissions, and so on. Earned income is taxed at the individual's tax bracket.

>> **Passive income:** This type of income comes from enterprises in which an individual isn't actively involved. Passive income includes income from limited partnerships (see Chapter 10) and rental property. When you see the words *passive income* on the SIE exam, immediately start thinking that the income comes from a limited partnership (DPP). Passive income is in a category of its own and can only be written off against passive losses.

>> **Portfolio income:** This type of income includes interest, dividends, and capital gains derived from the sale of securities. The following section tells you more about taxes on portfolio income. Portfolio income may be taxed at the investor's tax bracket or at a lower rate, depending on the holding period.

Noting Taxes on Investments

You need to understand how dividends, interest, capital gains, and capital losses affect investors. To make your life more interesting, the IRS has given tax advantages to people who hold onto investments for a long period of time, so familiarize yourself with the types of taxes that apply to investments and how investors are taxed.

Interest income

Interest income that bondholders receive may or may not be taxable, depending on the type of security or securities held:

>> **Corporate bond interest:** Interest received from corporate bonds is taxable on all levels (federal, state, and, local, where local taxes exist).

>> **Municipal bond interest:** Interest received from municipal bonds is federally tax free; however, investors may be taxed on the state and local levels, depending on the issuer of the bonds (see Chapter 8).

>> **U.S. government securities interest:** Interest received from U.S. government securities, such as T-bills, T-notes, T-STRIPS, and T-bonds, is taxable on the federal level but is exempt from state and local taxes.

REMEMBER

Even though T-bills, T-STRIPS, and any other zero-coupon bonds don't generate interest payments (because the securities are issued at a discount and mature at par), the difference between the purchase price and the amount received at maturity is considered interest and is subject to taxation.

Dividends

Dividends may be in the form of cash, stock, or product. However, cash dividends are the only ones that are taxable in the year that they're received. The following sections discuss dividends in cash, in stock, and from mutual funds.

Cash dividends

Qualified cash dividends received from stocks are taxed at a maximum rate of 0 percent, 15 percent, or 20 percent depending on the investor's adjusted gross income (AGI). Qualified dividends are ones in which the customer has held onto the stock for at least 61 days (91 days for preferred stock). The 61-day holding period starts 60 days prior to the *ex-dividend date* (the first day the stock trades without dividends). If the investor has held the stock for less than the 61-day holding period, the dividends are considered *nonqualified* and investors are taxed at the rate determined by their regular tax bracket.

Stock dividends

Stock dividends don't change the overall value of an investment, so the additional shares received are not taxed (for details, see Chapter 6). However, stock dividends do lower the cost basis per share for tax purposes. The cost basis is used to calculate capital gains or losses.

Dividends from mutual funds

Dividends and interest generated from securities that are held in a mutual fund portfolio are passed through to investors and are taxed as either *qualified* (see the earlier section "Cash dividends") or *nonqualified*. The type(s) of securities in the portfolio and the length of time the fund held the securities dictate how the investor is taxed. Here's how mutual fund dividends are taxed:

Federally Tax Free	0, 15, or 20 Percent	Ordinary Income
Municipal bond funds	Stock funds	Corporate bond funds
	Long-term capital gains	Short-term capital gains

REMEMBER

One of the great things about owning mutual funds is that they're nice enough to let you know what taxes you're going to be subject to. At the beginning of each year you will receive a statement from the mutual fund that lets you know how much you received the previous year in dividends, in short-term capital gains, and in long-term capital gains. The mutual fund also sends a copy of the statement to the IRS.

The mutual fund determines the long-term or short-term gains by its holding period, not the investors'. Also, remember that you'd be subject to capital gains tax and taxes on dividends even if the money were reinvested back into the fund.

At the sale: Capital gains and losses

Capital gains are profits made when selling a security, and *capital losses* are losses incurred when selling a security. To determine whether an investor has a capital gain or capital loss, you have to start with the investor's cost basis. The *cost basis* is used for tax purposes and includes the purchase price plus any commission (although on the SIE exam, the test designers usually don't throw commission into the equation). The cost basis remains the same unless it's adjusted for things like stock splits, stock dividends, accretion, amortization, and so on.

Note: Accretion and amortization come into play when an investor purchases a bond at a price other than par. The bond cost basis will be adjusted toward par over the amount of time until maturity. You won't be asked to calculate it on the SIE exam.

Incurring taxes with capital gains

An investor realizes capital gains when he sells a security at a price higher than his cost basis. Capital gains on any security (even municipal and U.S. government bonds) are fully taxed on the federal, state, and local level.

REMEMBER

A capital gain isn't realized until a security is *sold*. If the value of an investment increases, it's considered appreciation or an unrealized gain, and if the investor doesn't sell, the investor doesn't incur capital gains taxes.

Capital gains are broken down into two categories, depending on the holding period of the securities:

>> **Short-term capital gains:** These gains are realized when a security is held for *one year or less*. Short-term capital gains are taxed according to the *investor's tax bracket*.

>> **Long-term capital gains:** These gains are realized when a security is held for *more than one year*. To encourage investors to buy and hold securities, long-term capital gains are currently taxed at a rate in line with cash dividends (0, 15, or 20 percent depending on the investor's adjusted gross income). (For more information on capital gains and losses, visit the Internal Revenue Service's website at www.irs.gov/taxtopics/tc409).

Offsetting gains with capital losses

An investor realizes a capital loss when selling a security at a value lower than the cost basis. Investors can use capital losses to offset capital gains and reduce the tax burden. As with capital gains, capital losses are also broken down into short-term and long-term:

>> **Short-term capital losses:** An investor incurs these losses when he has held the security for *one year or less*. Investors can use short-term capital losses to offset short-term capital gains.

>> **Long-term capital losses:** An investor incurs these losses when he has held the security for *more than one year*. Long-term capital losses can offset long-term capital gains.

When an investor has a net capital loss, he can write off $3,000 per year against his earned income and carry the balance forward the next year.

The following question involves capital-loss write-offs.

EXAMPLE

In a particular year, Mrs. Jones realizes $30,000 in long-term capital gains and $50,000 in long-term capital losses. How much of the capital losses would be carried forward to the following year?

(A) $3,000

(B) $17,000

(C) $20,000

(D) $30,000

The correct answer is Choice (B). Mrs. Jones has a net capital loss of $20,000 (a $50,000 loss minus the $30,000 gain). Mrs. Jones writes off $3,000 of that capital loss against her earned income and carries the additional loss of $17,000 forward to write off against any capital gains she may have the following year. In the event that Mrs. Jones doesn't have any capital gains the following year, she can still write off $3,000 of the $17,000 against any earned income and carry the remaining $14,000 forward, which can be used to offset any capital gains the following year.

The wash sale rule: Adjusting the cost basis when you can't claim a loss

To keep investors from claiming a loss on securities (which an investor could use to offset gains on another investment — see the preceding section) while repurchasing substantially (or exactly) the same security, the IRS has come up with the *wash sale rule*; according to this rule, if an investor sells a security at a capital loss, the investor can't repurchase the same security or anything convertible into the same security for 30 days prior to or after the sale and be able to claim the loss. An investor doesn't end up in handcuffs for violating the wash sale rule; he simply can't claim the loss on his taxes.

However, the loss doesn't go away if investors buy the security within that window of time — investors get to adjust the cost basis of the security. For instance, if an investor were to sell 100 shares of ABC at a $2-per-share loss and purchase 100 shares of ABC within 30 days for $50 per share, the investor's new cost basis (excluding commissions) would be $52 per share (the $50 purchase price plus the $2 loss on the shares sold), thus lowering the amount of capital gains he would face on the new purchase.

The following question tests your understanding of the wash sale rule.

EXAMPLE

If Melissa sells DEF common stock at a loss on June 2, for 30 days she can't buy

  I. DEF common stock

  II. DEF warrants

  III. DEF call options

  IV. DEF preferred stock

(A) I only

(B) I and IV only

(C) I, II, and III only

(D) I, II, III, and IV

The answer you want is Choice (C). You need to remember that Melissa sold DEF at a loss; therefore, she can't buy back the same security (as in Statement I) or anything convertible into the same security (as in Statements II and III) within 30 days to avoid the wash sale rule. Warrants give an investor the right to buy stock at a fixed price (see Chapter 6), and call options give investors the right to buy securities at a fixed price (Chapter 11). However, Statement IV is okay because DEF preferred stock is a different security and is not convertible into DEF common stock (unless it's convertible preferred, which it isn't; if it were convertible, the question would have told you so). For Melissa to avoid the wash sale rule, she can't buy DEF common stock, DEF convertible preferred stock, DEF convertible bonds, DEF call options, DEF warrants, or DEF rights for 30 days. However, she can buy DEF preferred stock, DEF bonds, or DEF put options (the right to sell DEF).

REMEMBER

Putting it in simple terms, the cost basis is the price an individual paid for an investment. This cost includes brokerage fees, trading costs, and loads (sales charges for mutual funds). Now, things can get a little more complex in the event of stock splits, mergers, and dividend payments. The main thing that you will need to know for the SIE exam is that the cost basis is used for calculations to determine an investor's tax liability when selling securities. More recently, brokerage firms, mutual funds, and so on are required to provide investor's information on their tax liability such as amount of short-term capital gains, long-term capital gains, dividends, interest, and so on.

Exploring Retirement Plan Tax Advantages

I place retirement plans in with taxes because retirement plans give investors tax advantages. When you're reviewing this section, zone in on the differences and similarities among the different types of plans. The contribution limits are important but not as important as understanding the plan specifics and who's qualified to open which type of plan.

Qualified versus nonqualified plans

The IRS may dub employee retirement plans as qualified or nonqualified. The distinction concerns whether they meet IRS and Employee Retirement Income Security Act (ERISA) standards for favorable tax treatment.

Tax-qualified plans

A *tax-qualified plan* meets IRS standards to receive a favorable tax treatment. When you're investing in a tax-qualified plan, the contributions into the plan are made from pretax dollars and are deductible against your taxable income. Not only are contributions into the plan tax-deductible, but the account also grows on a tax-deferred basis, so you aren't taxed until you withdraw money from the account at retirement. Individual Retirement Accounts (IRAs) are an example of a tax-qualified retirement plan. The two types of corporate tax-qualified retirement plans are defined contribution and defined benefit plans. These include 401(k)s, profit-sharing plans, and money-purchase plans. Most corporate pension plans are tax-qualified plans.

REMEMBER

Because investors don't pay tax on the money initially deposited or on the earnings, the entire withdrawal from a tax-qualified plan is taxed at a rate determined by the investor's tax bracket, which is normally lower at retirement. Additionally, distributions taken before age 59½ are subject to a 10 percent tax penalty (10 percent is added to the investor's tax bracket) except in cases of death, disability, first-time home buying, educational expenses for certain family members, medical premiums for unemployed individuals, and so on.

Nonqualified plans

Obviously, a nonqualified plan is the opposite of a qualified plan. *Nonqualified plans,* such as deferred compensation plans, payroll deduction plans, and 457 plans do not meet IRS and ERISA standards for favorable tax treatment. If you're investing in a nonqualified retirement plan, deposits are not tax-deductible (they're made from after-tax dollars); however, because you're dealing with a retirement plan, earnings in the plan do build up on a tax-deferred basis. People may choose to invest in nonqualified plans because either their employer doesn't have a qualified plan set up or the investment guidelines are not as strict (investors may be able to contribute more and invest in a wider choice of securities).

REMEMBER

Because investors have already paid tax on the money initially deposited but not on the earnings, withdrawals from nonqualified plans are only partially taxed at the rate determined by the investor's tax bracket. The investor is taxed only on the amount that exceeds the amount of the contributions made.

IRA types and contribution limits

You'll likely be tested on a few different types of retirement plans and possibly the contribution limits. When you're looking at this section, understand the specifics of the types of plans and view the contribution limits as secondary. The contribution limits change pretty much yearly, and the SIE questions may not change that often. If you have a rough idea of the contribution limits, you should be okay. For updates and additional information, you can go to www.irs.gov/retirement-plans/plan-participant-employee/retirement-topics-ira-contribution-limits.

Traditional IRAs (individual retirement accounts)

IRAs are tax-qualified retirement plans, so deposits into the account are made from pretax dollars (they're tax-deductible). IRAs are completely funded by contributions that the *holder of the account* makes. Regardless of whether individuals are covered by a pension plan, they can still deposit money into an IRA. Here's a list of some of the key points of IRAs:

>> IRAs may be set up as *single life* (when the owner is the beneficiary of the account), *joint and last survivor* (when the sole beneficiary of the account is his or her spouse and the spouse is more than ten years younger than the owner), or *uniform lifetime* (when the spouse is not the sole beneficiary or the spouse is not more than ten years younger than the owner).

>> Permissible investments for IRAs include stocks, bonds, mutual funds, U.S. gold and silver coins, and real estate.

>> The maximum contribution per person is $5,500 per year, with an additional catch-up contribution of $1,000 per person allowed for investors age 50 or older. Excess contributions are taxed at a rate of 6 percent until withdrawn.

>> A husband and wife can have separate accounts with a maximum contribution of $5,500 per year each, whether both are working or one is working.

>> Contributions into the IRA are fully deductible for individuals not covered by employer pension plans.

   If investors are covered by an employer pension plan, deposits into an IRA may or may not be tax-deductible. Although I think that the chances of your being tested on the values are slim, if an individual is covered by an employer pension plan and earns up to $63,000 per year ($101,000 jointly), deposits made into an IRA are fully deductible. The deductions are gradually phased out and disappear when an individual earns more than $73,000 per year ($121,000 jointly).

>> When an investor starts to withdraw funds from an IRA, the investor is taxed on the entire withdrawal (the amount deposited, which was not taxed, and the appreciation in value). The withdrawal is taxed as ordinary income.

>> Withdrawals can't begin before age 59½, or investors have to pay an early withdrawal penalty of 10 percent added to the investor's rate according to his tax bracket. An investor isn't subject to the 10 percent tax penalty in cases of death, disability, first-time homebuyers, and a few other exceptions. Obviously, dead retirees won't be making withdrawals, but their beneficiaries will be. In this case, the beneficiaries aren't hit with the 10 percent penalty.

>> Withdrawals must begin by April 1 of the year after the investor reaches age 70½ (the *required beginning date*, or RBD). Investors who don't take their *required minimum distribution* (RMD) by that time are subject to a 50 percent tax penalty on the amount they should have withdrawn. The IRS provides minimum distribution worksheets to help you determine the amount that needs to be taken in order to avoid the penalty (you can find them at www.irs.gov/ retirement-plans/plan-participant-employee/required-minimum-distribution-worksheets).

>> Deposits into IRAs are allowed up to April 15 (tax day) to qualify as a deduction for the previous year's taxes.

Roth IRAs

Anyone who doesn't make too much money can open a Roth IRA. The key difference between a traditional IRA and a Roth IRA is that withdrawals from a Roth IRA are tax-free. However, deposits made into the Roth IRA are not tax-deductible (made from after-tax dollars). Provided that the investor has held onto the Roth IRA for over five years and has reached age 59½, he can withdraw money from the Roth IRA without incurring any taxable income on the amount deposited or on the appreciation in the account.

REMEMBER

The maximum that an individual may contribute to a traditional IRA and Roth IRA is $5,500 per year combined (or $6,500 if over age 50). There is also a catch-up contribution of $1,000 allowed for individuals age 50 and older.

Investors who have an adjusted gross income of more than $135,000 per year ($199,000 jointly) can't contribute to a Roth IRA.

Simplified employee pensions (SEP-IRAs)

An SEP-IRA is a retirement vehicle designed for small business owners, self-employed individuals, and their employees. SEP-IRAs allow participants to invest money for retirement on a tax-deferred basis. Employers can make tax-deductible contributions directly to their employees' SEP-IRAs. As of 2018, the maximum employer contribution to each employee's SEP-IRA is 25 percent of the employee's compensation (salary, bonuses, and overtime) or $55,000 (subject to cost-of-living increases in the following years), whichever is less. Employees who are part of the plan may still make annual contributions to a traditional or Roth IRA.

401(k) and 403(b)

There are certainly a number of qualified retirement plans besides IRAs. 401(k)s and 403(b)s are two that you should know a little about before taking the SIE exam.

401(k) plans

As stated previously, a 401(k) is a corporate retirement plan. With this type of plan, employees can contribute a percentage of their salary up to a certain amount each year (as such, it's a defined contribution plan). Since it's a qualified plan, the amount contributed by the employee into the 401(k) is deducted from the employee's gross income. In addition, in most cases, the employer matches the employee's contribution up to a certain amount (for example, 25 percent, 50 percent, and so on). The account grows on a tax-deferred basis, so everything withdrawn from the account at retirement is taxable.

403(b) plans

These are salary reduction plans for public school (elementary school, secondary school, college, and so on) employees. As with 401(k)s, employees can elect to have a portion of their pay put into the retirement plan that's tax deferred. However, unlike 401(k)s, the employer doesn't match a percentage of the contributions.

REMEMBER

Because the IRS wants to be able to collect taxes, the holders of IRAs (except for Roth IRAs) and other qualified plan participants must start withdrawing money at a certain point. Plan participants must take a required minimum distribution (RMD) by April 1 of the year after they turn age 70½. In addition, they must continue to take additional minimum distributions each subsequent year until all the money is out of the account.

TIP

You will not likely be asked to figure out the required minimum distribution amount on the SIE exam but for your, your family members', or clients' knowledge, you can work out the required minimum distribution right on the IRS website at www.irs.gov/retirement-plans/plan-participant-employee/retirement-topics-required-minimum-distributions-rmds.

Chapter **16**

No Fooling Around: Rules and Regulations

irst off, I'd like to apologize for having to include this chapter. Unfortunately, rules are a part of life and part of the SIE. When you're reading this, please remember that I didn't make the rules — but I do my best to make them as easy to digest as possible. Rules have become increasingly important on FINRA securities exams like the SIE, especially since the Patriot Act came into the picture.

In this chapter, I cover topics related to rules and regulations. First, I help you understand who the guardians of the market are and their roles in protecting customers and enforcing rules. I also place considerable emphasis on opening, closing, transferring, and handling customers' accounts. And of course, I provide practice questions to guide you on your way.

The Market Watchdogs: Securities Regulatory Organizations

To keep the market running smoothly and to make sure investors aren't abused (at least too much), regulatory organizations stay on the lookout. Although you don't need to know all the minute details about each of them, you do have to know the basics.

The Securities and Exchange Commission

The Securities and Exchange Commission, or SEC, is the major watchdog of the securities industry. Congress created the SEC to regulate the market and to protect investors from fraudulent and manipulative practices. All broker-dealers who transact business with investors and other broker-dealers must register with the SEC. And that registration means something: All broker-dealers have to comply with SEC rules or face censure (an official reprimand), limits on activity, suspension or suspension of one or more associated persons (such as a registered rep or principal), a fine, and/or having their registration revoked.

REMEMBER

SEC investigations may lead to a civil (financial) complaint being filed in a federal court. The SEC may seek disgorgement (taking away) of ill-gotten gains, civil money penalties, and injunctive relief (a cease-and-desist order from the court). If the matter is criminal in nature, the investigation is conducted by the U.S. Attorney's Office and the grand jury.

Among its other numerous functions, you need to be aware that the SEC also enforces the following acts:

>> **The Securities Act of 1933:** The Act of 1933 requires the full and fair disclosure of all material information about a new issue.

>> **The Securities Exchange Act of 1934:** The Act of 1934, which established the SEC, was enacted to protect investors by regulating the over-the-counter (OTC) market and exchanges (such as the NYSE). Chapter 14 tells you more about markets. In addition, the Act of 1934 regulates

- The extension of credit in margin accounts (see Chapter 12)

- The registration and regulation of brokers and dealers

- The registration of securities associations

- Transactions by insiders

- Customer accounts

- Trading activities

>> **The Trust Indenture Act of 1939:** This act prohibits bond issues valued at over $5 million from being offered to investors without an indenture. The trust *indenture* is a written agreement that protects investors by disclosing the particulars of the issue (the coupon rate, the maturity date, any collateral backing the bond, and so on). As part of the Trust Indenture Act of 1939, all companies must hire a trustee who's responsible for protecting the rights of bondholders.

>> **The Investment Company Act of 1940:** This act regulates the registration requirements and the activities of investment companies.

>> **The Investment Advisers Act of 1940:** This act requires the registration of certain investment advisers with the SEC. An investment adviser is a person who receives a fee for giving investment advice. Any investment adviser with at least $25 million of assets under management or anyone who advises an investment company must register with the SEC. All other investment advisers have to register on the state level. The Investment Advisers Act of 1940 regulates

- Record-keeping responsibilities

- Advisory contracts

- Advertising rules

- Custody of customers' assets and funds

Self-regulatory organizations

As you can imagine, due to the unscrupulous nature of some investors and registered representatives, the SEC's job is overwhelming. Fortunately, a few self-regulatory organizations (SROs) are there to take some of the burden off of the SEC's shoulders. Although membership isn't mandatory, most broker-dealers are members of one or more SROs. SRO rules are usually stricter than those of the SEC.

The four types of SROs you need to know for the SIE are the FINRA, MSRB, NYSE, and CBOE:

>> **The FINRA (Financial Industry Regulatory Authority):** The FINRA is a self-regulatory organization that's responsible for the operation and regulation of the over-the-counter market, investment banking (the underwriting of securities), New York Stock Exchange (NYSE) trades, investment companies, limited partnerships, and so on. The FINRA was created in 2007 and is a consolidation of the NASD (National Association of Securities Dealers) and the regulation and enforcement portions of the NYSE (New York Stock Exchange). FINRA is responsible for making sure that its members not only follow FINRA rules but also the rules set forth by the SEC. Additionally, the FINRA is responsible for the handling of complaints against member firms and may take disciplinary action, if necessary. The FINRA is also responsible for administering securities exams such as the SIE (now you know who to blame). FINRA has strict rules (as the other SROs do, I suspect) regarding filing of misleading, incomplete, or inaccurate information as to membership or registration regarding the firm's registration or registration of member associates.

>> **The Municipal Securities Rulemaking Board:** The MSRB was established to develop rules that banks and securities firms have to follow when underwriting, selling, buying, and recommending municipal securities (check out Chapter 8 for info on municipal bonds). The MSRB is subject to SEC oversight but does not enforce SEC rules.

REMEMBER

The MSRB makes rules for firms (and representatives) who sell municipal bonds but doesn't enforce them — it leaves that up to FINRA.

>> **The New York Stock Exchange:** The NYSE is the oldest and largest stock exchange in the United States. The NYSE is responsible for listing securities, setting exchange policies, and supervising the exchange and member firms. The NYSE has the power to take disciplinary action against member firms.

>> **The Chicago Board Options Exchange:** The CBOE is an exchange that makes and enforces option exchange rules.

REMEMBER

Although SROs may be independent, they do work together creating and enforcing rules. FINRA and NYSE can fine, suspend, censure (reprimand), and expel members; however, the FINRA and NYSE can't imprison members who violate the rules and regulations.

TIP

Look at SIE questions with the words *guarantee* or *approve* in them very carefully. The FINRA, SEC, NYSE, and so on do *not* approve or guarantee securities. Any statement that says that they do is false. In addition, because a firm is registered with (or didn't have its registration revoked by) an SRO it does not mean that the SRO approves of the firm, its financial standing, its business, its conduct, and so on. So, member firms and their associates may not claim that they've been approved by the SEC or any SRO.

Investor education and protection

As a way of keeping clients up to date, member firms must send info to customers yearly in writing (which may be electronic). Included in the yearly info is FINRA's BrokerCheck hotline number, FINRA's website address, and a statement as to the availability of an investment brochure.

State regulators

The North American Securities Administrators Association (NASAA) is devoted to investor protection. It is a voluntary association whose membership consists of 67 regulators. NASAA even predates the creation of the SEC (Securities and Exchange Commission). Its key roles include

>> Licensing stockbrokers, smaller investment advisor firms (ones managing less than $100 million in assets), and securities firms conducting business in the state.

>> Registering securities on the state level.

>> Investigating customer complaints and possible cases of investment fraud.

>> Enforcing state securities laws. As such, the NASAA may fine, penalize, provide restitution to investors, assist in prosecuting investment-related criminals, and impose new conduct laws to correct problems as they arise.

>> Examining investment advisor firms and broker-dealers to ensure compliance with securities laws and making sure they keep accurate client records.

>> Reviewing offerings that are not exempt from state law.

>> Providing education to investors regarding their rights and providing information so that they can make more informed financial decisions.

>> Advocating for the passage of state securities laws.

TIP

Don't go crazy trying to remember every minute detail regarding the NASAA; you'll have to know more when taking the Series 63, Series 65, or Series 66. Get a general feeling for what they do so that you're able to recognize them in a question.

Department of the Treasury/IRS

The United States Department of the Treasury (USDT) was established to manage U.S. government revenue. As such, the USDT oversees the printing of all paper currency and minting of all coins. In addition, it is responsible for collecting taxes through the Internal Revenue Service (IRS), it is responsible for managing U.S. government debt securities (T-bonds, T-notes, T-bills, and so on), it licenses banks, and it helps advise U.S. government branches regarding fiscal policy.

FINRA Registration and Reporting Requirements

Persons wanting to register as financial professionals with FINRA (like you) must submit a U4 form. The application includes things like a ten-year employment history and a five-year residential history; if you're registered with another firm, how you're registering (Securities Trader, Financial and Operations Principal, General Securities Representative, and a slew more); states you want to be registered in; and so on. In addition, applicants must submit their fingerprints.

All U4 forms (www.finra.org/file/form-u4-uniform-application-securities-industry-registration-or-transfer) must be thoroughly reviewed by a principal of the firm. Background checks must be performed, and the applicant's employers for the previous three years must be called to verify the applicant's employment history. The calls must be made within 30 days of the firm receiving the U4 form. Special scrutiny of the applicant is required if the applicant has previously worked in the securities industry. Information contained in the U4 form must be complete and not misleading.

The U4 form also contains an *arbitration disclosure*, which states that disputes between the applicant and the member firm will be settled by arbitration.

TIP

Although there is a lot of information listed here that can disqualify a person, most of the information follows a common theme, which makes sense, and you shouldn't have to memorize it all. However, I would suggest you be aware of the ten-year disqualification rule if an individual has been convicted of a felony or certain misdemeanors. In addition, if a registrant includes misleading information or omits information, her registration will be denied.

Note: Non-registered persons may not solicit customers or take orders. In addition, member firms are prohibited from paying commissions, fees, concessions, discounts, and so on to any person who is not registered. The failure of a member firm to register someone who should be registered will likely end in disciplinary action by FINRA.

Disqualification

A person will be *statutorily disqualified* from membership from FINRA under the following circumstances:

>> If he had a felony criminal conviction or certain misdemeanor convictions within the last ten years.

>> If he has had a temporary or permanent injunction (no matter what his age) issued by a court involving a long list of unlawful investment activities.

>> If he has been expelled, barred, or is currently suspended from membership or participation in another self-regulatory organization. This holds true even if the person has been barred with the right to reapply.

>> If he has been barred or current suspension orders are coming from the SEC (Securities and Exchange Commission), CFTC (Commodity Futures Trading Commission), or any other appropriate authority or regulatory agency. As with the preceding rule, this holds true even if the person has been barred with the right to reapply.

>> If he has been denied or had his registration revoked by the CFTC, SEC, or any other appropriate authority or regulatory agency.

>> If it has been found that a member or person has made certain false statements in his application, in reports, or in proceedings before the SEC, SROs, or any other appropriate regulatory authority or agency.

>> If any final order from a state securities commission (or from any agency or state officer performing similar functions), savings association, credit union, any state authority that examines or supervises banks, state insurance commission (or any office or agency performing similar functions), an appropriate federal banking agency, or the National Credit Union Administration

   • Bars said person from association with an entity (such as a broker-dealer, investment advisory firm, and so on) regulated by such commission, agency, authority, or officer, or from engaging in the business of banking, insurance, securities, savings association activities, or credit union activities

   • Constitutes a final order based on violations of any regulations or laws that prohibit manipulative, fraudulent, or deceptive conduct

>> If the SEC, CFTC, or any SRO finds that a person

1. "Willfully" violated federal securities laws, "willfully" violated commodities laws, or "willfully" violated MSRB (Municipal Securities Rulemaking Board) rules

2. "Willfully" aided, commanded, induced, abetted, counseled, or procured violations as set forth in the preceding rule

3. Failed to supervise another person who committed violations as set forth in rule number one

>> If he has certain associations with disqualified persons.

Fingerprints

Under SEC Rule 17f-2 (you don't have to remember the rule number), all employees of a brokerage firm are required to be fingerprinted if they are involved in any of the following activities:

>> Making sales

>> Handling assets (cash and/or certificates)

>> Accessing original books and records

>> Supervising any of the preceding activities

Fingerprints are always required when a person is applying for registration. The fingerprints must be submitted as well as the U4 form. If FINRA doesn't receive the fingerprints within 30 days of the U4 being submitted, the applicant's registration will be deemed inactive.

REMEMBER

The information you provide and your investment professional history don't remain in a bubble. The Central Registration Depository's (CRD's) BrokerCheck allows investors access to vital information that they may need to help them pick the right firm and the right professional, like you. Don't worry; it won't disclose your address, social security number, and the like. However, it will disclose complaints against you and your employer, where you and your employer are registered, exams you passed, if you were convicted or pled guilty to a crime, if you or your broker have been expelled from an SRO, and so on. If a member maintains a website, the site must provide a link to BrokerCheck.

Continuing education

Yes, even after you've passed your securities exams like this one, you're not done. You're required to take continuing education programs as required by FINRA. There are two different elements to continuing education that are a requirement: the firm element and the regulatory element.

Firm element

Member firms must have annual meetings covering the services and strategies offered by the firm. In addition, the meeting must cover any recent regulatory developments, if any. The meetings must be interactive and allow people to ask questions. All registered persons who have direct contact with the public must attend the meeting. All firms must have continuing and current education programs for their covered employees.

Regulatory element

All registered persons are required to take a computer-based training session covering FINRA regulations within 120 days of the registered person's second anniversary and every three years after that. In the event that the training isn't taken within the required period, the person's securities license(s) will be deactivated until it's completed. If the registered person's licenses have been deactivated for two years, the individual will be administratively terminated. If administratively terminated, the person must reapply for registration.

Resignation and termination

If you leave your firm for whatever reason, the member firm you were working for has to file a U5 form with the CRD within 30 days of the date you resigned or were terminated. You will also receive a copy for your records. The U5 form requires the member firm to provide an explanation of why you left or why you were terminated. If you're moving to a new member firm, your new employer must file a new U4 form and receive a copy of the U5 filed by your former employer.

REMEMBER

Things sometimes change, so, if something on your U4 or U5 form is or becomes inaccurate, your firm must update the information on the CRD. This could be something as simple as an address change or some sort of violation or felony conviction.

TIP

Don't wait too long going from one firm to another. After a U5 form has been filed on your behalf, you have up to two years to get registered with another firm or you'll have to take your securities exams all over again. You certainly don't want that to happen.

Associated persons exempt from registration

Certain individuals who work for a member firm are exempt from FINRA registration. These include

>> Persons whose functions are solely clerical or ministerial

>> Persons solely affecting transactions on the floor of a national securities exchange and who are registered with that exchange

>> Persons whose function is solely and exclusively involved in transactions of municipal securities

>> Persons whose function is solely and exclusively involved in transactions of commodities

>> Persons whose function is solely and exclusively involved in transactions in securities futures, as long as that person is registered with a registered futures association

Reporting requirements

Under FINRA Rule 4530, member firms must report specified events, including quarterly statistical and summary information regarding customer complaints, and copies of certain civil and criminal actions. Members must report promptly (no later than 30 days after the member knows or should've known about the event) if the member or associated person of the member

>> Has been found to have violated any securities-related or non-securities-related investment laws or standards of conduct by a U.S. or foreign regulatory organization

>> Is the subject of a written customer complaint involving allegations of theft or misappropriation of funds or securities

>> Is the subject of a written customer complaint involving allegations of forgery

>> Has been named as a defendant or respondent in a proceeding brought by a U.S. or foreign regulatory body alleging a violation of rules

>> Has been denied registration, suspended, expelled, or disciplined by a U.S. or foreign regulatory organization

>> Is indicted, convicted of, or pleads guilty to any felony or certain misdemeanors in or outside of the U.S.

REMEMBER

The preceding list includes firm reporting requirements under Rule 4530, but firms are required to report certain other events too. These include

>> Outside business activities (covered in the following section).

>> Private securities transactions, which are transactions outside the broker-dealer's normal business. For argument's sake, say that an associate of a firm has a client who wants to trade options, but his firm doesn't trade options because it doesn't have an options principal. In this case, with permission of his firm, he can accept the order from his client and do the trade through another firm.

>> Political contributions and consequences for exceeding dollar contribution thresholds (see "Avoiding violations" later in the chapter).

>> Felonies, financial-related misdemeanors, liens, bankruptcies.

Outside business activities

While you're building your business and getting new clients, you may feel the need to make a few extra bucks working another job. If so, you must notify your brokerage firm in writing. However, you don't need to receive written permission to work the other job. Your member firm may reject or restrict your outside work if it feels there is a conflict of interest.

Accounts at other broker-dealers and financial institutions

Although you probably won't do this, persons associated with a member firm may open an account at another member firm (executing firm) with prior written permission from the employing firm. The associated person must also let the executing firm know that she is working for another member firm. Duplicate confirmations and statements must be sent to the employing firm if requested.

Trading by the Book When the Account Is Open

After you've opened a new account, you have to follow additional rules and regulations to keep working in the business. You need to know how to receive trade instructions and how to fill out an order ticket, as well as settlement and payment dates for different securities.

Filling out an order ticket

When you're working as a registered rep, completing documents such as order tickets will become second nature because you'll have them in front of you. When you're taking the SIE, you don't have that luxury, but you still need to know the particulars about what to fill out.

Getting the particulars on paper (or in binary form)

When your customer places an order, you have to fill out an order ticket. Order tickets may be on paper or entered electronically. Regardless of how you enter the order, it needs to contain the following information:

>> The registered rep's identification number

>> The customer's account number

>> The description of the security (stocks, bonds, symbol, and so on)

>> The number of shares or bonds that are being purchased or sold

>> Whether the registered rep has discretionary authority over the account

>> Whether the customer is buying, selling long (selling securities that are owned), or selling short (selling borrowed securities — see Chapter 12)

>> For option tickets, whether the customer is buying or writing (selling), is covered or uncovered, and is opening or closing (see Chapter 11 for info on options)

>> Whether it's a market order, good-till-canceled (GTC) order, day order, and so on

>> Whether the trade is executed in a cash or margin account

>> Whether the trade was solicited or unsolicited

>> The time of the order

>> The execution price

Figure 16-1 shows you what standard paper order tickets may look like.

Designating unsolicited trades

Normally, you'll be recommending securities in line with a customer's investment objectives. If, however, the customer requests a trade that you think is unsuitable, it's your duty to inform him about it. You don't have to reject the order (it's the customer's money, and you're in the business to generate commission). If the customer still wants to execute the trade, simply mark the order as *unsolicited*, which takes the responsibility off your shoulders.

A trip to the principal's office: Securing a signature

Principals are managers of a firm. All brokerage firms must have *at least two principals* (unless the firm is a sole proprietorship). When you open or trade an account, you have to bring the new account form or order ticket to a principal to sign. Principals need to approve all new accounts, all trades in accounts, and all advertisements and sales literature; they also handle all complaints (lucky break for you!), oversee employees, and watch for potential red flags. A principal doesn't have to approve a prospectus or your recommendations to your customers.

BUY

B	EXCHANGE	BRANCH	ACCOUNT No.	TYPE	R.R. No.	DAY / OPEN
QUANTITY	SECURITY			PRICE LIMIT		EXECUTION PRICE

CUSTOMER NAME AND ADDRESS	SOLICITED _	CANCEL
	UNSOLICITED _	
	DISCRET'Y A/C _	
	AMOUNT	
FUNDS, LOCATION	INTEREST	
	COM.	
BOUGHT FROM		
	NET	

NEW			BROKERAGE	SOARING SECURITIES	CHECKED BY

SELL

S	EXCHANGE	BRANCH	ACCOUNT No.	TYPE	R.R. No.	LONG / SHORT	DAY / OPEN
QUANTITY	SECURITY			PRICE LIMIT			EXECUTION PRICE

CUSTOMER NAME AND ADDRESS	SOLICITED _	CANCEL
	UNSOLICITED _	
	DISCRET'Y A/C _	
	AMOUNT	
SECURITY LOCATION	INTEREST OR ST. TAX	
	SEC.	
SOLD TO	COM.	
	NET	

EXEC. BRKR.	BROKERAGE	SOARING SECURITIES	CHECKED BY

FIGURE 16-1: Buy and sell order tickets have spaces for the info you need to make a trade.

Although you'll generally bring an order ticket to a principal right after taking an order, the principal can sign the order ticket later in the day. If you're questioned about this on the SIE exam, you want to answer that the principal needs to approve the trade on the same day, not before or immediately after the trade.

REMEMBER

Proportionate sharing

Members or associated persons are prohibited from sharing in the profits or losses in a customer's account. An exception to this rule is if the associated person contributed to the account. In that case, the associated person needs a written authorization from the customer and principal, and the profits and/or losses are shared by the customer and associated member based on the percentage contributed. Exempt from the rule of proportional sharing are accounts of immediate family (parents, mother-in-law, father-in-law, spouse, or children) of the associated member.

Checking your calendar: Payment and settlement dates

Securities that investors purchase have different payment and settlement dates. Here's what you need to know:

>> **Trade date:** The day the trade is executed. An investor who buys a security owns the security as soon as the trade is executed, whether or not he has paid for the trade.

>> **Settlement date:** The day the issuer updates its records and the certificates are delivered to the buyer's brokerage firm.

>> **Payment date:** The day the buyer of the securities must pay for the trade.

TIP

Unless the question specifically asks you to follow FINRA or NYSE rules (which I doubt it will), assume the Fed regular way settlement and payment dates as they appear in Table 16-1. The FINRA and NYSE rules both require payment for securities to be made no later than the settlement date, but the Federal Reserve Board states that the payment date for corporate securities is five business days after the trade date.

TABLE 16-1 ## Regular Way Settlement and Payment Dates

Type of Security	Settlement Date (in Business Days after the Trade Date)	Payment Date (in Business Days after the Trade Date)
Stocks and corporate bonds	2 (T+2 — two business days after the trade date)	4
Municipal bonds	2 (T+2)	2
U.S. government bonds	1 (T+1)	1
Options	1 (T+1)	4

REMEMBER

Cash trades (which are same-day settlements) require payment for the securities and delivery of the securities on the same day as the trade date.

In certain cases, securities may not be able to be delivered as in the preceding chart. In these cases, the seller may specify that there's going to be a *delayed delivery*. There can also be a *mutually agreed upon* date in which the buyer and seller agree on a delayed delivery date prior to or at the time of the transaction.

The *when, as, and if issued (when-issued transaction)* method of delivery is used for a securities issue that has been authorized and sold to investors before the certificates are ready for delivery. This method is typically used for stock splits, new issues of municipal bonds, and Treasury securities (U.S. government securities). The settlement date for when-issued securities can be any of the following:

>> A date to be assigned

>> Two business days after the securities are ready for delivery

>> On the date determined by the FINRA

Regulation S-P

According to Regulation S-P, broker-dealers, investment companies, and investment advisors must "adopt written policies and procedures that address administrative, technical, and physical safeguards for the protection of customer records and information." This means that members must provide a way for securing customers' nonpublic information, such as social security numbers, bank account numbers, or any other personally identifiable financial information. Members must provide customers with a notice of their privacy policies. Members may disclose a customer's nonpublic information to unaffiliated third parties unless the customer opts out and chooses not to have his information shared. Members must make every effort to safeguard customers' information, including securing computers, encrypting emails, and so on.

Confirming a trade

A *trade confirmation* (receipt of trade) is the document you send to a customer after a trade has taken place. You have to send out trade confirmations after each trade, at or before the completion of the transaction (the settlement date). Here's a list of information included in the confirmation:

>> The customer's account number

>> The registered rep's ID number

>> The trade date

>> Whether the customer bought (BOT), sold (SLD), or sold short

>> A description of the security purchased or sold

>> The number of shares of stock or the par value of bonds purchased or sold

>> The yield (if bonds)

>> The Committee on Uniform Security Identification Procedures (CUSIP) number, a security ID number

>> The price of the security

>> The total amount paid or received, not including commission or any fees

>> The commission, which is added on purchases and subtracted on sales (if the broker-dealer purchased for or sold from its own inventory, the markdown or markup doesn't have to be disclosed)

>> The *net amount,* or the amount the customer paid or received after adding or subtracting the commission (if the investor purchased or sold bonds, the accrued interest is added or subtracted during this calculation)

>> Whether the trade was executed on a principal or agency basis (the capacity)

REMEMBER

You should recognize the items listed in the preceding list, which are required for most securities trades including municipal bonds. However, the MSRB tends to be a little stricter and also requires the following information:

>> Whether the member acted as an agent for both the customer and another person for the same trade

>> The time of execution for institutional accounts or transactions in municipal fund securities

>> The settlement date

- » Yield-to-maturity or yield-to-call, whichever is lower

- » Final monies, including the total dollar amount of the transaction and accrued interest if applicable

- » Whether there's any credit backing the securities (for revenue bonds, the source of revenue; or if there's insurance backing the bonds)

- » Any special features of the bonds (callable, puttable, stepped coupon, book-entry only, and so on)

- » Information on the status of the securities (pre-refunded, called, escrowed to maturity, securities in default, and so on)

- » Tax information (taxable, nontaxable, subject to alternative minimum tax, original issue discount)

Financial exploitation of specified adults

With people living longer and the number of seniors increasing, FINRA has recently created rules to help curb or handle cases of financial exploitations of specified adults (seniors — natural persons aged 65 or older — and natural persons aged 18 or older who have mental or physical impairments that render them unable to protect their own interests). In the event that a member believes that the financial exploitation of specified adults has or may be taking place, Rule 2165 allows the member to place a temporary hold on the specified adult's funds or securities.

The SIE and other FINRA exams cover topics related to protecting seniors, including

- » Firms' marketing and communications to investors aged 65 and older

- » Information required when opening an account for a senior

- » Any disclosures provided to senior investors

- » Complaints filed by senior investors as well as how the firm handles the complaints

- » Supervision of registered reps as they communicate with senior investors

- » The suitability and types of securities marketed and sold to senior investors

- » The training of a firm's representatives as to how they are to handle the accounts of specified adults

FINRA recently created a helpline for seniors to provide support and assistance.

PHYSICAL VERSUS BOOK ENTRY

Although many years ago almost all delivery of stock certificates and debt securities (bonds) was in physical form (meaning you actually received the certificate), most delivery and settlement now is in book-entry form. Even though your don't get to actually hold your oft-times cool-looking certificates, book entry helps save money and makes trading much easier. When purchasing securities via book entry, you will receive a receipt of trade, showing you own the securities but will not receive the actual certificates. A record of your trading activity is kept on the financial institution's books. When it comes time to sell the securities, nothing has to be transferred; it is just changed on the institution's books and you receive confirmation (receipt) of the trade.

Borrowing from or lending to . . .

Registered persons associated with a member firm are prohibited from borrowing money from a customer or lending money to a customer unless the member firm has written procedures allowing borrowing and lending money between registered persons and customers, and one of the following applies:

>> The customer is a member of the registered person's immediate family (spouse, mother, father, mother-in-law, father-in-law, children)

>> The customer is a financial institution such as a bank that is in the business of providing credit, financing, or loans

>> The customer and the registered person are both registered under the same member firm

>> The customer and the registered person have a personal relationship outside of the broker-customer relationship

>> The customer and the registered person have a business relationship outside of the broker-customer relationship

REMEMBER

This only works if the member firm allows borrowing from or lending to customers. The registered member would have to notify and get written approval from his firm prior to entering into a buying or lending arrangement unless it's not required in the firm's written rules.

Following up with account statements

An *account statement* gives the customer information about his holdings in the account along with the market value at the time the statement was issued. Customers are supposed to receive account statements on a regular basis. The timing for issuing account statements should be pretty easy for you to remember. Here's how often you have to send out statements, from most to least often (remember the acronym *AIM*):

>> **Active accounts:** If any trading was executed within the month, the customer must receive an account statement for that month.

>> **Inactive accounts:** If the customer is not actively trading his account and is just holding a position, an account statement must be sent out at least quarterly (every three months).

>> **Mutual funds:** No matter how much (or little) trading was done, a customer needs to receive an account statement semiannually (every six months).

REMEMBER

Customers may not only want to know how their accounts are doing, they may wonder about the condition of the firm that they're working with. So, upon request by a customer, a member firm must disclose its financial condition by delivering its most recent balance sheet (not income statement). The balance sheet may be delivered in paper form or in electronic form (email) if the customer agrees to the electronic delivery.

Keeping your dividend dates straight

When customers are purchasing securities of a company that's in the process of declaring or paying a dividend, you need to be able to tell those customers whether they're entitled to receive the dividend. Because stock transactions settle in three business days, the customers are entitled to the dividend if they purchase the securities at least three days prior to the *record date*. Here's a list of the four need-to-know dates for the SIE exam:

REMEMBER

>> **Declaration date:** The day that the corporation officially announces that a dividend will be paid to shareholders.

>> **Ex-dividend date:** The first day that the stock trades without dividends. An investor purchasing the stock on the ex-dividend date isn't entitled to receive the dividend; because stock transactions take two business days to settle, the ex-dividend date is automatically one business day before the record date.

The ex-dividend date is the day that the price of the stock is reduced by the dividend amount. (Chapter 6 tells you more about dividends and related calculations.) When a stock is purchased ex-dividend (on or after the ex-dividend date), the seller is entitled to the dividend, not the buyer. Because the dividend may not be paid for up to a month, the buyer is required to sign a *due bill* indicating that the dividend belongs to the seller. In the case of a cash dividend, the due bill is in the form of a *due bill check,* which is payable on the date the dividend is paid by the issuer. In addition, if an investor buys a stock on time to receive a dividend but for some reason will not receive the certificates on time (by the record date), the seller must send a *due bill* to the buyer. A due bill states that the buyer is entitled to the rights of ownership even though he's not yet receiving the certificates.

>> **Record date:** The day the corporation inspects its records to see who gets the dividend. To receive the dividend, the investor must be listed as a stockholder in company records.

>> **Payment (payable) date:** The day that the corporation pays the dividend.

As you can see from the diagram, the buyer receives the dividend if he purchases the stock before the ex-dividend date. If the stock is purchased on or after the ex-dividend date, the seller receives the dividend.

To help you remember the sequence of dates, use the phrase *Don't Eat Rubber Pickles.* I know it sounds ridiculous, but the more ridiculous, the easier it is to remember.

TIP

REMEMBER

The board of directors must announce three dates: the declaration date, the record date, and the payment date. The ex-dividend date doesn't need to be announced because it's automatically one business day before the record date. However, mutual funds have to announce all four dates because they may set their ex-dividend date at any time (even on the record date).

The following question tests your ability to answer a dividend question.

EXAMPLE

Wedgie Corp. has just announced a $0.50 cash dividend. If the record date is Tuesday, March 9, when is the last day an investor can purchase the stock and receive the dividend?

(A) March 4

(B) March 5

(C) March 7

(D) March 8

The answer you're looking for is Choice (B). In order for an investor to purchase the stock and receive a previously declared dividend, he must purchase the stock at least one business day before the ex-dividend date. This question is a little more difficult because you have a weekend to take into consideration.

The ex-dividend date is March 8, which is one business day prior to the record date. This investor has to buy the stock before the ex-dividend date in order to receive the dividend, so he has to buy it March 5 or before (because the 6th and 7th are Saturday and Sunday). The last day an investor can purchase the stock and receive the dividend is March 5.

REMEMBER

If a stock is sold short (if the investor is selling a borrowed security), the lender of the stock sold short is entitled to receive the dividend. (See Chapter 9 for details on margin accounts.) Also, the trades in the example problems are regular way settlement (three business days after the trade date); remember that cash transactions settle on the same day as the trade date. In the case of dividends, if an investor purchases stock for cash, he receives the dividend if he purchases the stock anytime up to and including the record date.

Handling complaints

It's bound to happen sooner or later, no matter how awesome you are as a registered rep: One of your customers is going to complain about something (like unauthorized trades, guarantees, and so on). Complaints aren't considered official unless they're in *writing*. If necessary, FINRA wants you to follow the proper procedure for handling complaints. The following sections cover formal and informal proceedings.

Code of procedure (litigation)

The *code of procedure* is the FINRA's formal procedure for handling securities-related complaints between public customers and members of the securities industry (broker-dealers, registered reps, clearing corporations, and so on). The public customer has the choice of resolving the complaint via the formal code of procedure or the informal code of arbitration (see the next section).

In the code of procedure, the District Business Conduct Committee (DBCC) has the first jurisdiction over complaints. If the customer or member isn't satisfied with the results, he can appeal the decision to the FINRA Board of Governors. Decisions are appealable all the way to the Supreme Court.

Code of arbitration

The *code of arbitration* is an informal hearing (heard by two or three arbiters) that's primarily conducted for disputes between members of the FINRA. Members include not only broker-dealers but also individuals working for member firms.

For example, if you (a registered rep) have a dispute with the broker-dealer that you're working for, you can take the broker-dealer to arbitration. If a customer has a complaint against a broker-dealer or registered rep, the customer has the choice of going through code of procedure (see the preceding section) or code of arbitration, unless the customer has given prior written consent (usually by way of the new account form) stating that he will settle disputes only through arbitration.

REMEMBER

The decisions in arbitration are binding and non-appealable, so they're less costly than court action. If a member firm or person associated with that member firm fails to comply with the terms of the arbitration (in the case of a loss) within 15 days of notification, FINRA reserves the right to suspend or cancel the firm's or person's membership.

Mediation

If an investor and/or broker-dealer are looking for a more informal way to handle disputes, they may voluntarily decide to go to mediation. Disputes settled through mediation are heard by an independent third party. Unlike arbitration, mediation is nonbinding.

REMEMBER

Not all complaints end up going to arbitration, to mediation, or through the court system. Sometimes, the complaints are the result of miscommunication, such as instances in which the customer made a mistake, a customer feels he was charged too much commission, and so on. A lot of these complaints can be handled internally without the need for progression. However, all complaints need to be kept on file along with any action taken.

Retail communications

To help promote their business and to keep customers up to date, member firms continually send out sales literature, publish ads, run commercials, send out research reports, have scripted seminars, and so on. As you can imagine, ads and such cannot omit material facts, exaggerate, or be fraudulent or misleading, and must also explain the potential risks along with the potential benefits. You've probably heard the old disclaimers "past performance does not indicate future performance" and "people can and do lose money" on radio ads. Believe me, they wouldn't put those in unless they had to. FINRA divides communication into three categories:

» **Correspondence:** Any written communication (including electronic) distributed or made available to *25 or fewer* retail investors (ones that are not institutional investors) within a 30-calendar-day period.

» **Retail communication:** Similar to correspondence (see the preceding bullet) but made available to *more than 25* retail investors within a 30-calendar-day period.

» **Institutional communication:** Any written communication (including electronic) distributed or made available only to institutional investors, but not including a member's internal communications. Institutional investors include government entities, member firms and registered persons, employee benefit plans, a person acting solely on behalf of any such institutional investor, and so on.

REMEMBER

As with just about everything that happens at a brokerage firm, retail communications must be approved by a qualified principal of the firm. Research reports on particular securities must be approved by a supervisory analyst who has expertise in the particular product. Testimonials (if any) must be made by a person who has the knowledge and experience to have a valid opinion. Member firms are in many cases required to file retail communications with FINRA ten business days prior to first use. Members are required to keep the communications for a minimum of three years.

Record-keeping

As you can imagine, member firms must keep certain records on file. Depending on which records they are, there are certain SEC retention requirements. The records do not necessarily need to be kept in written format; they can be kept digitally as long as they are in a non-erasable format.

Corporate or partnership documents of the member firm must be kept for the *lifetime* of the firm. The documents must contain the list of officers, partners, and/or directors of the firm. Additionally, U4 forms of all active employees must be kept as long as the firm is in business.

The following records must be kept for a minimum of *six years*:

>> **Blotters:** Records of all trades executed by the brokerage firm for clients and for their own inventory.

>> **Ledgers:** Customer account statements, which include trade settlement dates.

>> **General ledgers:** A firm's financial statements, which must be updated monthly. A general ledger includes the firm's assets, liabilities, and net worth.

>> **Position record:** A record of all the securities owned by the firm and its location.

>> **Account record:** Terms and conditions of margin accounts and cash accounts.

>> **Closed accounts:** Firms must keep records of customers who've closed accounts for a minimum of six years after the account has been closed.

Note: Like FINRA rules, MSRB rules require blotters, ledgers, closed accounts, and position records to be kept for six years. However, MSRB also requires records relating to the underwriting of municipal securities, complaints (FINRA, four years), supervisory records, and gift records to be kept for six years.

The following records must be kept for a minimum of *3 years*:

>> U4 forms, U5 forms, and fingerprints of former employees

>> Trade confirmations

>> Order tickets

>> Advertisements

>> Sales literature

>> Dividends and interest received in each account

>> Powers of attorney

>> Speeches/public appearances

>> Compliance procedure manuals

>> Gifts

>> Compensation records of associates

Note: MSRB rules require members to maintain certain records for *four years*. These include subsidiary ledgers, trades, confirmations, terms and conditions of customer accounts, checkbooks and canceled checks, delivery of official statements, public communications, and so on.

Whether the records have to be kept for three years, six years, or whatever, they have to be easily accessible for two years (FINRA and MSRB).

As you can imagine, there are strict penalties for falsification, improper maintenance, or improper retention of records. FINRA reserves the right to inspect the books, records, and accounts of all member firms and their associates. All regulatory requests by FINRA for specified books, records, or accounts should be supplied by the member firm *promptly*.

Committing Other Important Rules to Memory

Brokers and investors must follow numerous rules in order to keep themselves from facing fines or worse. In this section, I list a few of the more important rules.

Sticking to the 5 percent markup policy

The 5 percent policy (FINRA 5 Percent Markup Policy) is more of a guideline than a rule. The policy was enacted to make sure that investors receive fair treatment and aren't charged excessively for broker-dealer services in the over-the-counter (OTC) market. The guideline says that brokerage firms shouldn't charge commissions, markups, or markdowns of more than 5 percent for standard trades.

The following trades are subject to the 5 percent markup policy:

>> **Principal (dealer) transactions:** A firm buys securities for or sells securities from its own inventory and charges a markdown or markup.

>> **Agency (broker) transactions:** A firm acts as a middleman (broker) and charges a commission.

>> **Riskless (simultaneous) transactions:** A firm buys a security for its own inventory for immediate resale to the customer (riskless to the firm).

>> **Proceeds transactions:** A firm sells a security and uses the money to immediately buy another security. You must treat this transaction as one trade (you can't charge on the way out and on the way in).

The 5 percent markup policy covers *over-the-counter trades of outstanding, nonexempt securities with public customers.* If securities are exempt from SEC registration, or if they're new securities that require a prospectus, they're exempt from the 5 percent policy. Additionally, if a dealer pays $20 per share to have a security in inventory (dealer cost) and the market price is $8 per share, the dealer can't charge customers $20 per share so that it doesn't take a loss.

Under extenuating circumstances, the brokerage firm may charge more. Justifiable reasons for charging more (or less) than 5 percent include

>> Experiencing difficulty buying or selling the security because the market price is too low or too high

>> Handling a small trade — for example, if a customer were to place an order for $100 worth of securities, you'd lose your shirt if you were to charge only 5 percent ($5); in this case, you wouldn't be out of line if you were to charge 100 percent (by the same token, if a customer were to purchase $1 million worth of securities, 5 percent [$50,000] would be considered excessive)

- **»** Encountering difficulty locating and purchasing a specific security

- **»** Incurring additional expenses involved in executing the trade

- **»** Dealing with odd lot trades (trades for less than the normal unit of trading — typically 100 shares)

- **»** Trading non-liquid securities

- **»** Executing transactions on foreign markets

REMEMBER

The 5 percent markup policy is a guideline and not a hard and fast rule. There are situations where charging a customer 5 percent would be considered excessive. For argument's sake, say you're lucky enough to have a customer who routinely likes to make trades of $1 million and you charge her 5 percent — that would be $50,000 in commission for one trade. In that case, you would definitely be frowned upon, so you may charge that customer 1 percent or maybe half a percent.

Note: The 5 percent markup policy is a guideline that member firms should use when making trades. However, firms may also charge customers for services performed other than trading securities. These services include collection of monies due for principal, interest, or dividends. They may also charge for the exchange or transfer of securities or the safekeeping of customers' securities. The main thing for you to remember is that the charges should be reasonable and not unfairly discriminatory (in other words, all customers should be charged the same for the same services performed).

Avoiding violations

It's up to your firm and you to understand violations and avoid them. FINRA expects its members and their representatives to "observe high standards of commercial honor and just and equitable principles of trade."

REMEMBER

You need to be aware of some violations not only for the SIE exam but also so you stay out of trouble. Of course the entire book and this chapter are filled with rules and violations. However, some violations can be summed up in a sentence or two (or three) — that's what this section is for. Some of the violations are more connected with broker–dealers, some with registered reps, and some with investment advisors. Violators are subject to sanctions such as fines, censures, suspensions, expulsions, and so on.

- **»** **Commingling of funds:** Combining a customer's fully paid and margined securities or combining a firm's securities with customer securities.

- **»** **Interpositioning:** Having two securities dealers act as agents for the same exact trade, so that two commissions are earned on one trade.

- **»** **Giving (or receiving) gifts:** Giving or receiving a gift of more than $100 per customer per year. Business expenses (lunch, dinner, hotel rooms, and so on) are exempt from this MSRB rule (see "Self-regulatory organizations," earlier in this chapter).

- **»** **Making political contributions (paying to play):** Under the Investment Advisers Act of 1940, investment advisors are prohibited from providing investment advisory services for a fee to a government client for two years after a contribution is made. This rule applies not only to the advisor, executives, and employees making contributions to certain elected officials but also to candidates who may later be elected. In addition, investment advisors are prohibited from soliciting contributions for elected officials or candidates if the investment advisor is seeking or providing government business.

>> **Falsifying or withholding documents:** Firms cannot make up information or withhold needed documents from customers or any SRO.

>> **Signatures of convenience:** Basically, forging a customer's signature even if approved by the customer is a violation.

>> **Guarantees:** Members and associates are prohibited from making guarantees against loss in any securities transaction or in any securities account of a customer.

>> **Improper use:** Members and associates are prohibited from making improper use of a customer's securities or funds.

>> **Freeriding:** Allowing a customer to buy or sell securities without paying for the purchase.

>> **Backing away:** Failure on the part of a securities dealer to honor a firm quote.

>> **Churning:** A violation whereby a registered rep excessively trades a customer's account for the sole purpose of generating commission.

>> **Use of manipulative, deceptive, or other fraudulent devices:** Members are prohibited from inducing the sale or purchase of any security by means of manipulation, deception, or any other fraudulent device or contrivance.

>> **Trading ahead of research reports:** No member shall trade a security based on information received from a research report prior to that research report being released publicly.

>> **Trading ahead of customer orders:** Members are prohibited from placing their order ahead of a customer's order. Their job is to get their customer the best price, and placing their order ahead of the customer's will likely cause the customer to get a worse price.

>> **Not disclosing a financial relationship with the issuer:** It is a violation to not disclose if your firm has a financial relationship (it is controlled by, has controlling interest in, or is under common control with) the issuer. In the event that there is a financial relationship, it must be disclosed (given to or sent to) the customer prior to the completion of the transaction.

>> **Frontrunning:** A violation in which a registered rep executes a trade for himself, his firm, or a discretionary account based on knowledge of a block trade (10,000 shares or more) before the trade is reported on the ticker tape.

>> **Prearranging trades:** A prearranged trade is an illegal agreement between a registered rep and a customer to buy back a security at a fixed price.

>> **Paying for referrals:** Members or persons associated with a member (for example, registered reps) are prohibited from paying cash or noncash compensation to any person except those registered with the member firm or other FINRA members. A violation occurs in the event that compensation is paid to a nonmember for locating, introducing, or referring a client.

Some violations include some sort of *market manipulation.* These include

>> **Market rumors:** Members are prohibited from spreading false market rumors that may prompt others to either buy or sell a security.

>> **Pump and dump:** This is fake news that most often happens with penny stocks. In this case, the promoters send out mass emails or regular mail to paint a glowing report on a particular security, thus pumping it up. Because of the positive reports, many investors purchase the security and drive the price up. At that point, the promoters sell (dump) their shares for a nice profit.

>> **Excessive trading:** A violation whereby a trader places both buy and sell orders on the same security around the same time, thus making it look like there's a lot of trading activity on that security.

» **Marking the open/marking the close:** Executing a series of trades within minutes of the open or close to manipulate the price of a security.

» **Matching orders:** Illegally manipulating the price of a security to make the trading volume appear larger than it really is, such as two brokerage firms working in concert by trading the same security back and forth.

» **Painting the tape:** Creating the illusion of trading activity due to misleading reports on the consolidated tape — for example, reporting a trade of 10,000 shares of stock as two separate trades for 5,000 shares each.

» **Paying the media:** A violation in which brokerage firms or affiliated persons pay an employee of the media (website, newspaper, magazine, radio, TV show, and so on) to affect the price of a security; for example, paying a TV stock expert to recommend a security that the firm has in its inventory.

» **Anti-intimidation/Coordination:** Members may not intimidate (threaten, harass, coerce, and so on) other members into changing their price(s) on a security. In addition, a member may not coordinate with another member to adjust the price of a security.

Gifts and gratuities

It is considered a violation for a member firm to distribute cash or noncash compensation to the employees of another member firm regarding the sale and distribution of securities unless all of the following apply:

» The compensation is not conditional on sales by the other firm.

» It has prior approval from the other member firm.

» The total amount of compensation does not exceed the limit of $100 per year.

Noncash compensation could be season tickets for the Jets, sending someone on vacation, gift certificates, and so on. Providing an occasional meal, ticket to a sporting event, and such are considered acceptable business entertainment expenses as long as they're neither too expensive nor too frequent. And, certain noncash expenses are considered okay as long as they're business related — for example, paying for a business dinner, paying for a seminar, providing airline tickets, and so on. In addition, you don't have to keep track of things that provide advertising, such as pens with your name on them, coffee mugs with your picture, and so on.

Also, FINRA wants to make sure that members and their associates are making recommendations based on their belief that they fall in line with their customer's investment strategy and their belief that the product(s) recommended is/are the right ones. So, in order to curb potential conflict of interest, similar cash and noncash compensation rules are put in place for program sponsors, such as investment companies. FINRA just wants to make sure that recommendations are not based on the fact that members or their associates owe someone.

Following the money: Anti-money-laundering rules

The *Bank Secrecy Act* establishes the U.S. Treasury Department as the regulator for anti-money laundering programs. All broker-dealers are required to develop programs to detect possible money-laundering abuses. In addition, all broker-dealers must review the Office of Foreign Asset Control's (OFAC) Specially Designated National's (SDN) list to make sure that they're not doing business with individuals or organizations that are on the list. Anti-money-laundering programs are designed to help prevent dirty money that has been cleaned (made to look like it came from a legitimate source) from being used to fund terrorist activities, illegal arms sales, drug trafficking, and so on. Here are three stages of money laundering that you must be aware of for the SIE exam (please, don't try this at home):

1. **Placement**

In this initial stage of money laundering, the funds, derived from criminal activity, are transferred into the financial system (typically via banks and broker-dealers).

2. **Layering**

Layering is the money launderers' attempt to disguise the source of the funds, usually by moving the funds from one place to another through a series of transactions.

3. **Integration**

Integration is the final stage of money laundering, when illegal funds are mixed *(commingled)* with legitimate funds. Launderers usually accomplish this step through businesses that operate using cash, importing and exporting companies, and so on.

REMEMBER

Broker–dealers and other financial institutions must report any *cash or cash equivalent* deposits, withdrawals, or transfers of *$10,000* or more through a Currency Transaction Report (CTR) to FinCEN (the U.S. Treasury Financial Crimes Network). An institution must report suspicious activity of *$5,000 or more of any type of transaction* to FinCEN by filing a Suspicious Activity Report (SAR).

Here are some indications of money laundering at the opening of the account:

>> Concern with U.S. government reporting requirements

>> Reluctance to reveal information about business activities

>> Suspect ID such as a license or passport that looks like it was made in someone's basement

>> Irrational transactions that are inconsistent with objectives

>> A fiduciary (the person who can legally make decisions for another investor) who's reluctant to provide information about the customer

>> An individual's lack of general knowledge of his industry

And here are some shady signals to look out for after the account is open:

>> Making deposits of large amounts of cash or money orders

>> *Structuring* — making cash or cash-equivalent deposits (such as money orders) of just under $10,000 to avoid having them be reported to the U.S. government

>> Making wire transfers to non-cooperative countries

>> Engaging in sudden and unexplained wire activity

>> Making a deposit and transferring it to another party without any business purpose

>> Buying a long-term investment and liquidating it in the short term

>> Making transfers between multiple accounts for no apparent reason

>> Depositing bearer bonds and requesting the money immediately

>> Displaying a total lack of concern about risks and commissions

TIP

The signs of money laundering tend to make sense, so when answering an SIE exam question about money laundering, think to yourself, "If it looks like a duck and quacks like a duck, it's probably a duck" — or in financial terms, "If it looks and seems like money laundering, it's probably money laundering."

AML compliance program

Under the Bank Secrecy Act, all financial institutions, including broker-dealers, must develop and carry out anti-money laundering (AML) programs. These programs must be approved in writing by a firm's senior management. Financial institutions and broker-dealers must do the following:

>> Initiate and carry out policies and procedures designed to detect and report suspicious transactions

>> Initiate and carry out policies, procedures, and internal controls that are designed to comply with the Bank Secrecy Act's regulations

>> Set up annual independent testing to make sure that the firm is complying with the AML rules under the Bank Secrecy Act

>> Appoint and indicate to FINRA (by name, title, email address, phone number, and so on) the people responsible for implementing and overseeing the daily internal controls of its AML program

REMEMBER

AML programs are not necessarily static and are subject to change. Each firm is responsible for making sure that its AML programs remain current.

Insider trading rules

Insider trading is a violation that occurs when an individual trades a particular publicly traded security based on information that has not been released (or adequately released) to the public (known as *material nonpublic information*). According to the Insider Trading and Securities Fraud Enforcement Act of 1988, both the tipper (the one who shared the nonpublic information) and the tippee (the one who traded based on the tip) are liable.

Charges of insider trading have been brought against

>> Officers, directors, and employees of a corporation who traded the corporation's securities after learning of important, confidential corporate developments

>> Family members, friends, business associates, and other people (tippees) who received tips from the officers, directors, and employees who traded the corporate securities based on confidential information received

>> Government employees who traded based on confidential information received because of their employment with the government which has not (or not yet) been released to the public

>> Employees of brokerage, banking, law, and printing firms who executed trades based on confidential information received as part of their job

>> Political intelligence consultants who have given tips or traded based on material nonpublic information they received from government employees

>> Other persons who have taken advantage of or traded on confidential information they received from employers, friends, family, and others

REMEMBER

Putting it in simple terms, material nonpublic (inside) information is information that could affect the market value of a security but the information has not been released (or adequately released) to the public.

Penalties for insider trading

As you can imagine, the penalties for insider trading are pretty severe.

» The maximum criminal fine for an individual is $5 million per violation and $25 million per business per violation.

» The maximum prison sentence is 20 years per violation.

» The maximum civil sanctions are three times the gain or three times the loss avoided plus disgorgement of profits.

Contemporaneous traders

Persons who enter orders at or about the same time as the person trading on inside information on the opposite side of the market are called contemporaneous traders. So, for argument's sake, if the person with inside information sold shares of ABC common stock due to inside information, a contemporaneous trader would be one who bought shares of ABC common stock at or about the same time (and vice versa). In this case, the contemporaneous trader may actually sue the person who violated the insider trading rules. The suits may be initiated up to five years after the occurrence.

The Investor's Bankruptcy Shield: FDIC and SIPC

The Federal Deposit Insurance Corporation (FDIC) provides deposit insurance, which guarantees a certain level of safety to people who have money on deposit at a bank. FDIC protects accounts from bank failure (bankruptcy). At the present time, each depositor is protected up to $250,000.

The Securities Investor Protection Corporation (SIPC), which was created under the Securities Investor Protection Act of 1970, protects the customer against broker-dealer bankruptcy. Although it's not a government agency, this private, nonprofit organization was created by the government in 1970. The SIPC protects each separate customer's assets (securities and cash) up to $500,000 total, of which no more than $250,000 can be cash.

Although brokerage firms are required to follow *net capital rules* — specifically, SEC Rule 15c3-1 — that are designed to minimize the chances of broker-dealer failure and protect customer assets, broker-dealers occasionally (too often) declare bankruptcy.

All members must advise clients at the opening of the account of the availability of SIPC protection and must provide an SIPC brochure and info on contacting SIPC, including the SIPC's web address and telephone number. In addition, clients must receive all that same info in writing at least once a year.

The following question concerns SIPC coverage.

EXAMPLE

John Fredericks has a cash account with $150,000 in securities and $300,000 cash and a margin account with $50,000 in equity. Additionally, John has a joint cash account with his wife Mary with $250,000 in securities and $300,000 cash. If John's broker–dealer goes bankrupt, what is his coverage under SIPC?

(A) $450,000

(B) $500,000

(C) $850,000

(D) $950,000

The right choice is (D). If one of your customers has a cash and margin account titled under one name, as John does, it's treated as though it belongs to one customer. Therefore, John's cash and margin account is covered up to $500,000, of which no more than $250,000 can be cash. He's covered for the $200,000 in securities ($150,000 in securities plus the $50,000 equity) and $250,000 of the $300,000 cash for a total of $450,000. Next, the joint account with his wife is treated as though from a separate customer. Therefore, that account is covered for the $250,000 in securities and $250,000 in cash. Add the two together, and you see that John is covered for a total of $950,000 ($450,000 plus $500,000).

REMEMBER

If an investor is not fully covered under SIPC, the investor is still owed money by the bankrupt broker–dealer; therefore, the investor becomes a *general creditor* of the firm for the balance owed.

Holding a customer's mail

If one of your customers is not receiving mail at her usual address because she is traveling, moving, or whatever, your firm can hold her mail for a specified time period up to three months (or longer if for safety or security concerns). This typically has to do with confirmations and account statements that the firm would normally mail. The member firm must have a way to contact the customer in a timely manner (by phone, email, and so on) and the firm must provide a way for the customer to receive information regarding her account (typically via email or through the member's website). In addition, the member firm must verify at reasonable intervals that the customer's instructions still apply.

Business continuity plans and emergency contact information

FINRA requires that all member firms must set up and maintain business continuity plans to deal with the possibility of a business disruption. The idea is to make sure that customers will still be able to contact the firm and be able to access their securities and funds during an emergency. Although the plan is somewhat flexible depending on the member's business, some of the items the plan should address include the following:

» Hard copy and electronic data back-up and recovery

» Alternate communications between customers and members

» Alternate communications between members and their employees

» Alternate physical location of employees

>> Regulatory reporting

>> Communication with regulators

>> How the member firm will assure that customers will be able to have prompt access to their securities and funds in the event that the member is unable to continue business

TIP

There are a few other things that could be on this list such as "all mission-critical systems" (ways they would be able to handle customers' orders and such), "financial and operational assessments" (how a member's operations would change), and so on. However, the preceding list should be able to get you through SIE exam questions related to what needs to be on a firm's business continuity plan.

Members are required to have a member of senior management (who must be a principal) approve of their business continuity plan. That member is also responsible for conducting an annual review. The member's plan must be disclosed to customers in writing at the opening of their account, posted on the firm's website (if any), and mailed to customers upon request. In addition, besides providing the plan info to FINRA, they must also provide emergency contact information to FINRA (FINRA must receive the names of two principals and members of senior management to contact in the event of an emergency; if the contact info changes, it must be updated within 30 days). In the event that any info changes regarding the business continuity plan, the firm is responsible for updating its customers, employees, and FINRA.

5

Putting Your Knowledge to Good Use: Practice Exams

Chapter 17

Bring It On: Practice Exam 1

Τ his chapter is where you get your chance to shine like a star.

This part of the practice exam has 75 questions in random order, just as they are in the actual SIE exam. Please read carefully — many test takers make careless mistakes because they miss key words or read too quickly. Focus on the information you do need to know and ignore the information that you don't need. Read the last sentence twice to make sure you know what the question is asking.

Mark your answers on the answer sheet provided or on a separate piece of paper. You may use a basic calculator and scrap paper for notes and figuring. As you're taking the exam, be sure to circle the questions you find difficult. This step can help you determine what you really need to review.

To simulate the real exam, try to finish each practice exam in 1 hour and 45 minutes or less. Please resist the urge to look at the answers and explanations as you work through the exam; save the grading for later. After you finish the first practice exam, you can check your answers (you can find the answers and detailed explanations in Chapter 18, along with an answer key at the end of that chapter).

Good luck!

Practice Exam Answer Sheet

1. Ⓐ Ⓑ Ⓒ Ⓓ	16. Ⓐ Ⓑ Ⓒ Ⓓ	31. Ⓐ Ⓑ Ⓒ Ⓓ	46. Ⓐ Ⓑ Ⓒ Ⓓ	61. Ⓐ Ⓑ Ⓒ Ⓓ
2. Ⓐ Ⓑ Ⓒ Ⓓ	17. Ⓐ Ⓑ Ⓒ Ⓓ	32. Ⓐ Ⓑ Ⓒ Ⓓ	47. Ⓐ Ⓑ Ⓒ Ⓓ	62. Ⓐ Ⓑ Ⓒ Ⓓ
3. Ⓐ Ⓑ Ⓒ Ⓓ	18. Ⓐ Ⓑ Ⓒ Ⓓ	33. Ⓐ Ⓑ Ⓒ Ⓓ	48. Ⓐ Ⓑ Ⓒ Ⓓ	63. Ⓐ Ⓑ Ⓒ Ⓓ
4. Ⓐ Ⓑ Ⓒ Ⓓ	19. Ⓐ Ⓑ Ⓒ Ⓓ	34. Ⓐ Ⓑ Ⓒ Ⓓ	49. Ⓐ Ⓑ Ⓒ Ⓓ	64. Ⓐ Ⓑ Ⓒ Ⓓ
5. Ⓐ Ⓑ Ⓒ Ⓓ	20. Ⓐ Ⓑ Ⓒ Ⓓ	35. Ⓐ Ⓑ Ⓒ Ⓓ	50. Ⓐ Ⓑ Ⓒ Ⓓ	65. Ⓐ Ⓑ Ⓒ Ⓓ
6. Ⓐ Ⓑ Ⓒ Ⓓ	21. Ⓐ Ⓑ Ⓒ Ⓓ	36. Ⓐ Ⓑ Ⓒ Ⓓ	51. Ⓐ Ⓑ Ⓒ Ⓓ	66. Ⓐ Ⓑ Ⓒ Ⓓ
7. Ⓐ Ⓑ Ⓒ Ⓓ	22. Ⓐ Ⓑ Ⓒ Ⓓ	37. Ⓐ Ⓑ Ⓒ Ⓓ	52. Ⓐ Ⓑ Ⓒ Ⓓ	67. Ⓐ Ⓑ Ⓒ Ⓓ
8. Ⓐ Ⓑ Ⓒ Ⓓ	23. Ⓐ Ⓑ Ⓒ Ⓓ	38. Ⓐ Ⓑ Ⓒ Ⓓ	53. Ⓐ Ⓑ Ⓒ Ⓓ	68. Ⓐ Ⓑ Ⓒ Ⓓ
9. Ⓐ Ⓑ Ⓒ Ⓓ	24. Ⓐ Ⓑ Ⓒ Ⓓ	39. Ⓐ Ⓑ Ⓒ Ⓓ	54. Ⓐ Ⓑ Ⓒ Ⓓ	69. Ⓐ Ⓑ Ⓒ Ⓓ
10. Ⓐ Ⓑ Ⓒ Ⓓ	25. Ⓐ Ⓑ Ⓒ Ⓓ	40. Ⓐ Ⓑ Ⓒ Ⓓ	55. Ⓐ Ⓑ Ⓒ Ⓓ	70. Ⓐ Ⓑ Ⓒ Ⓓ
11. Ⓐ Ⓑ Ⓒ Ⓓ	26. Ⓐ Ⓑ Ⓒ Ⓓ	41. Ⓐ Ⓑ Ⓒ Ⓓ	56. Ⓐ Ⓑ Ⓒ Ⓓ	71. Ⓐ Ⓑ Ⓒ Ⓓ
12. Ⓐ Ⓑ Ⓒ Ⓓ	27. Ⓐ Ⓑ Ⓒ Ⓓ	42. Ⓐ Ⓑ Ⓒ Ⓓ	57. Ⓐ Ⓑ Ⓒ Ⓓ	72. Ⓐ Ⓑ Ⓒ Ⓓ
13. Ⓐ Ⓑ Ⓒ Ⓓ	28. Ⓐ Ⓑ Ⓒ Ⓓ	43. Ⓐ Ⓑ Ⓒ Ⓓ	58. Ⓐ Ⓑ Ⓒ Ⓓ	73. Ⓐ Ⓑ Ⓒ Ⓓ
14. Ⓐ Ⓑ Ⓒ Ⓓ	29. Ⓐ Ⓑ Ⓒ Ⓓ	44. Ⓐ Ⓑ Ⓒ Ⓓ	59. Ⓐ Ⓑ Ⓒ Ⓓ	74. Ⓐ Ⓑ Ⓒ Ⓓ
15. Ⓐ Ⓑ Ⓒ Ⓓ	30. Ⓐ Ⓑ Ⓒ Ⓓ	45. Ⓐ Ⓑ Ⓒ Ⓓ	60. Ⓐ Ⓑ Ⓒ Ⓓ	75. Ⓐ Ⓑ Ⓒ Ⓓ

TIME: 1 hour and 45 minutes for 75 questions

DIRECTIONS: Choose the correct answer to each question. Then fill in the circle on your answer sheet that corresponds to the question number and the letter indicating your choice.

1. Which of the following have ownership positions in a corporation?

    I. Convertible bondholders

    II. Convertible preferred stockholders

    III. Common stockholders

    IV. Mortgage bondholders

    (A) II and III

    (B) I, II, III, and IV

    (C) II and IV

    (D) II only

2. Common stockholders of PXPX Corporation have which of the following rights and privileges?

    (A) The right to receive an audited financial report weekly

    (B) The right to vote for cash dividends to be paid

    (C) A residual claim to assets at dissolution

    (D) The right to vote for stock dividends to be paid

3. Jake Hanson lives in New York and is considering purchasing a bond. He has settled on either a 5-percent municipal bond offered by New York or a 7-percent corporate bond offered by The Greenhorn Corporation, which has headquarters in New York. Jake needs some guidance and would like you to help him determine which bond will provide him with the greatest return. Which of the following information do you need to obtain before you can make the appropriate recommendation?

    (A) The business of his employer

    (B) His current tax bracket

    (C) How long he has lived in New York

    (D) His other holdings

4. An investor who is long a call option will realize a profit if exercising the option when the underlying stock price is

    (A) below the strike price minus the premium paid

    (B) above the strike price

    (C) above the strike price plus the premium paid

    (D) below the strike price

5. One of your clients is new to investing and has limited resources. Which of the following investments would you least likely recommend to this investor?

    (A) Growth funds

    (B) T-bills

    (C) Blue-chip stock

    (D) Oil and gas developmental program

6. Which of the following is required on the registration statement for a new issue?

    I. The capitalization of the issuer

    II. Complete financial statements

    III. What the money raised will be used for

    IV. The names and addresses of all of the issuer's control persons

    (A) I, II, and III

    (B) I, III, and IV

    (C) I, II, and IV

    (D) I, II, III, and IV

7. Under the Securities Act of 1933, which of the following securities must be registered with the SEC?

    (A) Closed-end funds

    (B) Variable annuities

    (C) Open-end funds

    (D) All of the above

GO ON TO NEXT PAGE

8. A customer's confirmation must include

    I. the markdown, if the member acted as a principal in a NASDAQ security

    II. the amount of any commission, if the member acted as an agent

    III. whether the member acted as an agent or a principal

    IV. the markup if the member acted as a principal in a NASDAQ security

    (A) I and III

    (B) II and IV

    (C) I, III, and IV

    (D) I, II, III, and IV

9. Which of the following would qualify as management companies?

    (A) Face-amount certificate companies

    (B) Unit investment trusts

    (C) Closed-end funds

    (D) None of the above

10. Which of the following is TRUE regarding qualified retirement plans?

    (A) Contributions are made with 100 percent pretax dollars.

    (B) Contributions are made with 100 percent after-tax dollars.

    (C) Distributions are taxable only prior to age 59½.

    (D) Distributions are subject to a 10 percent penalty.

11. Variable annuities must be registered with the

    I. Department of State

    II. State Banking Commission

    III. State Insurance Commission

    IV. Securities and Exchange Commission

    (A) I and II

    (B) I and III

    (C) I and IV

    (D) III and IV

12. All the following items must be included on a trade confirmation EXCEPT

    (A) the customer's account number

    (B) the customer's signature

    (C) the price of the security

    (D) the commission, if the trade took place on an agency basis

13. Which of the following is true of the Telephone Act of 1991?

    I. You cannot make calls before 8 a.m. or after 9 p.m. in the local time zone of the customer.

    II. You are required to provide your name, company name, company address, and phone number.

    III. Individuals who ask not to be called need to be placed on the company's do-not-call list.

    IV. You may not send unsolicited ads by fax machine.

    (A) I and III

    (B) II and IV

    (C) I, II, and III

    (D) I, II, III, and IV

14. If one of your clients wants to order municipal securities that you believe to be unsuitable for her investment objectives, what should you do?

    (A) Execute the order as long as you mark the order ticket as "unsolicited."

    (B) You must refuse the order unless the client changes her investment objectives.

    (C) You must obtain the permission of the firm's compliance officer before executing the order.

    (D) You may only execute the order with prior permission of a principal of the firm.

15. All broker-dealers need to maintain customer identification programs and should check the names of all new clients against

    (A) a list maintained by the SEC

    (B) a do-not-call list maintained by the firm

    (C) a list compiled by FINRA

    (D) a list of specially designated nationals (SDNs) maintained by OFAC

16. Which of the following statements is NOT true of life-cycle funds?

    (A) As life-cycle funds get nearer to their target date, the portfolio holdings will be adjusted to purchase more equity securities and less fixed-income securities.

    (B) These funds are usually set up as funds of funds.

    (C) The asset allocation of the fund will be rebalanced on a regular basis to make sure that the risk/reward balance is correct given the target date of the fund.

    (D) The objective of the fund assumes that most investors cannot tolerate as much risk as they get older.

17. The ex-date is

    (A) the date on which the corporation ceases paying a dividend

    (B) the date on and after the date the seller is entitled to the dividend

    (C) the third business day before the record date

    (D) the day the stock price is increased by the amount of the dividend

18. Investors who have international investments are subject to

    I. political risk

    II. currency risk

    III. regulatory risk

    (A) I and II

    (B) II and III

    (C) I and III

    (D) I, II, and III

19. Which of the following are factors that affect the marketability of municipal GO bonds?

    I. The quality

    II. Call features

    III. The issuer's name

    IV. Credit enhancements

    (A) I and II

    (B) II and III

    (C) I, II, and III

    (D) I, II, III, and IV

20. If a customer wants to open a new account but refuses to provide some of the financial information requested by the member firm, which of the following statements is TRUE?

    (A) The firm may open the account for the customer and make recommendations freely.

    (B) The firm may open the account if it can determine from other sources that the customer has the financial means to handle the account.

    (C) The firm may open the account and take unsolicited trades only.

    (D) The firm may not accept any trades for the account until the information is received from the customer.

21. Which of the following is included in a preliminary prospectus?

    I. The purpose for the funds being raised

    II. Financial statements

    III. A written statement in red citing that the prospectus may be amended and a final prospectus issued

    IV. The final offering price

    (A) I and II

    (B) I, II, and III

    (C) II and IV

    (D) I, II, III, and IV

GO ON TO NEXT PAGE

22. Which of the following is true of accredited investors?

    (A) They have had an annual income in excess of $200,000 for at least the last three years.

    (B) They have had an annual income in excess of $100,000 for at least the last two years.

    (C) They have a net worth of at least $1,000,000, excluding any equity they have in their primary residence.

    (D) They have a net worth in excess of $200,000.

23. The SEC and FINRA require customer statements to be sent out for inactive accounts at least

    (A) monthly

    (B) quarterly

    (C) semiannually

    (D) annually

24. Which of the following securities is traded on an exchange and is an entity that makes mortgage loans to developers and has a portfolio of properties?

    (A) DPPs

    (B) ETNs

    (C) Hybrid REITs

    (D) Mutual funds

25. Which of the following are needed to open a margin account for a corporation?

    I. Corporate charter and resolution

    II. New account form

    III. Hypothecation agreement

    IV. Credit agreement

    (A) I and II

    (B) I and IV

    (C) III and IV

    (D) I, II, III, and IV

26. Which of the following partnership documents needs to be filed with the secretary of state in the home state of the partnership?

    I. The certificate of limited partnership

    II. The partnership agreement

    III. The subscription agreement

    (A) I only

    (B) II and III

    (C) I and III

    (D) I, II, and III

27. Martina Martin is new to investing but has determined that her primary objective is making sure that she is prepared for retirement. Which of the following is the MOST important factor for you to consider when helping her set up her investment portfolio?

    (A) Age

    (B) Net worth

    (C) Education level

    (D) Previous investment history

28. An investor buys 100 shares of common stock of T-Prompters, Inc. at $15 per share. Six months later, T-Prompter Inc. is trading at $12.40–$12.65, and the registered representative offers to purchase the 100 shares back from the investor for his own account at $15 per share. This procedure is

    (A) permitted by FINRA rules

    (B) permitted with the written permission of a manager of the firm

    (C) prohibited because it violates the Code of Procedure

    (D) prohibited because it is a guarantee against a loss

29. Which of the following is rated by most securities rating services?

    (A) Market risk

    (B) Investment risk

    (C) Quantity

    (D) Quality

30. Which of the following items are required on an order ticket?

    I. The time of the order

    II. A description of the security (stocks, bonds, symbol, and so on)

    III. Whether the registered rep has discretionary authority over the account

    IV. The registered rep's identification number

    (A) I, III, and IV

    (B) I and III only

    (C) I, II, and IV

    (D) I, II, III, and IV

31. All of the following are important factors when determining the markup or commission on a municipal bond trade EXCEPT

    (A) the fact that you and the firm you work for are entitled to make a profit

    (B) the difficulty of the trade

    (C) the 5 percent markup policy

    (D) the market value of the securities at the time of the trade

32. When compared to statutory voting, cumulative voting provides an advantage to

    I. larger shareholders

    II. mortgage bondholders

    III. smaller shareholders

    IV. convertible bondholders

    (A) I only

    (B) II and IV

    (C) III only

    (D) II and III

33. Which of the following is NOT a benefit of investing in ADRs?

    (A) The dividends are received in U.S. currency.

    (B) The transactions are done in U.S. currency.

    (C) ADRs are subject to antifraud rules.

    (D) Currency risk is minimized.

34. Keith Coalburner has written a letter of complaint regarding his recent purchase of municipal bonds to his broker–dealer. Upon receipt of the complaint, the broker–dealer must first

    (A) immediately repurchase the securities at a price at or slightly above Keith's purchase price

    (B) guarantee to make the customer whole

    (C) return any markup or commission charged

    (D) accept the complaint and write down any action taken

35. John Dow and Jane Dough, who are engaged but unmarried, want to open a new account registered as joint tenants with rights of survivorship. Which of the following should occur?

    (A) A principal of the firm should be notified immediately about the account registration so that a report can be filed with FINRA.

    (B) The agent must refuse to open the account.

    (C) The agent must notify a principal of the firm and a report must first be filed with the SEC.

    (D) The agent may open the account but should first discuss the rules of a JTWROS account with the unmarried couple.

36. Which of the following occurs under the provisions of the Uniform Gifts to Minors Act (UGMA) when a minor reaches the age of majority?

    (A) The account must be transferred to the donor.

    (B) The account is automatically changed to a UTMA account.

    (C) The account is closed, and the new adult receives a check in the amount equal to the market value of the account less any commission.

    (D) The account must be transferred to the donee after she reaches adulthood.

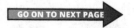 GO ON TO NEXT PAGE

37. Which type of margin account requires a minimum equity of $25,000?

   (A) A portfolio margin account
   (B) A short account
   (C) A day-trading account
   (D) A corporate account

38. Prior to buying or selling options, a customer must first receive a(n)

   (A) ODD
   (B) OCC
   (C) margin agreement
   (D) OPRA

39. The 5 percent markup policy applies to

   (A) riskless or simultaneous transactions
   (B) markdowns on stock sold from inventory
   (C) commissions charged when executing trades for a customer
   (D) all of the above

40. Skippy Barrier III has 1,000 shares of DIM common stock in his portfolio. Skippy would like to protect himself in the event that the market price of DIM drops. Which of the following orders would best meet Skippy's needs?

   (A) A buy stop order
   (B) A sell stop order
   (C) A buy limit order
   (D) A sell limit order

41. Which of the following is NOT an advantage for a customer adding REITs to her portfolio?

   (A) Having a professionally managed portfolio of real estate assets
   (B) Preferential dividend treatment
   (C) Being able to use a REIT as a potential hedge against a negative price movement in other equity securities
   (D) Liquidity

42. All the following items would be found on the official statement of a municipal bond issue EXCEPT

   (A) the markup
   (B) a description of the issuer
   (C) the coupon rate
   (D) a legal opinion

43. Which of the following are true about the annuitization of a variable annuity?

   I. The value of the annuity units is fixed.
   II. The number of annuity units is fixed.
   III. The value of the annuity units varies.
   IV. The number of annuity units varies.

   (A) I and II
   (B) II and III
   (C) II and IV
   (D) None of the above

44. Which of the following investments requires a registered representative to obtain written verification of an investor's net worth?

   (A) Hedge funds
   (B) Variable annuities
   (C) Direct participation programs
   (D) Triple-tax-free municipal bonds

45. The Federal Reserve Board is responsible for which of the following?

   (A) Easing the money supply
   (B) Setting Regulation T
   (C) Printing currency
   (D) All of the above

46. A registered representative may open all the following customer accounts EXCEPT

   (A) an account in the name of Mr. Wegner for Mrs. Wegner
   (B) a minor's account by a custodian
   (C) a corporate account by a designated officer
   (D) a partnership account by a designated partner

47. Exchange-listed securities trading over-the-counter takes place in the

(A) first market

(B) second market

(C) third market

(D) fourth market

48. Mutual funds must send financial statements to shareholders at least

(A) monthly

(B) bimonthly

(C) quarterly

(D) semiannually

49. Which of the following best defines selling dividends?

(A) Providing customers with a clear plan on how to invest dividends they receive

(B) Enticing customers to buy mutual fund shares just before the ex-dividend date so that they can receive a dividend

(C) Encouraging customers to sell stock just before a dividend is paid so that the stock will be easier to sell

(D) Encouraging customers to withdraw dividends from mutual funds and to invest in other securities so that you, as a registered rep, will receive additional commission

50. Which of the following establishes the U.S. Treasury Department as the regulator for anti-money-laundering programs?

(A) The Bank Secrecy Act

(B) OFAC

(C) SDN

(D) None of the above

51. Investing in a real-estate DPP program includes which of the following advantages?

I. Depreciation

II. Appreciation

III. Depletion

IV. Cash flow

(A) I and II

(B) III and IV

(C) I, II, and IV

(D) I, II, III, and IV

52. The Fed would be inclined to increase the money supply in which of the following conditions?

(A) Declining yields on bonds

(B) Declining gross domestic product (GDP)

(C) Declining interest rates

(D) Rising housing prices

53. The FDIC covers each

(A) depositor for up to $250,000

(B) investor for up to $250,000

(C) depositor for up to $500,000

(D) investor for up to $500,000

54. An investor owns the following investments:

50 New York 5 percent general obligation bonds maturing in 2020 and rated AA

50 Florida University 6.25 percent revenue bonds maturing in 2021 and rated AA

50 Nevada Turnpike 5.75 percent revenue bonds maturing in 2020 and rated AA

What type of diversification does this represent?

(A) Maturity

(B) Quality

(C) Quantity

(D) Geographical

55. An investor has shorted XYZ common stock at 55. XYZ common stock has recently dropped to 30, and the investor expects that the price will continue to decrease over the long term. If the investor would like to hedge against a possible increase in the price, the investor should

(A) buy an XYZ call

(B) sell an XYZ call

(C) buy an XYZ put

(D) buy an XYZ combination

56. If an investor buys an equity option contract on issuance, which expires unexercised, what is the investor's tax consequence at expiration?

(A) Short-term capital loss

(B) Long-term capital gain

(C) Long-term capital loss

(D) Short-term capital gain

GO ON TO NEXT PAGE

57. A customer, without giving written authorization, may permit a registered representative to exercise his judgment as to

(A) whether to buy or sell

(B) the security

(C) the price and timing to enter the order

(D) the number of shares

58. Which of the following are nonexempt securities?

  I. Municipal unit investment trust shares

  II. U.S. government bond fund shares

  III. Variable annuity accumulation units

  IV. Fixed annuities

(A) I and II

(B) III only

(C) III and IV

(D) I, II, and III

59. If Buddy Seagull has a limited amount of funds and wants to invest in the pharmaceutical industry but does not want to limit his investments to only one or two companies, which type of fund would be MOST suitable?

(A) A hedge fund

(B) A sector fund

(C) A balanced fund

(D) A money-market fund

60. What is the principal tax benefit for investing as a limited partner in an exploratory oil and gas drilling program?

(A) Tax credits

(B) Depreciation expenses

(C) Recourse loans

(D) Intangible drilling costs

61. If the U.S. dollar has fallen in comparison with foreign currencies, which of the following statements is TRUE?

(A) U.S. exports are likely to fall.

(B) Foreign currencies buy fewer U.S. dollars.

(C) U.S. products cost more for foreign consumers.

(D) U.S exports increase.

62. You have a new client who is in a high tax bracket and is looking for investments with a tax advantage. Which of the following securities would you LEAST likely recommend?

(A) Municipal bonds

(B) GNMAs

(C) Retirement plans

(D) Direct participation programs

63. Adjustable-rate preferred stock has a dividend that adjusts according to

(A) prevailing interest rates

(B) the amount of dividend given to common stockholders

(C) the coupon rate on the issuer's bonds

(D) the rate on CMOs

64. Which of the following items are found on an indenture of a bond?

  I. The maturity date

  II. Callable or convertible features

  III. The coupon rate

  IV. The name of the trustee

(A) II, III, and IV

(B) I, II, and III

(C) II and III

(D) I, II, III, and IV

65. The Legal List is for

(A) fiduciaries

(B) investment advisors

(C) municipal finance professionals

(D) corporate accounts

66. Which of the following are important to investors evaluating direct participation programs?

  I. The economic soundness of the program

  II. The expertise of the general partner

  III. The basic objectives of the program

  IV. The start-up costs

(A) I, II, and III

(B) I, II, and IV

(C) II, III, and IV

(D) I, II, III, and IV

67. What is the required beginning date (RBD) for traditional IRAs?

(A) The year after the investor reaches the age of 59½

(B) The year the investor turns the age of 70½

(C) April 1 of the year after the investor reaches the age of 70½

(D) April 15 of the year after the investor reaches the age of 70½

68. One of your clients is expecting to receive a lot of money over the next three years. Your client would like to shelter some of that money by investing in a DPP. Which of the following types of DPPs will help your client shelter the most money?

(A) Oil and gas income

(B) Oil and gas developmental

(C) Oil and gas combination

(D) Oil and gas wildcatting

69. Which of the following governmental bodies receives no revenue from ad-valorem taxes?

(A) County governments

(B) State governments

(C) School districts

(D) Local municipalities

70. According to MSRB rules, a customer confirmation must include

(A) the markup or markdown

(B) the location of the indenture

(C) the maturity date

(D) whether the trade was done on an agency or dealer basis

71. Which of the following disputes must be resolved using the Code of Arbitration?

I. A dispute between a member of FINRA and a registered rep

II. A dispute between a member of FINRA and a customer

III. A dispute between two members of FINRA

IV. A dispute between a bank and a member of FINRA

(A) IV only

(B) II and IV

(C) I and III

(D) I, III, and IV

72. Duke Wallwalker purchased an LTSBR Corporation convertible bond at 95 on January 20, 2019. The bond is convertible at $40, and the investor converts his bond into stock on January 21, 2022. If the bond is trading at 104 and the common stock is trading at $42, for tax purposes, these transactions will result in

(A) a $10 gain

(B) a $10 loss

(C) a $90 gain

(D) neither a gain nor a loss

73. RANs, BANs, TANs, and CLNs are issued by municipalities seeking

(A) to insure their municipal securities

(B) the approval of the SEC

(C) long-term financing

(D) short-term financing

GO ON TO NEXT PAGE

74. Which of the following statements regarding municipal revenue bonds is NOT true?

(A) Revenue bonds are not subject to a debt ceiling.

(B) Revenue bonds may be issued by interstate authorities.

(C) The maturity date of the issue will usually exceed the useful life of the facility backing the bonds.

(D) Debt service is paid from revenue received from the facility backing the bonds.

75. All of the following may be sources of revenue for a revenue bond EXCEPT

(A) property taxes

(B) user fees

(C) tolls

(D) airports

STOP

Chapter **18**

Answers & Explanations to Practice Exam 1

ongratulations! If you've reached this point, you've completed the first SIE practice exam. (If you haven't, flip back and take the test in Chapter 17. You don't want to spoil all the surprises, do you?) You should stop here and review your answers.

Review, review, review. And if I haven't mentioned this yet, reviewing is definitely a good idea. Look at the questions you had problems with, retake all the questions you got wrong, and make sure you get them right the second (or third) time around. If you're short on time but just can't wait to see how you fared, you can check out the abbreviated answer key (without the explanations) at the end of this chapter. I explain how the SIE is scored in the section "Making the Grade," just before the answer key. But I strongly suggest you come back later and — you guessed it — review.

Wait at least several days to a week before taking the same test again. Retaking the test won't help your cause if you're just memorizing the answers.

1. **A.** (Chapter 6) Common stockholders have equity (ownership) positions, as do preferred stockholders. However, bondholders are creditors, not owners.

2. **C.** (Chapter 6) Common stockholders of PXPX Corporation — or, for that matter, any publicly traded corporation — have a residual claim to the assets of the corporation at dissolution. PXPX Corp. common stockholders are entitled to receive a report containing audited financial statements on a yearly, not weekly, basis. Finally, PXPX Corp. stockholders never get to vote on dividends to be paid (whether stock or cash); dividends are decided by the board of directors.

3. **B.** (Chapter 8) In order to determine the best investment for Jake, you must do a tax-equivalent yield (TEY) calculation. To accomplish this, you need to know Jake's tax bracket. Remember, the interest received from municipal bond investments is tax-free, and investors in higher tax brackets save more money by investing in municipal bonds when compared to other investments. The SIE examiners are testing you to make sure you know that the other items listed here are not relevant to the question.

4. **C.** (Chapter 11) For an investor to profit when holding a long call, the investor has to exercise the option when the market price is above the strike (exercise) price plus the premium paid.

5. **D.** (Chapter 10) For this question, you can stop at the point where the investor has limited resources. Typically, DPPs such as oil and gas developmental programs require a large initial investment and a certain liquid net worth. A DPP would definitely not be right for this client.

6. **D.** (Chapter 5) When a company decides to go public, it must file a registration statement with the SEC. The registration statement must include

   - The issuer's name and a description of its business

   - The names and addresses of all of the issuer's control persons (in other words, officers, directors, and investors owning 10 percent or more of the issuer's securities)

   - What the money raised will be used for

   - The capitalization of the issuer

   - Complete financial statements

   - Whether there are any legal proceedings against the issuer

7. **D.** (Chapter 5) The securities listed in this question are all nonexempt, meaning that they all have to register with the SEC. The Securities Act of 1933 requires all new nonexempt issues of securities sold to the public to be registered. In general, exempt issues include municipal securities, U.S. government securities, bank issues, private placements, intrastate offerings, and securities issued by nonprofit organizations.

8. **D.** (Chapter 16) A confirmation sent to a customer must disclose the amount of markup or markdown charged for a principal transaction in a NASDAQ security, whether the member acted in an agency or a principal capacity, and, if the member acted as an agent, the amount of commission.

9. **C.** (Chapter 9) Open-end and closed-end funds are considered management companies because they have actively managed portfolios and are defined as such according to the Investment Company Act of 1940. Because face-amount certificate companies and unit trusts do not have actively managed portfolios, they're not considered management companies and have their own classification.

10. **A.** (Chapter 15) Qualified plans under IRS laws allow investors to invest money for retirement with *pre-tax dollars* (you can write qualified plan contributions off on your taxes). In addition, earnings accumulate on a *tax-deferred* basis (the investor isn't taxed until withdrawal). However, distributions (tax-deferred earnings and contributions) for which the participant receives a tax deduction are 100 percent taxable.

11. **D.** (Chapter 9) Tricky, tricky . . . the examiners want to make sure you know that a variable annuity is derived from two separate products: an insurance contract and securities held in a separate account. Consequently, a variable annuity must be registered with the State Insurance Commission (for the insurance contract) and the Securities and Exchange Commission (for the securities held in the separate account).

12. **B.** (Chapter 16) The customer's signature is not required on a trade confirmation. However, the customer's account number, the registered rep's ID number, the trade date, whether the customer bought or sold, the number of shares or par value of bonds, the yield (if bonds), the CUSIP number, the price of the security, the total amount paid, the commission (if on an agency basis), and the net amount are all required on the confirmation.

13. D. (Chapter 12) The Telephone Act of 1991 is designed to set standards for individuals soliciting business. All the choices listed are included in the act.

14. A. (Chapter 16) If a registered representative believes that a customer is making an unsuitable trade, the representative may enter the order but must mark the order ticket "unsolicited." In this question, the client is making a trade that you believe is unsuitable for her, but you can still execute the trade as long as you mark the order ticket as "unsolicited," which will protect you and make your client happy.

15. D. (Chapter 16) The Bank Secrecy Act establishes the U.S. Treasury Department as the regulator of anti-money-laundering programs. As such, all broker-dealers are required to have programs set up to help detect the possibility of money laundering. Broker-dealers must also review the OFAC's (Office of Foreign Asset Control's) SDN (Specially Designated Nationals) list to determine that they're not doing business with organizations or individuals who are on the list.

16. A. (Chapter 9) Life-cycle funds are actually funds of funds, which are based on an investor's age. Investors buy a life-cycle fund designed for people their age. Life-cycle funds adjust their holdings every so often so that investors are taking less risk as they get older. Because younger investors can afford to take more risk, a larger percentage of their portfolio is in equities and less is in fixed-income securities. As investors get older, they should have an increasing number of fixed-income securities and less equity securities. Life-cycle funds automatically take care of that for investors.

17. B. (Chapter 16) The *ex-date* or *ex-dividend date* is one business day before the record date and is the date that the buyer would be purchasing the stock without a dividend. On the ex-date, the stock is *reduced* by the amount of the dividend. The corporation is still responsible for paying the dividend, and because the buyer isn't entitled to it, the seller is.

18. D. (Chapter 13) Investors in foreign securities face all the risks listed along with a few others, depending on the type of securities held. Political (legislative) risk is the risk that the value of a security may suffer due to instability or political changes in a country. Currency risk is the risk that the value of an investment may be affected due to a change in exchange rates. Regulatory risk is the risk that legislative changes may affect the market.

19. D. (Chapter 8) Factors that affect the marketability (how easy it is to buy and sell) of municipal GO (general obligation) bonds are the quality, maturity date, call features, coupon rate, block size, dollar price, issuer's name, sinking fund, and credit enhancements (in other words, insurance).

20. B. (Chapter 12) You will find that this is not an unusual situation. When you're opening an account for a new customer, the customer may not feel comfortable sharing all her financial information with you. However, you can still do trading in the account and make recommendations if you can determine financial information from other sources, such as D&B cards. Say, for example, that the D&B card says that the customer is the CEO of a corporation that made $5 billion last year. You can assume the customer has a lot of money. The recommendations you make to a customer should be suitable to her investment objectives and financial situation. If you can't determine the information from other sources, you can still make trades and recommendations that would be suitable for all investors, such as mutual funds or U.S. government securities.

21. B. (Chapter 5) A preliminary prospectus includes the purpose for the funds and financial statements. Because a preliminary prospectus (red herring) is printed before the final price is established, it may include a projected price range that is subject to change.

22. **C.** (Chapter 5) Certain purchases, such as a Regulation D private placement, may require investors to be accredited (although they have a 35 unaccredited investor exclusion). Accredited investors are ones with a net worth of at least $1 million excluding any equity they may have in their primary residence, or ones with an annual income of at least $200,000 (or $300,000 for joint accounts) for the last two (not three) years that's expected to stay at least the same for the current year.

23. **B.** (Chapter 16) The SEC and FINRA require member firms to send customer account statements at least quarterly (once every three months) for inactive accounts. To help you remember how often account statements should be sent out, think "AIM":

   A = Active account (monthly)

   I = Inactive account (quarterly)

   M = Mutual fund (semi-annually)

24. **C.** (Chapter 10) Hybrid REITs (real-estate investment trusts) trade on an exchange, provide mortgage loans to developers, and hold a portfolio of securities. Hybrid REITs are a combination of equity (ownership) and mortgage REITs.

25. **D.** (Chapter 12) When a corporation opens a margin account, the corporation has to provide a corporate charter, which needs to say that the corporation can buy securities on margin, and a corporate resolution, which says who has the trading authority for the account. A new account form is always needed for any type of account. The corporation also needs a hypothecation agreement, which allows the broker–dealer to hold the securities in street name so that they can be used as collateral for a loan. In addition, the corporation needs a credit agreement, which sets the terms for the loan.

26. **A.** (Chapter 10) The certificate of limited partnership is the legal agreement between the general and limited partners and is the only partnership paperwork that needs to be filed with the secretary of state. The certificate of limited partnership includes the primary place of business, the names and addresses of the limited and general partner(s), the objectives of the partnership, the amount contributed by each partner, the roles of the partners, and so on.

27. **A.** (Chapter 12) Certainly, any information you can get about your client will help you set up a portfolio that fits the client's needs. However, because Martina's primary investment objective is making sure that she's prepared for retirement, you need to begin by looking at her age. Someone who is younger can take more risk than someone who is older.

28. **D.** (Chapter 16) Pursuant to Conduct Rules (not the SEC), registered representatives may never guarantee a customer against losses; therefore, this action is never permitted. If the investor wanted to sell the shares, he would have to sell them at the bid price of $12.40, not $15.

29. **D.** (Chapter 7) The expression "quality over quantity" applies here. Rating services are concerned with quality, defined as the issuer's (or guarantor's) default risk or ability to pay interest and principal on time. The two biggest rating services are Moody's and Standard & Poor's. The highest ratings for these rating services are Aaa and AAA, respectively.

30. **D.** (Chapter 16) All order tickets need to include the items listed in the question plus the customer's account number; the number of shares or bonds being purchased or sold; whether the customer is buying, selling, or selling short; whether the customer is covered or uncovered (option orders); and whether it's a market order, good-till-canceled, and so on.

31. C. (Chapter 8) Because municipal securities are exempt from SEC registration, they're not subject to the FINRA 5 percent markup policy.

32. C. (Chapter 6) Cumulative voting allows shareholders to aggregate (combine) their votes and vote for whomever they please. For argument's sake, if an investor owned 1,000 common shares and there were four members of the board of directors open for vote, the investor could use all of the 4,000 votes (1,000 shares × 4 members) for a single candidate, if desired. Cumulative voting can be used to make it easier for smaller shareholders to gain representation on the board of directors.

33. D. (Chapter 6) The purpose of ADRs (American Depositary Receipts) is to facilitate the trading of foreign securities in U.S. markets. ADRs carry currency risk because distributions on ADRs must be converted from foreign currency to U.S. dollars on the date of distribution. The trading price of the ADR is actually quite affected by currency fluctuation, which can devalue any dividends and/or the value of the stock.

34. D. (Chapter 16) After receiving Keith's written complaint, the municipal securities broker-dealer must accept the complaint and write down any action taken to resolve the complaint. All broker-dealers should keep a complaint file for each customer and keep accurate records of any communications or actions taken regarding a complaint.

35. D. (Chapter 12) No rules prohibit opening an account registered as joint tenants with rights of survivorship (JTWROS) for two unmarried persons. The registered representative should, however, take all steps to be sure that the unmarried individuals understand the resulting consequences should one party to the account die. For example, in an account registered JTWROS, if one of the engaged parties to the account (for example, John Dow) dies, the deceased party's ownership interest in the account passes to the surviving tenant (Jane Dough) rather than to the deceased party's (John Dow's) estate.

36. D. (Chapter 12) Under the terms of the Uniform Gifts to Minors Act, the account must be handed over to the new adult when a minor reaches the age of majority. You don't need to know the age of majority because it varies from state to state, but it's usually between the ages of 18 and 21.

37. C. (Chapter 12) A day-trading account requires an initial margin of $25,000, and the investor must keep $25,000 minimum equity in the account to keep trading. A portfolio margin account is relatively new and looks at the risk of the portfolio as a whole to determine the margin requirement. Only certain investors are able to take advantage of portfolio margin because it requires a certain degree of sophistication and a minimum equity of around $150,000.

38. A. (Chapter 11) Because of the additional risk involved when investing in options, such as the ability to lose all money invested or facing unlimited maximum loss, all investors must receive an ODD (options risk disclosure document) prior to the first transaction. The ODD is not an advertisement; it contains the pitfalls of investing in options. After the customer receives the ODD, the ROP (registered options principal) has to approve the account. Next, you can do the trade, and after that, the customer has to sign and return an OAA (options account agreement).

39. D. (Chapter 16) The 5 percent markup policy is a guideline for broker-dealers to use when executing trades of outstanding securities for public customers. In most cases, for a standard-sized trade of nonexempt securities, broker-dealers should not charge a commission, markup, or markdown that is in excess of 5 percent. The 5 percent policy applies to both commission charges on agency transactions and to markups and markdowns on principal transactions, including riskless and simultaneous transactions.

40. B. (Chapter 14) Remember that stop orders are used for protection. Because Skippy owns the stock, he would have to enter a sell stop order below the market price of the security. In the event that the price of the stock hits or drops below the stop price, the order would be triggered and the stock would be sold on the next transaction.

41. B. (Chapter 10) As with most other investment company products, REITs have a professionally managed portfolio. Many investors use REITs as a potential hedge against a downturn in the market because often there is an inverse relationship between the real-estate market and stock prices. In addition, REITs typically have a high degree of liquidity. However, there is no preferential dividend treatment for REITs.

42. A. (Chapter 8) The official statement for a municipal bond issue is similar to a prospectus for a corporate issue. The items that you find on an official statement include the offering terms, the underwriting spread, a description of the bonds, a description of the issuer, the offering price, the coupon rate, the feasibility statement, and the legal opinion.

43. B. (Chapter 9) When an investor of a variable annuity starts withdrawing money from the annuity, the accumulation units are converted into a fixed number of annuity units. However, the value of the annuity units varies based on the performance of the securities held in the separate account.

44. C. (Chapter 10) Because direct participation programs (limited partnerships) may require limited partners to come up with additional cash beyond their initial investment, investors must provide a written verification of net worth. After the general partner signs the subscription agreement, the investor is accepted as a limited partner.

45. D. (Chapter 13) The Federal Reserve Board was established in 1913 to stabilize the country's chaotic financial system. It performs all the services listed in Choices (A), (B), and (C), in addition to other duties it performs; therefore, Choice (D) is correct.

46. A. (Chapter 12) Here's that EXCEPT question type again! You're looking for a false answer here. Although a custodian may open an account with an agent for a minor, a designated officer may open a corporate account with an agent, and a designated partner may open a partnership account with an agent, an agent is not permitted to open an individual account in the name of a third person. This means that Choice (A) is the correct false answer that you're looking for.

47. C. (Chapter 14) First market is listed securities trading on an exchange. Second market is unlisted securities trading OTC (over-the-counter). Third market is listed securities trading OTC. Fourth market is institutional trading without using a broker-dealer.

48. D. (Chapter 16) Under the Investment Company Act of 1940, mutual funds must provide semiannual reports to shareholders. To help you remember how often account statements should be sent out, think "AIM":

A = Active account (monthly)

I = Inactive account (quarterly)

M = Mutual fund (semiannually)

49. B. (Chapter 16) Selling dividends is a violation in which a registered representative entices an investor to purchase a security in time to receive a previously declared dividend. Remember, there is no advantage to purchasing a security prior to the ex-dividend date (the first day the security trades without a dividend) because the price of the stock is reduced by the amount of the dividend on the ex-dividend date. Therefore, even though a customer might receive a $0.50 dividend, the price of the stock is reduced by $0.50, so there's no advantage.

50. **A.** (Chapter 16) The Bank Secrecy Act establishes the U.S. Treasury Department as the regulator for anti-money-laundering programs. All broker-dealers are required to develop programs to detect possible money-laundering abuses.

51. **C.** (Chapter 10) Real estate DPPs (direct participation programs — limited partnerships) provide advantages for investors such as depreciation deductions, appreciation potential, and cash flow, but not depletion. Depletion only applies to partnerships that deal in natural resources that can be depleted (used up), such as oil or gas.

52. **B.** (Chapter 13) In this question, if the GDP (gross domestic product) is declining, business is slowing down and possibly heading toward a recession, and the Fed would want to stimulate the economy by making more money available. Increasing the money supply through lower interest rates usually increases business activity. However, when there are declining yields and interest rates, and rising house prices, there is a danger of increased inflation if the Fed increases (eases) the money supply.

53. **A.** (Chapter 16) The FDIC (Federal Deposit Insurance Corporation) provides depositors insurance against failed (bankrupt) banks for up to $250,000. SIPC protects investors from broker-dealer failure up to $500,000, of which no more than $250,000 can be cash.

54. **D.** (Chapter 8) Because the investor bought 50 of each bond, they were all rated AA, and they mature around the same time, you can rule out maturity, quality, and quantity as your answers. The investor's funds are an example of geographic diversification because the bonds are from a variety of issuers around the United States.

55. **A.** (Chapter 11) To hedge means to protect. If the investor would like to hedge his position, he should buy a call on XYZ. Remember that the investor is short the stock and must buy XYZ back at some point to close his short position. Buying an XYZ call gives the investor the right to buy back XYZ at a fixed price, which would allow the investor to protect the position and not face an unlimited maximum loss potential.

56. **A.** (Chapter 15) Options are always taxed as capital gains or capital losses. This investor purchased an option that expired worthless, and, therefore, he lost money. Because the investor held the option for nine months (the typical expiration for an equity option), it's taxed as a short-term capital loss because it was held for one year or less.

57. **C.** (Chapter 16) Without having discretionary authority, registered representatives may not decide on whether to buy or sell, the security to purchase or sell, or the number of shares or dollar amount to purchase for the customer. Registered representatives may, however, without written power of attorney, choose the price or timing of an order.

58. **D.** (Chapter 5) You must distinguish a nonexempt security from an exempt security. A nonexempt security is one that is not exempt from SEC registration; in other words, it must be registered with the SEC. Variable annuities, which carry investment risk, are nonexempt securities under the Securities Act of 1933 and must be registered before public sale. Similarly, unit trusts and mutual funds are nonexempt even though the underlying securities may be exempt, such as municipals and U.S. government securities. However, a fixed annuity is an insurance product exempt from registration with the SEC. It's not considered a security because of the guaranteed payout.

59. **B.** (Chapter 9) A specialized or sector fund invests a minimum of 25 percent of its assets in a particular region or industry and would be the most suitable for Buddy.

60. **D.** (Chapter 10) Intangible drilling costs (IDCs), the costs involved in actually getting to the oil, provide a tax benefit to investors of an oil and gas exploratory (wildcatting) program. IDCs are items such as labor and surveys. IDCs are deductible expenses in the year in which they occur.

61. **D.** (Chapter 13) If you look at the answer choices carefully, you'll see that Choices (A) and (D) are opposite, which tells you that one of them has to be true. When the U.S. dollar loses value compared to a foreign currency, U.S exports increase because foreign currency strengthens in comparison and now buys more dollars. As a result, U.S. goods are cheaper than normal for foreign consumers.

62. **B.** (Chapter 7) GNMAs (Ginnie Maes) offer no tax advantages to buyers because they are taxed on all levels. However, the interest received on municipal bonds is federally tax-free and sometimes state-tax-free. In addition, retirement plans allow investors to deposit money tax-free (in most cases), and the money grows on a tax-deferred basis. DPPs (direct participation programs) allow for additional write-offs, such as depreciation and depletion, which provide for a cash flow that's greater than the net income.

63. **A.** (Chapter 6) Adjustable (floating rate) preferred stock receives a dividend that adjusts according to prevailing interest rates.

64. **D.** (Chapter 7) The bond indenture (deed of trust) is the legal agreement between the issuer and investors. The bond indenture includes the maturity date, the par value, the coupon rate, any collateral securing the bond, any callable or convertible features, and the name of the trustee.

65. **A.** (Chapter 12) The Legal List is for fiduciaries (a *fiduciary* is someone who can legally make decisions for another investor). Fiduciaries are subject to the "Prudent Investor Rule," which means that they must invest in securities on the state's legal list or, if there isn't one, invest in securities that only a prudent investor would purchase.

66. **D.** (Chapter 10) All the choices listed are important to evaluate for investors of direct participation programs.

67. **C.** (Chapter 15) Withdrawals must begin by April 1 of the year after the investor turns age 70½. At that point, the investor has to take a required minimum distribution (RMD), which can be determined by looking at the IRS's required minimum distribution worksheet.

68. **D.** (Chapter 10) An oil and gas wildcatting (exploratory) program would best suit your client's needs. Oil and gas wildcatting programs drill in unproven areas and create quite a lot of write-offs in the early years. However, if oil is hit, a wildcatting program will bring in a lot of money.

69. **B.** (Chapter 8) Remember that state governments do not collect ad-valorem (property) taxes. Ad-valorem taxes are assessed by local governments (for example, towns and counties). Generally, state governments receive the most income from income taxes and sales taxes.

70. **D.** (Chapter 16) The SIE examiners may try to trip you up by throwing in an irrelevant answer choice (like the date of maturity) to find out whether you know your MSRB (Municipal Securities Rulemaking Board) rules. MSRB rules require that confirmations include whether the trade was executed on a principal (dealer) or agency basis. The amount of the dealer's markup or markdown on a principal trade does not have to be disclosed, but the commission on an agency trade does need to be disclosed.

71. **C.** (Chapter 16) As you can see, the one common denominator is that all the answer choices have the acronym "FINRA" in them, which tells you that being a FINRA member must be pretty important. The Code of Arbitration is mandatory in member-against-member disputes including a member firm and one of its registered reps. However, FINRA has no jurisdiction over banks or over disputes between nonmembers such as customers or issuers; in cases such as these, the nonmember decides whether to use arbitration or a Code of Procedure hearing to settle a dispute.

72. **D.** (Chapter 15) There are no tax consequences to Duke for converting a bond into shares of common stock. In order for Duke to have a taxable gain or loss, the shares Duke received as a result of his conversion to common stock must be sold.

73. **D.** (Chapter 8) Municipal short-term notes such as RANs (revenue anticipation notes), BANs (bond anticipation notes), TANs (tax anticipation notes), and CLNs (construction loan notes) are used to provide short-term (interim) financing until a permanent, long-term bond issue is floated, until tax receipts increase, or until revenue flows in.

74. **C.** (Chapter 8) You need to be careful in this case because the examiners are asking you for a false statement. The maturity of revenue bonds may be 25 to 30 years, but the facility being built by the income received from the revenue bond issue is usually expected to last a lifetime. Revenue bonds may be issued by interstate authorities, such as tolls, and the debt service (interest and principal) on the bonds is paid from revenue received from the facility backing the bonds. In addition, revenue bonds are not subject to a debt ceiling; general obligation bonds are.

75. **A.** (Chapter 8) The SIE examiners want to make sure you can distinguish funds raised for municipal revenue bonds from those raised for general obligation bonds. Tolls, fees, airports, power plants, water, wastewater, and so forth may all be fund generators that subsidize revenue bonds. Property taxes (ad valorem taxes) support general obligation bonds.

Making the Grade

Here's how the SIE exam is scored:

» You get 1⅓ points for each correct answer.

» You get zero points for each incorrect answer.

A passing score is 70 percent. To calculate your grade for this exam, multiply the number of correct answers by 1.33 or divide it by 75. Whatever grade you get, make sure you round down, not up. For example, a grade of 71.6 is a 71 percent, not a 72.

REMEMBER

The actual test contains ten additional experimental questions that don't count toward your actual score. You can't tell these questions apart from the questions that do count, so you may have to answer a few more questions right to get your 70 percent. Don't sweat it. Simply come prepared, stay focused, and do your best.

Answer Key for Practice Exam 1

1.	A	20.	B	39.	D	58.	D
2.	C	21.	B	40.	B	59.	B
3.	B	22.	C	41.	B	60.	D
4.	C	23.	B	42.	A	61.	D
5.	D	24.	C	43.	B	62.	B
6.	D	25.	D	44.	C	63.	A
7.	D	26.	A	45.	D	64.	D
8.	D	27.	B	46.	A	65.	A
9.	C	28.	D	47.	C	66.	D
10.	A	29.	D	48.	D	67.	C
11.	D	30.	D	49.	B	68.	D
12.	D	31.	C	50.	A	69.	B
13.	D	32.	C	51.	C	70.	D
14.	A	33.	D	52.	B	71.	C
15.	D	34.	D	53.	A	72.	D
16.	A	35.	D	54.	D	73.	D
17.	B	36.	D	55.	A	74.	C
18.	D	37.	C	56.	A	75.	A
19.	D	38.	A	57.	C		

Chapter 19

Nothing But Net: Practice Exam 2

If you've just finished the first practice exam and are planning on continuing to this practice exam, please thoroughly review the first exam first. Just like Practice Exam 1, this practice exam has 75 questions. For those of you who couldn't wait to take the second exam and bypassed the first one, I review the test basics here.

As in the real SIE exam, the questions in both practice exams are in random order. Please read carefully. You can limit your careless mistakes by focusing in on the key words. Zone in on the information you do need to know to answer the question and ignore the information that doesn't help you. I suggest reading the last sentence twice to make sure you know what the question's asking. You may use scrap paper and a basic calculator for figuring.

Mark your answers on the answer sheet provided in this chapter or on a separate piece of paper. As you're taking the exam, circle or highlight the questions that you find troublesome. After taking and grading the exam, look over the questions that you got wrong and the questions that you circled or highlighted. Review the test, retake all the questions that you circled or answered wrong, and make sure that you get them right this time. To simulate the real exam, try to finish this part in one hour and 45 minutes or less. Please resist the urge to look at the answers and explanations until you've finished the exam. You can check your answers and get detailed explanations in Chapter 20. Good luck!

Practice Exam Part 2 Answer Sheet

1. Ⓐ Ⓑ Ⓒ Ⓓ
2. Ⓐ Ⓑ Ⓒ Ⓓ
3. Ⓐ Ⓑ Ⓒ Ⓓ
4. Ⓐ Ⓑ Ⓒ Ⓓ
5. Ⓐ Ⓑ Ⓒ Ⓓ
6. Ⓐ Ⓑ Ⓒ Ⓓ
7. Ⓐ Ⓑ Ⓒ Ⓓ
8. Ⓐ Ⓑ Ⓒ Ⓓ
9. Ⓐ Ⓑ Ⓒ Ⓓ
10. Ⓐ Ⓑ Ⓒ Ⓓ
11. Ⓐ Ⓑ Ⓒ Ⓓ
12. Ⓐ Ⓑ Ⓒ Ⓓ
13. Ⓐ Ⓑ Ⓒ Ⓓ
14. Ⓐ Ⓑ Ⓒ Ⓓ
15. Ⓐ Ⓑ Ⓒ Ⓓ

16. Ⓐ Ⓑ Ⓒ Ⓓ
17. Ⓐ Ⓑ Ⓒ Ⓓ
18. Ⓐ Ⓑ Ⓒ Ⓓ
19. Ⓐ Ⓑ Ⓒ Ⓓ
20. Ⓐ Ⓑ Ⓒ Ⓓ
21. Ⓐ Ⓑ Ⓒ Ⓓ
22. Ⓐ Ⓑ Ⓒ Ⓓ
23. Ⓐ Ⓑ Ⓒ Ⓓ
24. Ⓐ Ⓑ Ⓒ Ⓓ
25. Ⓐ Ⓑ Ⓒ Ⓓ
26. Ⓐ Ⓑ Ⓒ Ⓓ
27. Ⓐ Ⓑ Ⓒ Ⓓ
28. Ⓐ Ⓑ Ⓒ Ⓓ
29. Ⓐ Ⓑ Ⓒ Ⓓ
30. Ⓐ Ⓑ Ⓒ Ⓓ

31. Ⓐ Ⓑ Ⓒ Ⓓ
32. Ⓐ Ⓑ Ⓒ Ⓓ
33. Ⓐ Ⓑ Ⓒ Ⓓ
34. Ⓐ Ⓑ Ⓒ Ⓓ
35. Ⓐ Ⓑ Ⓒ Ⓓ
36. Ⓐ Ⓑ Ⓒ Ⓓ
37. Ⓐ Ⓑ Ⓒ Ⓓ
38. Ⓐ Ⓑ Ⓒ Ⓓ
39. Ⓐ Ⓑ Ⓒ Ⓓ
40. Ⓐ Ⓑ Ⓒ Ⓓ
41. Ⓐ Ⓑ Ⓒ Ⓓ
42. Ⓐ Ⓑ Ⓒ Ⓓ
43. Ⓐ Ⓑ Ⓒ Ⓓ
44. Ⓐ Ⓑ Ⓒ Ⓓ
45. Ⓐ Ⓑ Ⓒ Ⓓ

46. Ⓐ Ⓑ Ⓒ Ⓓ
47. Ⓐ Ⓑ Ⓒ Ⓓ
48. Ⓐ Ⓑ Ⓒ Ⓓ
49. Ⓐ Ⓑ Ⓒ Ⓓ
50. Ⓐ Ⓑ Ⓒ Ⓓ
51. Ⓐ Ⓑ Ⓒ Ⓓ
52. Ⓐ Ⓑ Ⓒ Ⓓ
53. Ⓐ Ⓑ Ⓒ Ⓓ
54. Ⓐ Ⓑ Ⓒ Ⓓ
55. Ⓐ Ⓑ Ⓒ Ⓓ
56. Ⓐ Ⓑ Ⓒ Ⓓ
57. Ⓐ Ⓑ Ⓒ Ⓓ
58. Ⓐ Ⓑ Ⓒ Ⓓ
59. Ⓐ Ⓑ Ⓒ Ⓓ
60. Ⓐ Ⓑ Ⓒ Ⓓ

61. Ⓐ Ⓑ Ⓒ Ⓓ
62. Ⓐ Ⓑ Ⓒ Ⓓ
63. Ⓐ Ⓑ Ⓒ Ⓓ
64. Ⓐ Ⓑ Ⓒ Ⓓ
65. Ⓐ Ⓑ Ⓒ Ⓓ
66. Ⓐ Ⓑ Ⓒ Ⓓ
67. Ⓐ Ⓑ Ⓒ Ⓓ
68. Ⓐ Ⓑ Ⓒ Ⓓ
69. Ⓐ Ⓑ Ⓒ Ⓓ
70. Ⓐ Ⓑ Ⓒ Ⓓ
71. Ⓐ Ⓑ Ⓒ Ⓓ
72. Ⓐ Ⓑ Ⓒ Ⓓ
73. Ⓐ Ⓑ Ⓒ Ⓓ
74. Ⓐ Ⓑ Ⓒ Ⓓ
75. Ⓐ Ⓑ Ⓒ Ⓓ

TIME: 1 hour and 45 minutes for 75 questions

DIRECTIONS: Choose the correct answer to each question. Then fill in the circle on your answer sheet that corresponds to the question number and the letter indicating your choice.

1. Mark Schwimmerr owns 2,500 shares of TP Corporation. Which of the following actions would dilute Mark's equity?

   I. Primary share offerings (registered)

   II. A stock split

   III. Payment of a stock dividend

   IV. Secondary share offerings (registered)

   (A) I only

   (B) II only

   (C) I, II, and IV

   (D) I, II, III, and IV

2. Mike Smith is one of your clients. Mike is 55 years old, has a wife, two young adults going to college, and two children living at home. You have helped Mike determine his investment profile and how much risk he should be willing to take. However, Mike is hot on a particularly speculative security that doesn't fit his investment profile. Mike calls you saying he wants to purchase $20,000 worth of this security. What should you do?

   (A) Accept the order and mark it as unsolicited.

   (B) Refuse the order because it doesn't fit his investment profile.

   (C) Do nothing until talking to a principal.

   (D) Limit Mike's exposure by making sure that he doesn't purchase more than $5,000 worth of this speculative security.

3. An investor has a child who will be going to college in 15 years. Which of the following is a suitable investment?

   (A) T-bills

   (B) T-notes

   (C) Treasury receipts

   (D) AAAA aggressive growth fund

4. Which of the following statements is TRUE about revenue bonds?

   (A) Their value is measured by the municipal project's capacity for generating revenue.

   (B) They are secured by a mortgage-backed bond.

   (C) They are a type of general obligation bond.

   (D) They are subject to the statutory debt limitations of the issuing jurisdiction.

5. Which of the following is the balance sheet equation?

   (A) assets = liabilities + shareholder's equity

   (B) assets + liabilities = shareholder's equity

   (C) shareholder's equity + assets = liabilities

   (D) None of the above

6. Regarding the taxation of dividends from corporate securities, which TWO of the following are TRUE?

   I. Qualified dividends are taxed at the investor's income tax rate.

   II. Qualified dividends are taxed at a maximum rate of 15 percent.

   III. Nonqualified dividends are taxed at the investor's tax rate.

   IV. Nonqualified dividends are taxed at a maximum rate of 15 percent.

   (A) I and III

   (B) I and IV

   (C) II and III

   (D) II and IV

GO ON TO NEXT PAGE

7. Where can an investor find the most information about a new municipal issue?

(A) In a prospectus

(B) In an official statement

(C) In a tombstone ad

(D) In a registration statement

8. Which of the following statements made by a registered rep is not prohibited?

(A) "The stock will double in price."

(B) "The earnings of the company will be better than expected."

(C) "I can guarantee that you will not lose money on this stock."

(D) "A research report shows that the company's financial performance may be better than expected."

9. Which two of the following are true of Roth IRAs?

I. Contributions are made from after-tax dollars.

II. Contributions are made from pretax dollars.

III. Distributions are tax-free.

IV. Distributions are taxed on the amount above the amount of the contribution.

(A) I and III

(B) I and IV

(C) II and III

(D) II and IV

10. Which of the following are true of broker-dealer business continuity and disaster recovery plans?

I. They must be in written form.

II. Firms must have backup of data (both hard copies and electronic).

III. Firms must have some sort of alternative communication between the firm and its employees.

IV. They must be approved by a principal.

(A) I, II, and III

(B) II, III, and IV

(C) I, II, and IV

(D) I, II, III, and IV

11. One of your clients wants to start adding some diversity to her portfolio by investing in mutual funds. Which of the following is the most important consideration when choosing a mutual fund?

(A) Whether the fund is load or no-load

(B) Management fees

(C) Investment objectives

(D) 12b1 fees

12. Common stockholders in a corporation can do which of the following?

(A) Elect the corporation's board of directors

(B) Make decisions about the day-to-day dealings, such as the office supply dealer used by the corporation

(C) Receive interest payments

(D) Expect to be paid par value for their stock if the corporation goes out of business

13. Which of the following investments are suitable for a 21-year-old investor who has limited resources but would like to start investing on a regular basis?

I. Growth funds

II. Raw land DPP

III. Call options

IV. Hedge funds

(A) I only

(B) II and IV

(C) I, II, and III

(D) I, III, and IV

14. According to the Investment Adviser's Act of 1940, which of the following are considered investment advisers?

(A) Securities lawyers talking to clients about investments

(B) Economics professors giving investment advice to students

(C) Registered reps giving paid advice on investments

(D) All of the above

15. Which of the following statements is TRUE regarding municipal revenue bond issues?

    (A) The bonds are backed by the issuer's unlimited taxing power.

    (B) User fees provide revenue for bondholders.

    (C) The bonds' feasibility is not dependent on the earnings potential of the facility or project.

    (D) Revenue bonds are most suitable for investors with high risk tolerance.

16. Jameson and Johnson Securities sent Art a confirmation of his latest trade of Johnstone Corporation common stock. Which of the following items should be on the confirmation?

    I. The trade date and the settlement date

    II. Whether Jameson and Johnson acted as an agent or a principal

    III. The name of the security and how many shares were traded

    IV. The amount of commission paid if Jameson and Johnson acted as an agent

    (A) I and III

    (B) I, II, and III

    (C) I, III, and IV

    (D) I, II, III, and IV

17. If a customer, Jessica James, decides to give limited power of attorney to her registered representative, which of the following is TRUE?

    (A) The registered representative still needs verbal authorization from Jessica for each trade.

    (B) Jessica must sign a power-of-attorney document.

    (C) The registered representative must sign a power-of-attorney document.

    (D) Jessica must initial each order before it is entered.

18. Which of the following is NOT a characteristic of a real estate investment trust (REIT)?

    (A) Pass-through treatment of income only

    (B) Pass-through treatment of income and losses

    (C) At least 75 percent of the assets must be invested in real-estate-related projects

    (D) Ownership of real property without management responsibility

19. A principal is responsible for approving new accounts opened for

    I. individuals

    II. corporations

    III. banks

    IV. trusts

    (A) I only

    (B) I and II

    (C) I, II, and III

    (D) I, II, III, and IV

20. George Lincoln opens a margin account and signs a loan consent, hypothecation, and credit agreement. Which of the following statements are TRUE?

    I. George's stock may not be kept in street name.

    II. A portion of George's stock may be pledged for a loan.

    III. George will be required to pay interest on the money borrowed.

    IV. George's stock must be cosigned by the broker/dealer.

    (A) I and IV

    (B) II and III

    (C) I and II

    (D) None of the above

21. To protect investors of variable life insurance policies who become disabled, there is a rider called a(n)

    (A) disability rider

    (B) waiver of premium

    (C) early withdrawal rider

    (D) none of the above

GO ON TO NEXT PAGE

22. As a client's investment objectives change, a registered rep should keep track of those changes so that he can rebalance the client's portfolio and make proper recommendations. Which of the following changes may affect a customer's investment objectives?

    I. Growing older

    II. Getting divorced

    III. Having triplets

    IV. Getting a higher paying job

    (A) I and III

    (B) I, II, and III

    (C) II, III, and IV

    (D) I, II, III, and IV

23. JKLM Corporation has declared a $0.40 dividend payable to shareholders of record on Thursday, September 14. What would happen to the opening price of JKLM on Tuesday, September 12?

    (A) It would be reduced by the amount of the dividend.

    (B) It would remain the same.

    (C) It would be increased by the amount of the dividend.

    (D) Cannot be determined

24. Larry Eagle is a resident of Michigan. Mr. Eagle purchased a Michigan municipal bond. What is the tax treatment of the interest that Larry earns on his Michigan bond?

    I. It is exempt from local taxes.

    II. It is exempt from state taxes.

    III. It is exempt from federal taxes.

    (A) III only

    (B) I and III

    (C) II and III

    (D) I, II, and III

25. Who is responsible for paying the taxes when securities in a Uniform Gifts to Minors Act (UGMA) account are sold at a profit?

    (A) The minor

    (B) The donor

    (C) The custodian

    (D) The parent or guardian

26. An investor wants to invest in a DPP that's relatively safe. Which of the following are you LEAST likely to recommend?

    (A) A real-estate partnership that invests in raw land

    (B) An oil and gas developmental program

    (C) An oil and gas income program

    (D) An equipment leasing program

27. Which of the following is a function of a transfer agent?

    (A) Underwriting shares in new corporate stock offerings

    (B) Preparing corporate balance sheets

    (C) Advising municipalities regarding the debt structure of new issues

    (D) Sending out proxies

28. All the following information is required on a preliminary prospectus EXCEPT

    (A) the final offering price

    (B) the purpose for which the issuer is raising the funds

    (C) a statement in red lettering stating that items on the preliminary prospectus are subject to change before the final prospectus is issued

    (D) the issuer's history and financial status

29. Which of the following situations requires a broker-dealer to file a currency transaction report?

    (A) A customer purchases $20,000 worth of stock with a check from a joint account.

    (B) A customer opens an account with $14,000 cash.

    (C) A customer opens an account with a wire transfer from his personal account for $25,000.

    (D) A customer deposits corporate bonds with a par value of $30,000.

30. A mutual fund has a NAV of $9.30 and a POP of $10. What is the sales charge of this fund?

    (A) 5 percent

    (B) 6 percent

    (C) 7 percent

    (D) 8 percent

31. Investments that move in the opposite direction of the economic cycles are known to be counter-cyclical. Historically, investments that are known to be counter-cyclical include

    (A) gold stock
    (B) utility stock
    (C) pharmaceutical stock
    (D) food company stock

32. On a competitive bid for a new municipal underwriting, the difference between the syndicate bid and the reoffering price is the

    (A) discount price
    (B) offering price
    (C) spread
    (D) bid price

33. If a customer wants to open a cash account at a brokerage firm, the signature(s) of which of the following is/are required?

    I. The registered representative
    II. The customer
    III. The principal
    IV. The guarantor

    (A) IV only
    (B) I and III
    (C) I, II, and III
    (D) I, II, III, and IV

34. A sell stop order is entered

    I. below the support level of the stock
    II. above the resistance level of the stock
    III. to limit the loss on a long stock position
    IV. to limit the loss on a short stock position

    (A) I and III
    (B) I and IV
    (C) II and III
    (D) II and IV

35. The indenture of a corporate bond includes all of the following EXCEPT

    (A) the coupon rate
    (B) the credit rating
    (C) the name of the trustee
    (D) the maturity date

36. Which of the following items can be found in the certificate of limited partnership?

    I. The goals of the partnership and how long it's expected to last
    II. The authority of the general partner to charge a fee for making management decisions for the partnership
    III. How the profits are to be distributed
    IV. The amount contributed by each partner, plus future expected investments

    (A) I, II, and III
    (B) II, III, and IV
    (C) I, III, and IV
    (D) I, II, III, and IV

37. All the following securities may pay a dividend EXCEPT

    (A) warrants
    (B) common stock
    (C) American depositary receipts (ADRs)
    (D) participating preferred stock

38. Which of the following is/are true of a REIT?

    I. It must invest at least 75 percent of its assets in real-estate-related activities.
    II. It must be organized as a trust.
    III. It must distribute at least 90 percent of its net investment income.
    IV. It must pass along losses to shareholders.

    (A) I, II, III, and IV
    (B) I, II, and III
    (C) I only
    (D) II and IV

39. An investor purchases 100 shares of DUD Corp. at $45 per share and purchases 1 DUD Oct 40 put at 6. What is the customer's break-even point?

    (A) 39
    (B) 45
    (C) 46
    (D) 51

GO ON TO NEXT PAGE

40. Under the Securities Act of 1933, which of the following securities are exempt from registration and disclosure provisions?

(A) Railroad equipment trust certificate

(B) Municipal bonds

(C) Commercial paper maturing in 270 days or less

(D) All of the above

41. One of your customers is interested in investing in an oil and gas limited partnership. As his registered rep, which of the following steps are you required to take?

I. Prescreen the customer.

II. Determine the economic soundness of the program.

III. Explain the risks of investing in limited partnerships.

IV. Have your customer fill out a partnership agreement.

(A) I and III

(B) I, II, and III

(C) II, III, and IV

(D) I, II, III, and IV

42. Which of the following funds changes its balance to hold more fixed-income securities and less equity securities as the years pass?

(A) A balanced fund

(B) A hedge fund

(C) A life-cycle fund

(D) A growth fund

43. The first time a company ever issues securities is called a(n)

(A) IPO

(B) first-market trade

(C) rights offering

(D) None of the above

44. Bearish strategies include

I. selling short

II. buying put options

III. selling uncovered call options

IV. selling covered call options

(A) I and IV

(B) II and IV

(C) I, II, and III

(D) I, II, and IV

45. One of your customers wants to add some diversity to his portfolio by investing in some defensive stocks. Which of the following stocks would you recommend?

I. CCCold Refrigerator Corporation common stock

II. Smoky Tobacco Inc. common stock

III. Forgetful Vodka Corp. common stock

IV. ImpeeAuto Corporation common stock

(A) I and IV

(B) II and III

(C) I, III, and IV

(D) II, III, and IV

46. Mr. Smith has an inactive account with stocks and bonds at a broker-dealer. How often is the firm required to send Mr. Smith an account statement?

(A) Once a month

(B) Once a week

(C) Once every three months

(D) Once every six months

47. All the following orders are reduced on the order book for a cash dividend on the ex-date EXCEPT

(A) buy limit

(B) sell stop

(C) sell stop limit

(D) buy stop

48. All of the following impact the marketing of a municipal bond issue EXCEPT

(A) the rating

(B) the interest

(C) the date of maturity

(D) the dated date

49. An investor who purchases a variable life insurance policy faces which of the following risks?

(A) The insurance company may have to increase the premium if the securities held in the separate account underperform the market.

(B) The insurance company may decrease the premium if the securities held in the separate account outperform the market.

(C) The policy may have no cash value if the securities held in the separate account perform poorly.

(D) The death benefit may fall below the minimum in the event that the securities held in the separate account underperform.

50. All of the following are nonfinancial influences that may help determine an investor's investment profile EXCEPT

(A) the investor's age

(B) the amount of marketable securities the investor owns

(C) the number of dependents

(D) investment experience

51. Ginny Goldtrain is a wealthy investor who is in the highest income bracket. Ginny is looking for an investment that would limit her tax liability and put her on equal footing with investors in lower income-tax brackets. Which of the following securities would you MOST likely recommend?

(A) High-yield bonds

(B) CMOs

(C) Municipal bonds

(D) Hedge funds

52. Which of the following bonds most likely has the highest coupon rate?

(A) DEF Corp. mortgage bonds

(B) DEF Corp. collateral trusts

(C) DEF Corp. debentures

(D) DEF Corp. equipment trusts

53. Your client, Dana Griffin, is about to retire and she wants predictable income. Which of the following would NOT be a good investment for Dana?

I. AA rated IDB

II. U.S. Treasury note

III. AA rated debenture

IV. Income bonds

(A) II only

(B) I and III

(C) II and IV

(D) IV only

54. Sal Gold is new to investing and wants to purchase a security that will provide him with current income with minimal risk. Which of the following are you LEAST likely to recommend?

(A) An income fund

(B) Treasury bonds

(C) An international fund

(D) AA rated municipal bonds

55. Which of the following is the issuer and guarantor of all listed options?

(A) The OCC

(B) The OAA

(C) The ODD

(D) The CBOE

56. If your customer, William Goate, purchases shares in a municipal bond fund, which of the following statements is TRUE?

(A) Dividends are subject to alternative minimum tax.

(B) Dividends are taxable to all investors.

(C) Capital gains distributions are taxable.

(D) Capital gains distributions are not taxable.

57. These municipal notes provide interim financing for a municipality that's waiting for a grant from the U.S. government.

(A) BANs

(B) TRANs

(C) GANs

(D) CLNs

GO ON TO NEXT PAGE

58. Use the following exhibit to answer this question:

Balance Sheet of ABCD Corp.

Assets		Liabilities	
Cash	$300,000	Accounts payable	$300,000
Accounts receivable	$1,500,000	Taxes payable	$250,000
Inventory	$1,200,000	Bonds maturing this year	$800,000
Goodwill	$2,000,000	Bonds maturing in 5 years	$2,000,000
Machinery	$1,500,000		
Land	$5,000,000		

What is the net worth of ABCD Corporation?

(A) $3,150,000

(B) $1,650,000

(C) $8,150,000

(D) $10,150,000

59. One of the advantages of portfolio margin is that it allows

(A) smaller investors the opportunity to purchase securities on margin

(B) less sophisticated investors a chance to purchase securities on margin

(C) investors to avoid maintenance calls

(D) investors greater leverage

60. Which of the following statements regarding municipal bonds with call provisions is TRUE?

(A) Bonds are likely to be called when interest rates fall.

(B) Call provisions favor investors.

(C) Bonds are likely to be called when interest rates rise.

(D) Call provisions are not advantageous to issuers.

61. Sam Smith sends an email to his registered rep, John Johnson, complaining about the amount of commission he was charged on his last trade. According to FINRA rules, what should John Johnson do with the complaint?

(A) Ignore it because the complaint needs to be in writing

(B) Print it out and give it to his principal

(C) Print it out and send it to FINRA

(D) Forward it to FINRA's complaint department

62. All of the following are types of blue-sky registration EXCEPT

(A) registration by cooperation

(B) registration by coordination

(C) registration by qualification

(D) registration by filing

63. A TUV Oct 60 call is trading for 9 when TUV is at $65. What is the time value of this option?

(A) 0

(B) 4

(C) 5

(D) 9

64. Which of the following need approval from a brokerage firm's principal?

I. New accounts

II. Recommendations

III. Handling of complaints

IV. Trades in all accounts

(A) I and II

(B) I, III, and IV

(C) II, III, and IV

(D) I, II, III, and IV

65. Which of the following municipal bonds is backed by lease payments made by an underlying facility?

(A) IDR

(B) LTGO

(C) LRB

(D) BAB

66. All of the following are included on a confirmation for noncallable municipal bonds that were purchased on a yield basis EXCEPT

    (A) the purchase price
    (B) the par value
    (C) the yield to maturity
    (D) the taxable equivalent yield

67. A customer wants her registered representative to purchase a security that is incompatible with her investment objectives. What action should the registered representative take under FINRA rules?

    (A) Enter the order and note that it was unsolicited.
    (B) Enter the order only if the customer puts her request in writing.
    (C) Obtain the approval of the firm's compliance officer before entering the order.
    (D) The registered representative cannot enter the order.

68. Which of the following are money market securities?

    (A) Commercial paper
    (B) Treasury bonds
    (C) American depositary receipts (ADRs)
    (D) Warrants

69. Income derived from an investment in a real-estate limited partnership is termed

    (A) earned income
    (B) passive income
    (C) portfolio income
    (D) capital gains

70. What is the primary objective for an individual who invests in undeveloped land?

    (A) Depletion deductions
    (B) Depreciation deductions
    (C) Appreciation potential
    (D) Tax-deferred income

71. An investor purchased 1,000 shares of WXY at $40. If WXY announces a 5-for-4 split, what is the investor's position after the split?

    (A) 1,250 WXY at $32
    (B) 1,250 WXY at $50
    (C) 800 WXY at $32
    (D) 800 WXY at $50

72. The economic theory that supports controlling the money supply in order to stimulate economic growth is called

    (A) the Federal Reserve Board
    (B) the Keynesian theory
    (C) supply-side economics
    (D) the monetarist theory

73. Which of the following is characteristic of commercial paper?

    (A) It is quoted as a percent of par.
    (B) It is proof of ownership of the corporation.
    (C) It is issued to raise capital for a corporation.
    (D) It is junior to convertible preferred stock.

74. A mutual fund that invests only in securities within a specific industry is called a

    (A) Balanced fund
    (B) Growth fund
    (C) Hedge fund
    (D) Sector fund

75. At what time must an individual begin withdrawals from a Roth IRA?

    (A) At age 59½
    (B) At age 70½
    (C) On April 1 of the year after turning 70½
    (D) None of the above

STOP

Chapter **20**
Answers & Explanations to Practice Exam 2

Congratulations! You've just completed the second exam (unless you're just randomly flipping through the book). After grading both the first and second exams, you should have an idea of where you stand regarding the SIE exam. Kudos if you did really well on both practice exams.

As with the first exam, review all the questions that you got wrong and the ones you struggled with. Test yourself again by answering all the questions you highlighted and the questions you answered incorrectly, and make sure you get them right this time! Please give yourself a few days to a week before taking the same test again. Memorizing answers can give you a false sense of security, and you won't get an accurate forecast of how well you'll do on the SIE exam (you certainly don't want your score to be as unpredictable as the weather). I encourage you to take as many SIE practice exams as possible (there will be more available online). I could only cover so many potential practice test questions in this book. Make sure you have a good handle on *everything* in the book, even if you didn't see it in the practice tests. FINRA's test banks have thousands of questions and the test will spit them out randomly, so be prepared.

If you're short on time but just can't wait to see how well you did, you can check out the abbreviated answer key (without the explanations) at the end of this chapter. I explain how the SIE is scored in the section "Knowing the Score," just before the answer key. But I strongly suggest you come back later and do a more thorough review.

1. **A.** (Chapter 5) Another primary issue of shares would dilute Mark's ownership because new shares would be coming to the market. Don't forget that when a corporation issues stock dividends, splits its stock, or makes a secondary offering, the percent of equity does not change.

2. **A.** (Chapter 16) You can accept the trade and mark it as unsolicited. Even if a customer wants to purchase a security that doesn't fit his investment profile, you can still accept it in most cases by marking it as unsolicited. I call this the CYD (cover your derriere) rule. As long as you mark the ticket as unsolicited, you save yourself some aggravation (and maybe arbitration) if Mike loses money on the deal.

3. **C.** (Chapter 7) T-strips or Treasury receipts are long-term zero-coupon bonds backed by the full faith and credit of the U.S. government. Zero-coupon bonds are ideal investments to plan for future events because investors don't face reinvestment risk. In addition, the purchase price for long-term zero-coupon bonds is comparatively low.

4. **A.** (Chapter 8) The SIE examiners want to see that you can distinguish revenue bonds from general obligation bonds. In this question, Choice (A) is the correct answer. Revenue bonds are backed by a project's earning capacity. Choices (B), (C), and (D) are incorrect because revenue bonds are not secured by a specific pledge of property, are not a type of general obligation bond, and are not subject to debt limitations the way that many general obligation bonds are.

5. **A.** (Chapter 13) When you look at a corporation's balance sheet, the left-hand side lists all the assets and the right-hand side lists all the liabilities plus the shareholders' equity. The left side and the right side balance out (equal the same amount of money).

6. **C.** (Chapter 15) Dividends are profits shared by corporations. Dividends can be taxed as either qualified (up to a maximum rate of 15 percent) or nonqualified (according to the investor's tax bracket). In order for the dividends to be qualified, the investor must have held onto the stock for at least 61 days. The 61-day holding period starts 60 days prior to the ex-dividend date.

7. **B.** (Chapter 8) An official statement includes all relevant information about a new municipal bond. Municipal bonds don't have a prospectus, but an official statement is along the same lines. An official statement gives information about the municipal issue, such as the reason the bonds are being issued, what revenues are going to be used to pay the bonds, the issuer's payment history, and so forth. A tombstone ad is a brief advertisement that does not go into detail about the security being issued, and a registration statement is used by corporations when they are filing with the SEC.

8. **D.** (Chapter 16) This question is a double negative ("not prohibited"), so it's asking which statement a registered representative can make. The answer is pretty much a matter of logic. Choices (A), (B), and (C) are all guarantees. A registered rep who makes guarantees may get into trouble. However, Choice (D) is not a guarantee and may be said to an investor as long as it's true.

9. **A.** (Chapter 15) The main difference between traditional IRAs and Roth IRAs is the tax implications. Contributions to traditional IRAs are made from pretax dollars (you can write them off on your taxes), whereas contributions to Roth IRAs are made from after-tax dollars (you can't write them off on your taxes). However, distributions (withdrawals) from traditional IRAs are taxed on the amount above contribution, whereas withdrawals from Roth IRAs are tax-free. When withdrawing from a Roth IRA, neither the amount invested, which was already taxed, nor the amount the account has gone up in value (appreciation) is taxed, which is a great benefit to Roth IRA holders.

10. **D.** (Chapter 16) All firms must now have business continuity and disaster recovery plans to be prepared in the event of a significant disruption in their business. These plans must be in written form, be approved by a principal, and address the following information:

    - The existence of back-up data

    - A means of alternative communication between a firm and its employees, customers, and regulators

    - The creation of an alternative location for all employees

    - A means of giving customers fast access to their securities and funds

11. **C.** (Chapter 9) Certainly all the choices listed are important, but the most important one is the investment objectives of the mutual fund. In other words, you need to know whether the investor is looking for a growth fund, an income fund, a municipal bond fund, an international fund, and so on. When comparing funds with the same investment objectives, all the other things, such as comparing management fees, whether the fund is load or no-load, and so on, come into play.

12. **A.** (Chapter 6) Common stockholders may cast votes for candidates to be members of the board of directors; therefore, Choice (A) is the correct answer. Choice (B) is incorrect because while common stockholders may vote on important issues that affect the welfare of the corporation, they do not have voting rights on the day-to-day operations of the corporation, like buying office supplies. Choice (C) is incorrect because a stockholder doesn't receive interest payments, bondholders do. Finally, Choice (D) is incorrect because a common stockholder's initial investment can be lost if a corporation fails; therefore, par value is not guaranteed.

13. **A.** (Chapter 9) The clues in this question are that the investor is 21 years old, has limited resources, and would like to start investing on a regular basis. This investor is screaming out to be put in a mutual fund. Typically, investors of mutual funds are in it for the long haul; they're not in and out like they may be with other investments. Ideally, this investor should probably be set up on a dollar cost averaging plan whereby he invests x amount of dollars every so often (for instance, once a month). Because this investor is young, he can take a little more risk, so a growth fund would be ideal. DPPs, buying call options, and hedge funds are too risky, require too much money, and/or require a certain degree of sophistication.

14. **C.** (Chapter 16) Lawyers, accountants, teachers, and engineers are not advisors unless they're offering advice outside of their job descriptions. In Choice (A), the lawyer is a securities attorney. In Choice (B), the teacher is an economics professor. A registered rep of a brokerage firm must become licensed as an advisor or advisor representative to be able to offer advice for a fee. In most cases, registered reps may only be paid for executing trades.

15. **B.** (Chapter 8) The answer is Choice (B). Choices (A), (C), and (D) are incorrect. Revenue bonds are generally considered low-risk because they're issued by municipalities. The riskiest municipal bonds are IDRs (industrial development revenue bonds), which are backed by a corporation, not the municipality.

16. **D.** (Chapter 16) When a client receives a trade confirmation (receipt of trade), the confirmation must show the trade date, settlement date, the name of the security, how many shares were traded, whether the broker-dealer acted as an agent or principal, and the amount of commission if traded on an agency basis.

17. **B.** (Chapter 12) The correct answer is Choice (B) because when Jessica grants her registered representative a limited power of attorney, she is the one who must sign the document. Although a principal must approve before the registered representative exercises his discretionary authority, the registered representative does not have to sign the document, and Jessica's approval of each order is not required.

18. **B.** (Chapter 10) Real estate investment trusts pass through income earned by the real-estate investments, but not losses. Real-estate limited partnerships pass through income and losses to investors because DPPs aren't responsible for paying business taxes.

19. **D.** (Chapter 16) I hope this was an easy one for you. Principals must approve all new accounts and must sign all new account forms.

20. **B.** (Chapter 12) Because George is borrowing money through a margin account to purchase securities, he must leave the stock in the broker-dealer's safekeeping, pay interest on the loan, register the stock in street name, and agree to allow the broker-dealer to pledge the securities because he signed a loan consent agreement.

21. **B.** (Chapter 9) Variable life insurance policies often have a rider or statement of condition that allows individuals to keep their policy in force if they become disabled. This waiver of premium forgives policyholders of paying additional premiums if they become totally disabled.

22. **D.** (Chapter 12) Certainly just about anything you can think of could change a client's investment objectives. As people get older, they usually can't take as much risk. Conversely, investors who get higher-paying jobs are likely to want to take additional risk. Someone who is getting (or has gotten) divorced is likely to have less money (due to alimony payments, one person paying for the house instead of two, child support payments, and so on). Obviously, having triplets puts a financial burden on an investor (unless she gets a reality show).

23. **A.** (Chapter 6) Remember, the ex-dividend date (the first day the stock trades without the dividend) is two business days before the record date. In this case, the record date is Thursday, September 14, which makes the ex-dividend date Tuesday, September 12. The opening price on the ex-dividend date is reduced by the amount of the dividend ($0.40 in this case).

24. **D.** (Chapter 8) When you purchase a municipal bond issued within your home state, the interest you receive is triple tax-free (exempt from federal, state, and local taxes). In addition, if you purchase a bond issued by a U.S. territory (such as Puerto Rico, U.S. Virgin Islands, Guam, Samoa, and Washington, D.C.), the interest is triple-tax free. However, if you purchase a bond issued by another state, the interest is exempt from federal taxes only.

25. **A.** (Chapter 12) The correct answer is Choice (A). All taxes on the account are the responsibility of the minor because the UGMA account was opened for the benefit of the minor and the account is registered with the minor's Social Security number.

26. **A.** (Chapter 10) Of the choices listed, a real-estate partnership that invests in raw land is the riskiest. Partnerships that invest in raw land are considered speculative, as are oil and gas wildcatting programs. The risk of investing in raw land is that even though the property is purchased at a low price, developers may not be interested in that area and the partnership may be stuck with relatively worthless property.

27. **D.** (Chapter 6) Hopefully the word "transfer" in "transfer agent" led you to the correct answer. Yes, the transfer agent is responsible for transferring or sending things. Typically, the transfer agent is responsible for sending out proxies (voting by mail), cancelling old shares and sending out new shares, distributing dividends, and so on.

28. **A.** (Chapter 5) The final offering price would not be found on the preliminary prospectus (red herring) because the price hasn't been finalized at this point. After the issuer and the syndicate manager come up with a final offering price, they place it on the final prospectus.

29. **B.** (Chapter 16) When determining whether a broker-dealer has to file a currency transaction report (CTR), you need to look at the size of the trade first. Any cash or cash-equivalent (for example, a money order) transaction of $10,000 or more requires that you file a CTR to FinCEN (the U.S. Treasury Financial Crimes Network) to determine whether it may be money laundering. In Choice (B), the investor is depositing $14,000 in cash, which is over the $10,000 threshold. In addition, an SAR (Suspicious Activity Report) must be filed for any transaction of $5,000 or more for any trade or transfer that just looks suspicious.

30. **C.** (Chapter 9) To determine the sales charge percentage of a fund, use the following equation:

$$\text{Sales charge \%} = \frac{\text{POP} - \text{NAV}}{\text{POP}} = \frac{\$10.00 - \$9.30}{\$10.00} = \frac{\$0.70}{\$10.00} = 7\%$$

The POP is the public offering price, which is the price that investors pay, including the sales charge. The NAV is the net asset value and is where the fund should be trading, excluding the sales charge.

31. **A.** (Chapter 13) The correct answer is Choice (A). Historically, precious metals, like gold, are counter-cyclical and move opposite of the economic cycles. Choices (B), (C), and (D) are incorrect because utility, pharmaceutical, and food companies are defensive or noncyclical, and their movement isn't tied to the economic cycle.

32. **C.** (Chapter 8) On a competitive bid for a new municipal underwriting, the difference between the bid to the issuer and the dollar price at which the underwriter reoffers the bonds to the public is the spread, which, importantly, is also the underwriter's compensation.

33. **B.** (Chapter 16) Remember, when a customer opens a cash account, the only signatures that are required are that of the registered rep and a principal of the firm. However, if a customer were to open up a margin account, she'd have to sign a margin agreement.

34. **A.** (Chapter 14) Sell stop orders are used for protection. A sell stop order is placed below the support level of the stock and limits the loss on a long position. For argument's sake, say that a stock has a trading range of 30 to 32. An investor may enter a sell stop order at 29.50 to protect herself if the stock drops to 29.50 or below. If the price of the stock hits 29.50, the sell stop order becomes a market order for immediate execution at the next available price.

35. **B.** (Chapter 7) The *indenture* (trust indenture or deed of trust) of a bond is a legal contract between the issuer and the trustee representing the investors. The bond indenture includes the coupon rate (nominal yield), the maturity date, the name of the trustee, collateral that may be backing the bond, and so on. However, the credit rating isn't found on the indenture because that's something that would change if the financial condition of the issuer changes.

36. **C.** (Chapter 10) The certificate of limited partnership is the legal agreement between the limited and general partners and has to be filed with the secretary of state. The certificate of limited partnership includes the name of the partnership, the partnership's primary place of business, the names and addresses of the limited and general partners, the goals of the partnership and how long it's expected to last, the amount contributed by each partner, how the profits are to be distributed, the roles of the participants, how the partnership can be dissolved, and whether a limited partner can sell or assign his interest in the partnership. The authority that allows the general partner to charge a fee for making management decisions is found in the partnership agreement.

37. **A.** (Chapter 6) The correct answer is Choice (A). Because warrants are basically long-term options to buy stock at a fixed price from the issuer, they can't pay dividends.

38. **B.** (Chapter 10) Choice (B) is the correct answer because three components are true about a REIT. As indicated by its acronym, a REIT is a real estate investment trust. REITs engage in real-estate activities and are organized as trusts. In order to qualify for favorable tax treatment, a REIT must pass through at least 90 percent of its net investment income to its shareholders. Statement IV is false because, although a REIT can pass through income to investors, it can't pass through losses.

39. D. (Chapter 11) The easiest way to calculate the break-even point for stock/option problems is to take a look at what's happening. This investor purchased the stock for $45 per share and then purchased the option for $6 per share. The investor paid $51 ($45 + $6) per share out of pocket, so the investor needs the stock to be at $51 per share in order to break even.

40. D. (Chapter 5) All the securities listed are exempt from the registration and disclosure provisions under the Securities Act of 1933.

41. B. (Chapter 10) Investors of limited partnerships bear additional risks, such as the possibility of money being tied up for a long period of time, little or no liquidity, the making of additional loans to the partnership, and so on. As a registered rep, you need to prescreen your customers to see whether they're a good match for the partnership. You should also look at the partnership and management itself to see whether they have a good track record and whether the partnership makes sense. You need to explain the risks to your customer and have your customer fill out a subscription agreement, not a partnership agreement. The subscription agreement needs to include a check, a signature giving the general partner power of attorney, financial statements, and so on.

42. C. (Chapter 9) Life-cycle funds are ideal for investors of any age. The idea behind them is that investors buy into life-cycle funds that are targeted for their age. The percentage of equities held by the fund decreases over time, whereas the percentage of fixed-income securities increases, because investors should hold a higher percentage of fixed-income securities as they age. For example, say a 45-year-old investor buys into a life-cycle fund that's targeted for investors who are currently between the ages of 44–47. At this particular point, the fund may have a nearly 50-50 split between equity securities and fixed-income securities. The fund rebalances every so often so that ten years into the future, the fund may have 40 percent invested in equity securities and 60 percent invested in fixed-income securities. Ten years after that, the fund may have a 30-70 split between equity and fixed-income securities. This fund is designed to take the guesswork out of the equation for investors.

43. A. (Chapter 14) An *IPO* (initial public offering) is the first time a corporation ever sells securities to the public. A first-market trade is a trade of exchange-listed securities trading on an exchange. A rights offering is when a company offers new shares to existing shareholders at a discount.

44. C. (Chapter 13) When someone is bearish on the market or an individual security, she believes that the price is going down. Investors who believe that they can capitalize on their bearish feelings can sell securities short, buy bearish funds (ones that generally increase in value in a declining market), purchase inverse ETFs (exchange-traded funds), sell uncovered (naked) options, buy put options, and so on.

45. B. (Chapter 13) Defensive stocks perform consistently no matter how poorly the economy's doing. Stock of corporations that sell goods such as alcohol, tobacco, pharmaceutical supplies, food, and so on issue defensive stocks. However, companies that sell appliances, automobiles, and so on aren't defensive because they sell items that don't sell well in a weak economy.

46. A. (Chapter 16) The broker-dealer must send out account statements at least once every three months (quarterly) for an inactive account. If there has been any activity during a particular month, the brokerage firm must send out an account statement that month. Mutual funds must send out account statements once every six months (semiannually).

47. **D.** (Chapter 14) Here's another question where you must find the false answer. Choices (A), (B), and (C) are wrong because only orders placed below the market price are reduced for cash dividends on the order book. Buy limits and sell stops (BLiSS orders) are entered below the market price. Buy stops are entered above the market price, so Choice (D) is the false — and therefore, correct — answer.

48. **D.** (Chapter 8) Because this is an "except" question, you must find the false answer. The correct answer is Choice (D). Even if you didn't know what the "dated date" was, you should know that the rating (the higher the better), the interest received (the more the better), and the maturity date (the shorter the more marketable) affect a bond's marketability. The dated date of a bond issue is the date on which the issue begins to earn interest, which has little impact on marketability of a bond.

49. **C.** (Chapter 9) Similar to variable annuities, variable life insurance policies have a separate account of securities. All variable life insurance (VLI) policies have a set premium and a minimum death benefit. However, if the securities held in the separate account perform well, the policy will build up cash value, which will increase the death benefit.

50. **B.** (Chapter 12) Certainly, all the choices listed are important when determining a client's investment profile. However, this is an "except" question, which means that you're looking for an investment influence that is financial. The amount of marketable securities an investor owns is part of her financial profile as well as other things like net worth, money available for investing, current income, expenses, home ownership, and so on.

51. **C.** (Chapter 8) The interest received on municipal bonds is federally tax-free. Because Ginny is in the highest income tax bracket, she can save more tax money by investing in municipal bonds. This strategy will put her on equal footing with other investors because neither high-income nor low-income investors have to pay taxes on the interest received from municipal bonds. Therefore, municipal bonds are more advantageous to investors in high income-tax brackets.

52. **C.** (Chapter 7) Mortgage bonds, collateral trusts, and equipment trusts are all forms of secured bonds. Because these bonds are secured with collateral, the collateral securing the bonds is sold to satisfy the bondholders if the issuer defaults. However, debentures are not backed with collateral and are therefore riskier. Because more risk equals more reward, debenture holders can expect a coupon rate that's higher than that of the secured bonds.

53. **D.** (Chapter 7) Of the answer choices given, Choice (D) is the least preferable and, therefore, the correct answer. AA rated bonds, U.S. treasury notes, and AA rated debentures can yield predictable income. By contrast, income bonds are issued when a corporation is coming out of bankruptcy and trying to reorganize. Therefore, income bonds only pay interest if the corporation can meet the interest payment and normally trade without accrued interest. Income bonds are not suitable for Dana because she's seeking predictable income.

54. **C.** (Chapter 9) Although international funds may be okay to help diversify a portfolio, they're certainly the riskiest of all the choices given. International funds invest in securities outside of the investor's home country. International funds have additional risks that many other securities don't have, such as currency risk (the risk that the currency exchange rate will be bad). Also, the investor faces political risk (the risk that political changes in a country may adversely affect the price of securities). You should definitely steer this investor away from international funds.

55. **A.** (Chapter 11) The OCC (Options Clearing Corporation) is the issuer and guarantor of all listed options. The OCC determines which options will be traded and guarantees that option holders can always exercise their options.

56. **C.** (Chapter 9) Dividends that are distributed by municipal bond funds are federally tax-free, but any capital gain distribution is taxable. Choice (C) is the right answer.

57. **C.** (Chapter 8) Hopefully, the "G" in "GANs" was enough to help you get the correct answer. GANs are *grant anticipation notes,* which a municipality issues to provide temporary financing while waiting for a grant from the U.S. government.

58. **C.** (Chapter 13) To determine the net worth of a company, use the following equation:

    net worth = assets – liabilities

    net worth = $11,500,000 – $3,350,000 = $8,150,000

59. **D.** (Chapter 12) *Portfolio margin* looks at the risk of an investor's portfolio as a whole when determining margin requirements. Portfolio margin allows investors greater leverage but is only available to more sophisticated investors, and those investors must keep a minimum equity in their account of around $150,000.

60. **A.** (Chapter 7) The correct answer is Choice (A) because issuers call bonds when interest rates are falling. Choice (B) is incorrect because after the notes are called, new bonds at the lower rate are issued to raise funds in order to call the outstanding bonds with the higher rate. Choice (D) is incorrect because municipal bond call provisions are advantageous to issuers; the call provisions reduce fixed costs by providing issuers with the ability to redeem bonds before maturity.

61. **B.** (Chapter 16) All written complaints need to be handled by a principal and kept on file. Even though the complaint was sent via email, it's still considered a written complaint. The complaint does not need to be forwarded or sent to FINRA.

62. **A.** (Chapter 5) All securities sold in a state must be registered in that state (also known as blue-sky registration). Coordination, qualification, and notification (filing) are all types of state registration; registration by cooperation is not. If an agent wants to sell in a state, the security, the registered rep, and the broker-dealer must be registered in that state.

63. **B.** (Chapter 11) The easiest way to figure out the answer to this question is to use the equation P = I + T, where

    » P = the Premium of the option

    » I = the Intrinsic value of the option (how much it is in the money)

    » T = the Time value of the option (how much the investor is paying for the time to use the option)

    $$P = I + T$$
    $$9 = 5 + T$$
    $$T = 4$$

First, put the premium of 9 into the equation. Next, because the option is 5 points in the money (call options go in the money when the price of the stock goes above the strike price), insert the intrinsic value of 5 in the equation. Because the premium is 9 and the option is 5 points in the money, the time value is 4.

64. **B.** (Chapter 16) Principals of a firm must approve all new accounts, advertising used by the firm, handling of complaints, trades in all accounts, and so on. However, as far as the SIE exam goes, principals don't need to approve recommendations made by registered reps. In real life, I would get approval before making recommendations if I were you. You have to remember that principals must sign all order tickets, and if you don't clear a recommendation with them first, they may be reluctant to do so.

65. **C.** (Chapter 8) LRBs (lease revenue bonds) are similar to IDRs (industrial development revenue bonds), but instead of the bonds being backed by corporations, they're backed by lease payments made by office buildings, universities, prisons, and so forth. LTGOs (limited tax general obligation bonds) are a type of GO (general obligation) bond that's backed by taxes that aren't used to back other bonds. BABs (build America bonds) are taxable municipal bonds in which the U.S. Treasury either reimburses the issuer or gives a tax credit to investors for up to 35 percent of the interest cost.

66. **D.** (Chapter 8) Remember that an "except" question is looking for a false answer. The correct answer is Choice (D). Taxable equivalent yields cannot be shown because every investor has a unique tax issue and bracket.

67. **A.** (Chapter 16) Under FINRA rules, the representative should execute the trade in accordance with the customer's request and note on the trade ticket that the order was unsolicited.

68. **A.** (Chapter 7) Money market securities are short-term debt securities. Remember that commercial paper, as well as negotiable certificates of deposit, are money market securities.

69. **B.** (Chapter 10) Any income derived from an investment in a limited partnership is termed passive. Passive gains can only be written off against passive losses. Earned income includes money made from salary, bonuses, tips, and so on. Portfolio income includes money made from interest, dividends, and capital gains made from investing in securities.

70. **C.** (Chapter 10) The primary reason for investing in undeveloped land is appreciation potential. People who invest in undeveloped land either privately or by way of a real-estate DPP are hoping that their land will be of more value sometime in the near future.

71. **A.** (Chapter 6) After the split, stockholders are going to have 5 shares for every 4 that they had before. If the number of shares is going to increase, the price of the stock is going to decrease to make up for the additional shares. After the split, the investor should have the same overall market value of securities. Use the following equation to determine the number of shares and the stock price after a split:

$$LMV - DR = EQ$$
$$\$30,000 - \$12,000 = \$18,000$$
$$Reg\ T \times LMV = \underline{\$15,000}$$
$$\$3,000\ \text{excess equity}$$

72. **D.** (Chapter 13) The correct answer is Choice (D) because controlling the money supply implies a hands-on approach that's referred to as the *monetarist theory*. Choice (A) is incorrect because, although the Federal Reserve Board (FRB) controls the money supply, it isn't not an economic theory. Choice (B) is incorrect because the *Keynesian theory* is about big (some say stifling) government intervention; it's more about raising taxes and government control over businesses. Choice (C) is incorrect because the *supply-side economic theory* calls for low taxes and low government spending to stabilize the economy.

73. **C.** (Chapter 7) Commercial paper is generally issued for the purpose of raising capital for a corporation. Choice (A) is incorrect because commercial instruments are not quoted as a percent of par. Choice (B) is incorrect because a commercial instrument is proof of a debt, not ownership. Choice (D) is incorrect because commercial instruments are a debt security; therefore, if a claim is filed against the issuing corporation, the commercial instrument holds a senior position to preferred stock.

74. **D.** (Chapter 9) A specialized or *sector* fund invests within a single industry or geographical area.

75. **D.** (Chapter 15) Withdrawals from a Roth IRA may begin any time after the investor reaches age 59½. However, there's no required beginning date (RBD) or required minimum distribution (RMD) for Roth IRAs like there is for other retirement plans. You need to remember that the money withdrawn from a Roth IRA is tax-free, so the IRS doesn't care when these investors take their money because it isn't getting any of it.

Knowing the Score

Here's how the SIE exam is scored:

>> You get 1⅓ points for each correct answer.

>> You get zero points for each incorrect answer.

A passing grade is 70 percent. In other words, you need at least 53 correct answers on each practice test to get one step closer to your Nobel Prize in stockbrokerage (okay, economics).

To calculate your score, multiply the number of correct answers by 1.33 or divide it by 75. Whatever grade you get, make sure you round down, not up. For example, a grade of 71.6 is a 71 percent, not a 72.

Answer Key for Practice Exam 2

1.	A	20.	B	39.	D	58.	C
2.	A	21.	B	40.	D	59.	D
3.	C	22.	D	41.	B	60.	A
4.	A	23.	A	42.	C	61.	B
5.	A	24.	D	43.	A	62.	A
6.	C	25.	A	44.	C	63.	B
7.	B	26.	A	45.	B	64.	B
8.	D	27.	D	46.	A	65.	C
9.	A	28.	A	47.	D	66.	D
10.	D	29.	B	48.	D	67.	A
11.	C	30.	C	49.	C	68.	A
12.	A	31.	A	50.	B	69.	B
13.	A	32.	C	51.	C	70.	C
14.	C	33.	B	52.	C	71.	A
15.	B	34.	A	53.	D	72.	D
16.	D	35.	B	54.	C	73.	C
17.	B	36.	C	55.	A	74.	D
18.	B	37.	A	56.	C	75.	D
19.	D	38.	B	57.	C		

6

The Part of Tens

Discover ways to avoid the ten most common traps on the SIE exam.

Start your career as a financial professional the right way with ten job-related tips.

Chapter **21**

Ten SIE Exam Traps to Avoid

After all the time, effort, and sacrifice you put into studying, elevating the importance of the SIE exam to an unrealistically high level is easy. Step back for a moment. Keep it in perspective. This situation is not life or death. If you don't pass the test the first time, the worst thing that happens is that you have to retake it.

On the other hand, getting tripped up by some trivial exam traps after you've come this far would be a shame. This chapter lists some common mistakes and gives you some last-minute advice to help you over the last hurdles that stand between you and your first million dollars as a stockbroker.

Easing Up on the Studying

Perhaps you stop studying because you're getting good scores on practice exams and your confidence is high. If you're scoring 80s on exams that you're seeing for the first time, shoot for 85s. If you're getting 85s, shoot for 90s. The point is that you should continue to take exams until the day before your scheduled exam day. I firmly believe that every day away from studying ultimately costs you points on your exam that you can't afford to lose.

By the same token, make sure you don't wait too long before taking the exam. If you have to wait several weeks before you can take the exam, you lose your sense of urgency, and it's almost impossible to keep up the intense level of preparation needed for many months at a time. If you're taking a prep course before you schedule your SIE, follow your instructor's advice as to when you should take the exam. If you're directing your own course of study, after you're passing practice exams consistently with 80s or better, take the test as soon as possible. The longer you wait to take the exam, the more likely you are to forget the key points and complex formulas. If your test date is too far in the future, you also risk falling into the I'll-study-later trap, where you think you can double your efforts later to make up for any wasted time. Overall, losing your sense of urgency leads to complacency and a lack of motivation, which probably aren't characteristics broker-dealers are looking for in their employees.

Assuming the Question's Intent

You glance at the question quickly and incorrectly anticipate what the exam question is really asking you. You pick the wrong answer because you were in such a rush, you didn't see the word *except* at the end of the question. What a shame.

You don't want to fail the exam when you really know the material. Read each question carefully and look for tricky words like *except, not,* and *unless.* Then read all the answer choices before making your selection. (For more info on test-taking strategies that apply to certain question types, see Chapter 3.)

Reading into the Question

You're thinking *but what if* before you even look at the answer choices. When reviewing questions with students, I constantly get questions like "Yeah, but what if he's an insider?" or "What if he's of retirement age?" The bottom line is that you shouldn't add anything to the question that isn't there. Don't be afraid to read the question at face value and select the right answer, even if it occasionally seems too easy. Eliminate answer choices that are too much of a stretch, and remember that when two answer choices are opposites, one of them is most likely correct.

Becoming Distracted When Others Finish

You haven't even started looking over the questions you marked for review when the woman next to you leaps from her seat, picks up her results (with a little victory dance), and makes a break for the door.

Don't let people who are taking the exam with you psych you out. If others finish ahead of you, perhaps they're members of Mensa or maybe this is the fifth time they've taken the exam — practice makes perfect. They may even be taking a totally different exam. Besides the SIE, the testing centers also offer other securities exams with fewer questions. Keep focused and centered on taking your own exam. The only time you need to be concerned with is your own — whether you're on track.

Not Dressing for Comfort

You're trying to calculate the taxable equivalent yield on Mr. Dimwitty's GO bond, but the pencil keeps slipping out of your sweaty hand. You swear the test center has the heat cranked up to 80 degrees. Hmm. Maybe wearing your warmest wool sweater wasn't the best idea.

Dress comfortably. Don't wear a tie that's so tight it cuts off the circulation to your brain. You're under enough stress just taking the exam. Dress in layers. A T-shirt, a sweatshirt, and a jacket are great insulation against the cold. Another advantage is that you can shed layers of clothing (without ending up sitting in your underwear) if the exam room is too warm.

Forgetting to Breathe

You walk into the test center brimming with confidence. All of a sudden, the exam begins and some of the words look like they're in a foreign language. Your heart starts pounding, and you feel like you're going to pass out.

If stress becomes overwhelming, your breathing can become shallow and ineffective, which only adds to your stress level. Focus yourself before the exam by closing your eyes and taking a few deep breaths. This same process of closing your eyes and breathing deeply is a great way to calm yourself if you become stressed or anxious at any time during the exam.

Trying to Work Out Equations in Your Head Instead of Writing Them Down

While taking the exam, your memory starts to cloud and, somehow, the fact that two plus two equals five begins to make sense to you and the only formula you can remember is that there are 12 inches in a foot.

Certainly there aren't a real lot of equations you'll need for the SIE exam (not as much as for the Series 7 exam). However, don't throw away easy questions — memorize your equations while you're studying for your SIE exam so you know them cold before you arrive at the test site. If your nerves are getting the best of you and clouding your memory, jotting down the equations that you want to remember as soon as you receive permission to start the exam may be helpful (this process is known as a *brain dump*). When working out the math problems, you have scrap paper to work with (and a basic calculator). Use them. For example, some formulas, such as determining the value of a right (cum rights), require you to find sums and differences before you can divide. Even simple calculations, such as finding averages, can involve quite a few numbers. In problems with multiple parts, it's easy for you to accidentally skip steps, plug in the wrong numbers from the question, or forget values that you calculated along the way. Writing things out helps you keep things in place without cluttering your short-term memory.

Spending Too Much Time on One Question

Although the questions are weighted (a little more points for more difficult questions and less for easy questions), you don't want to get bogged down on one question. If you spend too much time on one question, you may lose points for many questions you didn't have time to even look at because you wasted so much time on the one that gave you trouble. If you find yourself taking too long to answer a question, take your best guess, mark it for review, and return to it later.

Changing Your Answers for the Wrong Reasons

You change an answer just because you already selected that same letter for the preceding three or four questions in a row. Just a touch of paranoia, right?

You've probably been told from the time you first started primary school not to change your answers. Trust your instincts and go with your original reaction. You have only two good reasons to change your answer:

>> You find that you initially forgot or didn't see the words *not* or *except* and you initially chose the wrong answer because you didn't see the tricky word.

>> You find that the answer choice you originally selected is not the best answer after all.

Calculating Your Final Score Prematurely

You waste valuable time concentrating on the number of questions you think you got wrong instead of focusing on the SIE exam questions you still have to answer.

Just read each question carefully, scrutinize the answer choices, and select the best answer. You'll find out whether you passed right after you complete the exam; it's not like you need to figure out your possible grade in advance to avoid sleepless nights until you receive your score. If you have additional time, use it to check your answers to the questions you marked for review.

Chapter **22**

Ten Ways to Start Your Career Off Right

Passing the SIE and one of the co-requisite exams can be one of the high points in your life. You've dedicated yourself to attaining your goal, put your life (and partying) on hold while you studied, and fulfilled your commitment to long hours of studying and hard work. You're now ready to reap the rewards. As you begin your new profession, you'll encounter many new hurdles. I give you this chapter to help prepare you for what to expect and, hopefully, to maximize your chances of a long, successful career.

Win at the Numbers Game

A majority of you will start out as cold callers. As with any other sales job, selling securities to investors is a numbers game. Some people actually track the number of calls it takes to open a new account, but I'm not among them. There are no specific economic benchmarks; however, you may have to make 500 cold calls to get to talk to 150 people. Out of these 150 people, you may generate ten leads. Out of every ten leads, you may open up one account.

The point is that you have to pick up that phone day in and day out and make the calls. If you're making 200 to 300 phone calls per day, you're likely to open an account every few days. However, if you're making 50 phone calls a day, you'll probably open up an account every couple weeks, and unless you hook a whale (a huge investor who likes to trade), you'll have trouble paying for gas for your new car. Remember that you're participating in a numbers game and that every "no" brings you one call closer to a "yes."

Be an Apprentice

There's no better way to hit the ground running than to have a top producer as a role model. Find the person in your firm with sales techniques that are most comfortable for you and invest as much time as possible watching how this mentor conducts herself on a daily basis. Top producers earn the most income because they've found a way to stand out in a competitive market.

Maybe this person can take you under her wing and show you the ropes in return for leads you develop while under her supervision. You can even have a contract between you and your mentor that sets forth the agreed-upon terms for each of you for a fixed period of time.

Do Your Homework

Take time to find out as much as possible about your job and the securities you're trying to sell. When you know what you're talking about, you inspire confidence from potential new customers. Spend some of your free time watching investing programs and reading the *Wall Street Journal* or any other trade magazines or newspapers you can get your hands on. The more you learn, the more comfortable you'll be on the phone, and the more sales you'll make.

Treat the Minnow like a Whale

More often than not, new customers don't disclose all their financial background to you. However, whether a customer has $10,000 or $10 million to invest, the money is important to her. Treat every customer as though she's the most valuable person in the world. Who knows? You may be speaking to someone with a lot of money to invest now or someone who will have a lot of money to invest in the future, or your customer may be a friend or family member of someone with substantial resources. Remember, a strong referral is a most influential lead.

Smile When You Dial

Be positive. You're going to have good days and bad days. You have to accept that as part of the business, but don't let it get you down. If you need to, take a five-minute break to gather your thoughts. If you aren't in a positive state of mind, you'll reflect that in the way you talk to existing or potential customers.

When a Security Falls, Don't Be a Stranger

You can't guarantee success, and that's okay. Savvy investors know that not every investment can end up a winner, no matter how good the situation looks in the beginning. If you recommend a security and it gets beaten down, call your customer. The customer is just waiting to hear from you. This call may be right up there with the most uncomfortable tasks you'll ever have to perform. Remember, however, that a savvy customer is most likely aware of what's going on, and your news won't be a surprise. Customers just want to be comforted and reassured that you'll be there with them — in good times and bad. Hopefully, the other seven or eight securities that you recommended are doing well.

Put In the Hours

Of course, you have to educate yourself about selling your products and cold-calling. In the beginning, be prepared to put in approximately ten hours each day. As you grow more experienced, you'll receive more leads and open more accounts in a shorter period of time, but in the beginning, you have to play the numbers game in order to earn money while you develop a more confident sales pitch.

Broaden Your Horizons

Consider obtaining other licenses to increase your skills and your ability to compete in the securities and financial industry. For example, the Series 65 or 66 (investment advisor exams) allow you to receive a fee for giving investment advice; Series 24 (the principal's license exam) allows you to manage other registered reps; and a Life, Accident, and Health Insurance license allows you to sell insurance policies and variable annuities to customers. If you take prep courses to obtain these licenses, you may also be exposed to a network of professionals who can become a source of future referrals.

Pay Yourself First

The stock market (and you with it) will have many peaks and valleys, but your financial security doesn't have to be quite so uneven. In the peak times, put away half your earnings when you receive your big paychecks. Tell yourself that you aren't going to make a big purchase until you have a certain amount socked away (see the upcoming section on setting goals). I've seen too many new brokers go out and buy a new car, a new boat, or whatever with their first big paycheck, expecting to make that much every month. The first time they have a bad month, they're wondering how they're going to make the payments (and possibly pay the rent). Remember, stockbrokers are supposed to be good with money. Burying yourself in debt looks kind of bad.

KEEP HUNGER IN YOUR EFFORTS, NOT YOUR STOMACH

When I first began my career as a stockbroker, the sales manager at the securities firm where I worked began the staff meetings by introducing himself and stating that he'd earned $100,000 his first year in the business and spent $150,000 of it — and he considered that to be a good thing! Somehow that just doesn't make sense either mathematically or logically (no matter how much your spending stimulates the economy). Some of the other trainees at the meeting were very impressed with the sales manager's suggestion, especially when he told us that he stayed hungry by spending so much more than he earned.

I remember looking at the sales manager and the other trainees who were attending this meeting and thinking, "What an idiot!" You'll get a lot of foolish suggestions along the way. If you want to stay hungry in your efforts, work hard, sock away (or invest) half your earnings, and pretend that money isn't there. Otherwise, you may be hungry for another reason: You can't afford to buy food!

Set Some Goals: The Brass Ring

Focus on your goals. Successful people have realistic short-term and long-term goals and a plan to achieve them. Whether your short-term goal is to put $5,000 away per month or to open ten new accounts, identifying what you want to do is the first step in creating a plan for your future.

What's the first thing every broker wants to do with the first big paycheck? You guessed it — buy a new car. Although that glistening Porsche can be an awesome incentive, set yourself smaller milestones to reach prior to making a big purchase. You can break down long-term goals, such as paying for a wedding, buying a new car, or purchasing your first house, into monthly income goals after you figure out the costs involved. Take a picture of your dream car or house and put it in a frame on your desk to remind you of the reward that awaits you.

Whatever your plan is, setting your mind on what you want, defining the steps you have to take to get there, and focusing your efforts on accomplishing each goal are the essential elements of a lucrative and rewarding career. Remember, you control your destiny.

Index

Numbers

A

About the Author

After earning a high score on the Series 7 exam in the mid '90s, **Steven M. Rice** began his career as a stockbroker for a broker dealership with offices in Nassau County, Long Island, and in New York City. In addition to his duties as a registered representative, he also gained invaluable experience about securities registration rules and regulations when he worked in the firm's compliance office. But only after Steve began tutoring others in the firm to help them pass the Series 7 did he find his true calling as an instructor. Shortly thereafter, Steve became a founding partner and educator in Empire Stockbroker Training Institute (www.empirestockbroker.com).

In addition to writing the *Securities Industry Essentials Exam For Dummies with Online Practice* and multiple editions of *Series 7 Exam For Dummies*, Steve developed and designed the Empire Stockbroker Training Institute online (*Series 7, Series 6, Series 63, Series 65, Series 66, Series 24*, and more) exams. Steve has also co-authored a complete library of securities training manuals for classroom use and for home study, including the *Series 4, Series 6, Series 7, Series 11, Series 24, Series 63, Series 65*, and *Series 66*. Steve's popular and highly acclaimed classes, online courses, and training manuals have helped tens of thousands of people achieve their goals and begin their lucrative new careers in the securities industry.

Dedication

I dedicate this book to my beautiful wife, Melissa. Melissa was the love of my life, my inspiration, and my best friend. Sadly, my soulmate lost her eight-year battle with cancer in 2017, and there remains a hole in my heart that will never be filled. However, I carry her undying love with me every single day.